THE ROYAL HORTICULTURAL SOCIETY

ESSENTIAL
GARDENING
TECHNIQUES

THE ROYAL HORTICULTURAL SOCIETY

ESSENTIAL GARDENING TECHNIQUES

Compiled and edited by Barbara Haynes
and Richard Bird

Editor-in-Chief
Christopher Brickell

TED SMART

**Royal Horticultural Society
Essential Gardening Techniques**

First published in 2002 by Mitchell Beazley,
an imprint of Octopus Publishing Group Ltd,
2–4 Heron Quays, London E14 4JP

Copyright © Octopus Publishing Group Ltd 2002

This edition produced for The Book People Ltd,
Hall Wood Avenue, Haydock, St Helens WA11 9UL

ISBN 1 8400 0711 7

A CIP catalogue copy of this book is available
from the British Library

Project Editor **Michèle Byam**
Executive Art Editor **Christie Cooper**
Designer **Terry Hirst**
Editors **Richard Bird and Barbara Haynes**
Production Controller **Alix McCulloch**
Picture Researcher **Nick Wheldon**
Indexer **Phyllis Van Reenen**

Set in Meta

Printed and bound in China by
Toppan Printing Company Limited

NOTE ON SEASONS

In this book seasons are used to denote
months as follows:

NORTHERN HEMISPHERE
Spring: March to May
Summer: June to August
Autumn: September to November
Winter: December to February

SOUTHERN HEMISPHERE
Spring: September to November
Summer: December to February
Autumn: March to May
Winter: June to August

No definition of seasons can be exact
as local climatic and growing conditions
affect the rate at which plants grow.
They should therefore be considered
as a general guideline only.

Contents

Introduction

The various elements of *Royal Horticultural Society Essential Gardening Techniques* have been drawn from the very popular series that comprise the *RHS Encyclopedia of Practical Gardening*. Between its various volumes this work covers in great depth all the principles and techniques vital to successful gardening. In this new and completely updated compilation, techniques have been selected and drawn together to give a basic, but nonetheless, remarkably comprehensive guide to looking after your garden. Because it takes a "hands-on" approach, the techniques are copiously illustrated step-by-step, and amplified by textual introductions.

ABOUT THE BOOK

The book is divided into 12 sections: Tools and Equipment; Soil Management; Growing Flowers; Growing Ornamental Trees, Shrubs, Roses, and Climbers; Growing in Containers; Lawns; Growing Vegetables and Herbs; Growing Fruit; Plant Care; Construction Work; Avoiding Problems; and The Year in the Garden – a checklist of essential tasks.

The book begins by looking at gardening tools, both manual and electrical, and a range of other basic gardening equipment. There is advice on how to use them and look after them as once you've got the right tools you can tackle the soil.

Soil needs managing, and you only get out of it what you put in. Plants extract much food and all their moisture from the soil, and fruits and vegetables have particularly high demands. It is vital, therefore, to replenish the soil regularly with home-made garden compost, or other sources of organic matter, to maintain a good structure, its moisture-retaining capacity and nutrient balance, further supplemented by judicious use of fertilizers. Good drainage and a near neutral pH are also desirable. If you have a poor draining soil there are solutions, for it can be drained, physically improved or planted to exploit the situation. Acid soils can be "sweetened" with lime, or made the most of by planting acid-loving plants like rhododendrons. Soil-testing is easily done with a kit and should be carried out every few years as soil pH does change.

Growing plants is what gardeners most enjoy, and all the techniques of growing your annuals, perennials, bulbs, shrubs, and trees are covered. Propagation methods, from seed or cuttings or by division, are also explained. There is also coverage of pruning, with plant examples given for every method. Sometimes there may be several equally acceptable methods of pruning the same plants, and this is recognised. Remember that, when following the diagrams, your own plants may not be exactly like the example illustrated. The diagrams are in all cases designed to show the basic principles.

Plants in containers have never been more popular and details on how to grow them successfully this way are covered. The practical aspects of planting window boxes and hanging baskets are illustrated, as well as their day-to-day care.

A smartly striped lawn is an asset gained only by regular care and a considerable effort. We show

how this can be achieved, although there is a more basic lawn-care and renovation programme. Full details are also given of how to create a new lawn from seed and how to lay turf.

The rewards of fruit and vegetable gardening have been justifiably proclaimed many times. It is not only worthwhile, but also can be extremely enjoyable. A major incentive to grow your own produce is its superior flavour, plus the fact that you know how it has been grown. Any chemical treatments are of your own choice.

There are many aspects of gardening that apply to all plants – watering and feeding, for example. Then there are the methods of protecting vulnerable plants from frost and wind damage. Siting plants incorrectly means they are handicapped from the start. The information on microclimates will enable you to understand the range or conditions found in your garden. It is a rare garden that does not have both sunny and shady areas. There are other slight variations that can be taken advantage of if they can be identified and correctly planted.

Growing the right plant in the right place is a good start to avoiding problems in the garden. Plants growing strongly are far less likely to be affected by pests and diseases, than those struggling, for example, due to poor planting in the wrong soil, shortage of water or an essential nutrient. *Royal Horticultural Society Essential Gardening Techniques* urges a "whole garden" approach and takes the line that the easiest way of dealing with a problem is to prevent it occurring in the first place.

The section on construction work deals with basic hard-landscape elements of the garden. There are instructions on how to build a pond, a millstone fountain with a sunken reservoir, and a rock garden. Although many gardeners prefer to bring in professional help for construction jobs, the basic skill required to erect a fence or lay a path can be learned by almost anyone. This "do-it-yourself" approach is invariably less expensive than employing someone else, and there is a great deal of satisfaction to be gained from making something yourself.

SAFETY IN THE GARDEN

Accidents are mostly due to carelessness – tools, hoses and cables left lying about where they can be tripped over, or supporting canes with unprotected ends. Getting into the habit of putting away all equipment neatly after use is a simple way of making the garden a safer place.

Although there is no need to be wary of using power tools provided you take sensible precautions, take special care when using electrical equipment near water. Installing electricity in the garden should always be done by a qualified electrician.

Wear sensible clothing, in particular stout footwear. The less skin exposed the better when pruning, and especially when using garden chemicals. With any chemical it is vital to follow the manufacturer's instructions to the letter. Remember that all chemicals must be kept in their original container with the label intact, and stored under lock and key out of the way of children and pets.

TOOLS AND EQUIPMENT

Before you can start to garden you need a few basic tools and equipment. Good quality tools may cost more but they are worth the extra money as they not only last longer but they are usually better balanced and make the job easier. The basic starter tool kit is a spade and border fork, a trowel and hand fork, hoe and rake, watering cans, and a pair of secateurs. Lawn-owners obviously need a mower and a pair of shears. Beyond this most basic starter kit are various other tools that will make your gardening life easier and more thorough, and these are described and illustrated on the following pages. Sometimes these extras tools – such as edging irons – are passed down through families, used maybe once or twice a year and carefully oiled by an uncle or grandfather. New is not necessarily better so if your budget is tight look for second-hand tools that have been well-cared for, or even share tools among your family.

To get the best out of your tools look after them. Clean them after use. This may seem a chore but you will appreciate it when you come to use them again. Usually all it means is washing off any soil and wiping the blade – whatever the tool – with an oily rag. Put tools away after use and don't leave them laying about where they will deteriorate and quite possibly be a hazard.

SHEDS AND STORAGE

From this you will realise that storage is important. The best solution for storage is a garden shed. A shed is an essential garden feature in which to store tools and equipment, as well as bulky items such as bags of compost and pots. Many types of shed are available and it is not difficult to erect

them yourself or, if you prefer, manufacturers or garden centres will erect them for you. Sheds come in different sizes. One measuring 2 x 1.5m (6 x 5ft) should give ample space for storage plus room for a shelf and folding workbench. If you have space go for a slightly larger one you will have more room to move. A window is desirable, although most sheds come with one. Wooden sheds are pressure treated and you can further treat them with wood stain or preservative in the colour of your choice. Metal sheds are also available but they cost more than wooden ones. Whatever size or type you choose, your shed needs a firm foundation of cast concrete or concrete slabs. Make the foundation exceed the size of the shed by at least 10cm (4in) all round. The foundation should also slope gently and consistently in one direction, with a fall of about 2–3cm (1in), to ensure rapid drainage. A hard standing area in front of the shed will be useful and prevent the ground becoming rutted and muddy in wet weather. It is also a good idea to fit a gutter and down pipe to a water butt.

Store tools neatly in the shed, hanging them up on tool racks. Roll up garden hoses and electrical cables so that you don't trip over them. If you use garden chemicals it is sensible to have a small lockable cupboard to store them out of reach of children and pets. As garden thefts are on the increase it is also wise to fit your shed with a secure padlock.

For those with gardens too small for a conventional shed there are more compact alternatives. Some storage areas double up as a garden bench, while others are more like garden cupboards and can be fitted against a wall or fence.

Basic tools

Always choose tools to match your height and build. When buying a spade or fork, in particular, pick up several types and go through the motions of digging to make certain that the balance and weight suit you, and that they are comfortable to use. A 75cm (30in) handle on a spade or fork is about right for a person of average height who likes to dig with a straight back; and a 70cm (27½in) handle often suits those who prefer to bend their back slightly when digging.

Avoid flimsy, poorly made tools however cheap they may be. Badly designed tools made of materials that bend after a little use or with a rough finish or narrow spaces between the tines, where the soil clogs, are a waste of money. Also avoid trowels, handforks, and other tools made of aluminium as it blunts quickly and stains the hands. Conventional good quality steel tools with a smooth finish should be used to obtain the best results with the least physical effort. Stainless steel tools are durable and require only minor maintenance, but they are expensive and sometimes heavy and exhausting to use. If the weight and balance are suitable they are undoubtedly the best buy because they are easy to clean and they will last for many years. Good quality second-hand tools are worth considering if they have been looked after properly.

Specially designed tools are available for the elderly and disabled, and some of these may be useful for gardeners who suffer from back troubles or find that conventional tools do not suit them for some other reason.

The shafts of tools can be made from several materials including wood, metal, and plastic. Wood is the traditional material. It is long lasting and comfortable to use. Metal shafts are heavy if made of steel, but aluminium alloy ones coated with plastic on rakes and hoes are light. Plastic polypropylene shafts are light and strong as well as being durable.

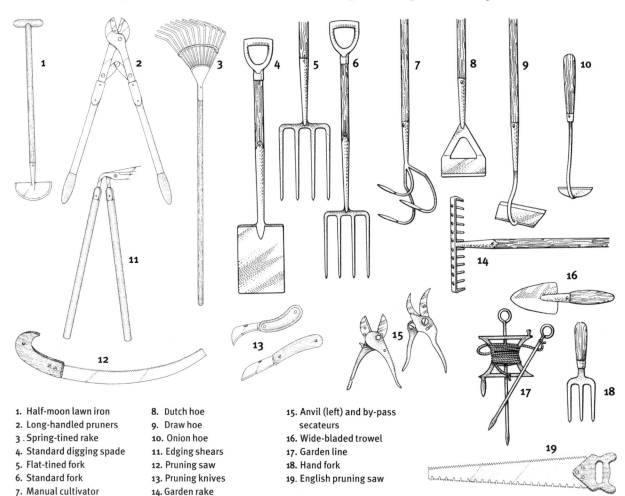

1. Half-moon lawn iron
2. Long-handled pruners
3. Spring-tined rake
4. Standard digging spade
5. Flat-tined fork
6. Standard fork
7. Manual cultivator
8. Dutch hoe
9. Draw hoe
10. Onion hoe
11. Edging shears
12. Pruning saw
13. Pruning knives
14. Garden rake
15. Anvil (left) and by-pass secateurs
16. Wide-bladed trowel
17. Garden line
18. Hand fork
19. English pruning saw

Wheelbarrows

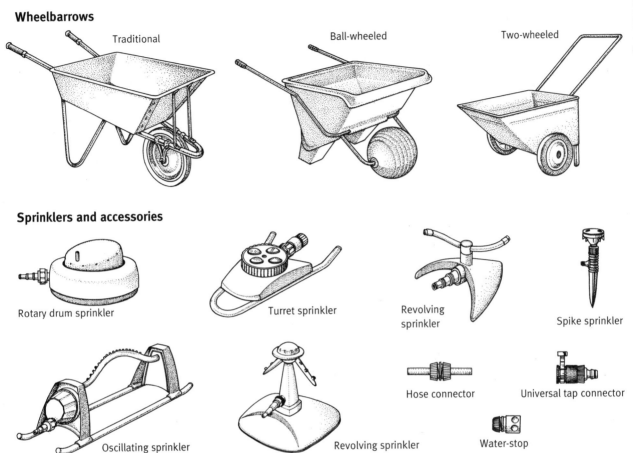

Traditional

Ball-wheeled

Two-wheeled

Sprinklers and accessories

Rotary drum sprinkler

Turret sprinkler

Revolving sprinkler

Spike sprinkler

Oscillating sprinkler

Revolving sprinkler

Hose connector

Universal tap connector

Water-stop

Watering cans, hosepipe, and accessories

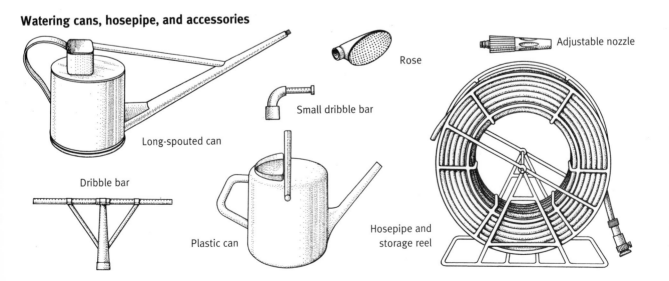

Rose

Adjustable nozzle

Long-spouted can

Small dribble bar

Dribble bar

Plastic can

Hosepipe and storage reel

Using the tools

Generally speaking most tools are easy to use and the feel of the tool in the hand and common sense will normally indicate how they are operated. Many tools have more than one function. For example, a spade is primarily for digging but it can be used as a shovel for moving soil or compost. By using tools for different purposes the gardener can start with a small selection and add to it as the years pass.

The main use of a spade is as a digging tool, but it can also be used for skimming weeds off the soil before digging, moving soil or compost, and making holes for planting larger plants such as trees. Forks are used for digging and breaking down soil as well as moving compost, manure, and heaps of vegetation. Although not as essential a tool as an ordinary fork, flat-tined forks can be used for lifting root vegetables. Handforks are used for loosening soil around plants as well as for general handweeding. Trowels can have a similar role, but they can also be used for skimming off weeds, digging planting holes, and for moving potting compost and other materials in small quantities.

Ordinary rakes are used for levelling cultivated ground as well as breaking down the soil into a fine tilth. Wide wooden rakes are useful for clearing up leaves and long cut grass. Spring-tined rakes are also useful for clearing up leaves and minor debris as well as scarifying lawns. There are several different types of hoe (see page 14) of which the draw hoe is probably the most versatile for the majority of gardeners. Wheelbarrows are useful for moving material, including weeds. However, in a small garden a large bucket may be sufficient. A garden line is essential for planting straight rows and a measuring stick with measurements marked on it is useful for getting planting distances right. No gardener can work without secateurs for cutting and pruning, while a pruning saw will be required once shrubs and trees reach a certain size. A folding knife is always useful to have in your pocket. The other cutting tool that is generally required is a pair of shears for cutting hedges, grass, and occasionally for trimming over plants. For watering a watering can is essential, preferably with a detachable rose.

Always clean garden tools and oil the metal parts as soon as possible after use. Store them in a dry shed or garage. Always protect from the wet to prevent rust. This is not simply an aesthetic consideration because rusty tools mean harder work and they will need replacing more quickly than tools that are cared for by washing, drying, and rubbing over with an oily rag.

When digging keep the blade as vertical as possible, which means that the handle will lean forward slightly. This will ensure that the ground is dug to its full depth. There is no need to lift the soil high.

A fork is used in a similar way to a spade, keeping the blade as vertical as possible. Some gardeners prefer forks to spades in heavier soils, such as clay, others restrict their use to lighter soils.

A hand fork is useful for a variety of small-scale jobs. It is most useful for hand-weeding, loosening the weed in the earth. It can be used for opening the soil around plants to aerate them. Hold back the plants while the earth is forked over, being careful not to harm any roots. It can also be used for lifting small plants from the ground.

A trowel is useful for similar small-scale tasks. Most importantly, it is used for digging small holes for planting purposes, as well as for pushing the soil back into the hole again, before firming it with the hands. A trowel can be used for loosening the soil and for digging up seedlings and small plants.

A rake is an essential tool for any gardener. Its basic use is to level the soil, by moving it forwards and backwards. It is also used to break down the soil into a fine tilth. To do this, first tamp down the soil by holding the rake vertically and gently pounding the soil with the back of the tines, and then rake across the surface.

A spring-tine, or wire-toothed, rake is used to gather up dead material, particularly from lawns, such as fallen leaves and other debris. Another use is to scratch out dead grass, or thatch, from a lawn. The action requires some force so that the debris is pulled away, leaving the living grass with more light and space to grow.

Using the tools

In a small garden it is possible to make do with one hoe, the draw hoe, as it can be used not only for clearing off weeds, but also for drawing up soil around plants. The corner of the hoe's blade can also be used for drawing out seed drills. It has the disadvantage, however, that the gardener walks forwards over the ground he has just hoed. Dutch or push hoes on the other hand are used walking backwards and are also easier to control, especially when weeding amongst plants. A Canterbury hoe has three solid prongs (sometimes two) and is used for heavy cultivation work in the vegetable garden. It is useful for breaking down clods of soil as well as earthing up such plants as potatoes and celery.

A Dutch hoe is operated by pushing the blade slightly into the soil's surface. While doing this the gardener walks backwards down the row. This type of hoe is especially useful for weeding amongst plants.

A draw hoe is pulled towards the operator with the blade at an angle to the soil and works with a chopping or scraping motion. The operator walks forwards, or works on a small area before moving backwards.

An onion hoe is like a minature Dutch hoe. Designed for hoeing amongst onions, it is also useful for careful hoeing in rock gardens or between any plants where a larger hoe might cause damage.

A Canterbury hoe is not as popular as it once was. It is primarily used in the vegetable garden for breaking down soil and for drawing up soil into ridges, such as when earthing up potatoes.

Using the tools

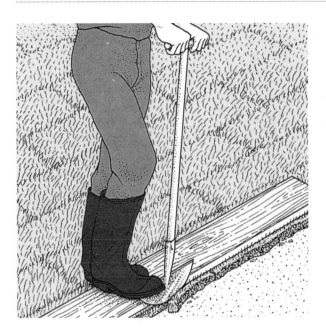

A half-moon lawn iron is used for cutting turf, such as the edges of newly-laid turf lawns, and recutting the edges of existing lawns. It can also be used for cutting out damaged turf within a lawn. Either hold it vertically against the side of a flat board, or against a garden line. For curved edges use a hosepipe as a guide.

Edging shears, as their name suggests, are for trimming the grass at the edges of a lawn. Hold the handle attached to the bottom blade steady at all times and move the handle of the top blade to and fro to make a cutting motion. This method produces an even cut faster and more easily than if both handles are moved.

Although they can be used for grass, shears are mainly used for cutting hedges. Their handles have a slight crank to allow the blades to be kept flat against the top or sides of the hedge. Check that a flat cut is being made all the time. Avoid digging the tips in.

Secateurs can be used for cutting herbaceous or thin woody material in the garden. Position the stem to be cut close to the blade where it can be held firmly, rather than at the tip which may strain the blades. Cut cleanly, never twist secateurs during a cut to get better leverage.

Using the tools

A variety of tools can be used for planting. For large scale operations, such as planting trees and shrubs, a spade is necessary. For smaller plants use a trowel or hand fork for digging the hole. They can also be used for filling in round the plant, although many gardeners prefer to use their hands. For smaller plants with little root spread a dibber is used. This is especially useful with vegetables, such as leeks or cabbages. A garden line, which can simply consist of two pegs and some string is essential for keeping rows straight and a measuring stick is useful for planting distances. Modular trays have simplified the job of raising plants from seeds and cuttings because small plants can develop without disturbance as pricking out is unnecessary.

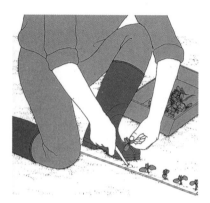

It is useful to have several sizes of dibbers, and some can be home made. A small one using 1.5cm (½in) of wooden dowelling is useful for planting small seedlings.

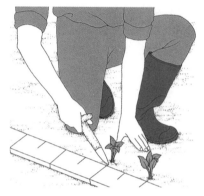

A large dibber can be made from a thicker dowel, a broom handle or even the remains of a broken spade handle. Dibbers work best when used in a loose soil .

Use a trowel to transplant plants from modular trays. Water the plant a couple of hours beforehand so the rootball remains intact during the operation.

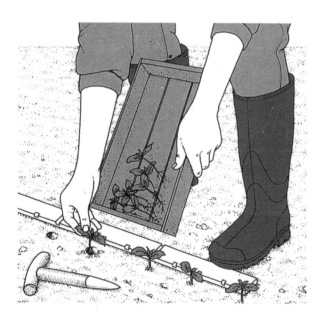

A measuring stick is indispensible. Any piece of wood about 1–1.5m (3–5ft) long will do. Mark off in 2.5cm (1in) intervals by making shallow cuts with a saw. Make deeper cuts at 15 and 30cm (6 and 12in).

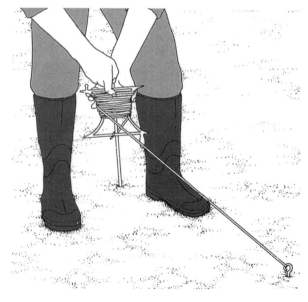

Traditional garden lines have a reel on one of the pegs. When in use the string must be stretched taut, and looped under the winding handle to prevent it slackening.

While it is perfectly feasible to garden using only hand tools, there is no doubt that power tools are a great boon to gardeners. Lawn mowers and hedge cutters are probably the most widely used. The two main sources of power are electricity and petrol. For smaller gardens, electricity is usually more convenient. Electrical equipment is lighter and cheaper and yet it has enough power to cope with most demands. Cables need to reach without being over-extended and must always be used with a circuit breaker (Residual Current Device). Keep cables over one shoulder, well clear of the machine during use, and after use wind them up. Not all electrical tools need a connecting cable, many cordless ones are now available giving them a greater range, but more limited operation time.

Petrol driven machines are usually more expensive and heavier but more robust and powerful. They are not restricted by cables and are more suitable for large gardens, especially if there is heavy work to be done on a regular basis.

It is essential that all power tools are regularly maintained. Even the least mechanically-minded gardener should keep equipment clean and store it properly. All equipment should have a professional service once a year. It is vital to take notice of safety precautions recommended when purchasing the machine. *Never ignore or cut back on safety measures.*

Cylinder mower

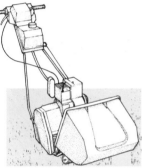

Cylinder mowers cut grass by means of a multi-bladed cylinder which revolves against a fixed blade.

Rotary mower

Rotary mowers power one or two horizontal blades which spin around a drive shaft beneath a cowl.

Hover mower

A hover mower creates a cushion of air on which the machine floats. The cutting action is rotary.

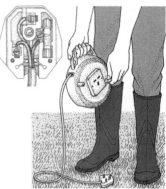

Store cables on a drum. Wire plugs with the brown wire (live) on the right, blue (neutral) left, and green and yellow centre.

When using electric tools with a power cable, drape the cable over one shoulder so that it does not accidentally get in the way and get cut. Wear gloves , goggles, and close-fitting clothes when cutting hedges.

Strimmers and brushwood cutters are useful for cutting grass alongside walls, long grass, and weedy growth. Some can be flipped over and used to edge lawns. Keep the nylon line well clear of trees as it will damage the bark.

Use a large metal funnel to transfer fuel to fill a tank. Do not re-fuel a machine while it is running. Petrol should only be stored in proper permitted containers. Avoid petrol spilling on the grass as it will burn it.

Potting equipment

Not everybody has space for a potting shed, but if you can possibly fit one in your garden it is worth it. A relatively small shed will do as long as there is room to stand, to have a bench on which to work, shelves on which to keep equipment, and a lockable cupboard in which to store chemicals and blades safely away from children. Place the bench below a window and, if possible, install a light for winter evening work. It is important to keep the shed, and the bench in particular, clean and tidy.

POTTING POSTURE

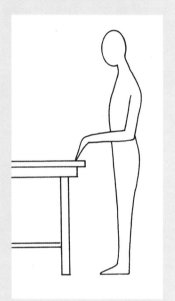

If you intend to work at your bench for more than a few minutes it is essential to have it at the right height. To find this correct height, stand up straight next to the bench, drop your arms to your side, and then raise your forearms at right angles to your body. Drop your wrist and the surface of the bench should be at the height indicated by your finger tips.

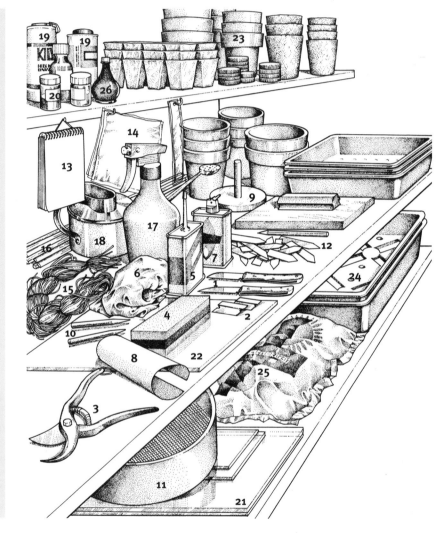

Potting shed contents

1. Knives
2. Safety razor blades
3. Secateurs
4. Sharpening stones
5. Oil for lubrication
6. Cleaning rags
7. Solvent
8. Emery paper
9. Pressers for firming compost
10. Dibbers
11. Sieve
12. Labels and pencil
13. Notebook
14. Polythene bags and tape
15. Raffia and twine
16. Split canes
17. Hand sprayer
18. Watering can
19. Garden chemicals – must be stored out of reach of pets and children
20. Rooting powders
21. Glass for covering seed
22. Spare glass
23. Pots
24. Seed trays
25. Composts
26. Fertilizer

Right: A large, corrugated plastic cloche, used here for producing early lettuces.

Below: A small, home-made coldframe, suitable for growing early crops or hardening off plants.

Right: Spotlights will illuminate a selected area such as this entrance to a pergola.

Below: Floodlights dramatically light up a summerhouse and the surrounding shrubs.

Seed and potting composts

A compost is a soil substitute for propagating and establishing plants. To carry out this function a compost needs to be well-aerated, to retain water, to hold nutrients, and to conduct warmth. Thus the components of a compost should be chosen to establish these particular conditions as well as maintaining them for a period of time. In order to prevent the occurrence of pests, diseases and weeds the component materials should also be sterile. There is a wide range of composts on the market formulated for general and specific purposes, but they all fall into one of two groups depending on whether they are loam- or soil-based or soilless.

The best known loam-based composts are those in the John Innes range. In these sterilised loam is mixed in varying proportions with peat, sharp sand, ground limestone, and fertilizer. The advantages of loam-based composts is that they retain moisture and nutrients for longer than soilless compost. The quality of the compost depends on the quality of loam and is verified by the John Innes Manufacturers' Association seal. In recent years there has been difficulty in obtaining loam of a consistent standard and sterilising it effectively, and in consequence soilless composts have become increasingly popular.

In the past peat has been widely used as the main component of soilless composts, generally in combination with other inert ingredients such as vermiculite, perlite, expanded polystyrene granules, or sand. However, increasing concern at the environmental consequences of large-scale peat extraction for horticulture has led to the development and use of various peat substitutes in composts. Coir and granulated bark are some of the most widely used. The formulation of soilless composts varies considerably. Ground limestone and trace elements are generally added with the base fertilizer. Soilless composts have several advantages. They are light, clean, naturally sterile, and easy to handle. Their disadvantages are that the nutrients they contain are exhausted four to six weeks after potting, after which the plants need regular feeding. Because they are so light the composts do not provide adequate support for top-heavy plants. Heavy firming at planting will destroy the open texture of the composts. Another point worth remembering is that plants grown in pots of soilless compost are often difficult to establish in garden soil. Watering requirements vary greatly and it is a case of trial and error until you get the measure of the particular compost you are using; peat-based composts are difficult to rewet once they dry out.

Take note of the storage facilities at your garden supplier; some compost bags hare small ventilation holes, which, if they are not covered, allow rain to enter and saturate the contents.

BASIC COMPOST MIXTURES

Compost	Properties
Seed	Loam-based (John Innes seed compost) and soilless; formulated to provide optimum conditions for germination, but low in nutrients; seedlings will starve unless transplanted at early stage into a richer mix (e.g. John Innes potting compost no. 1)
Cuttings	Must be sterile, chemically inactive and well aerated but sufficiently moisture retentive to prevent desiccation. A mix of equal parts peat, or peat alternative, and sharp sand is widely used, bur perlite, vermiculite, and rock wool give good results.
Potting	Loam-based (John Innes potting compost no. 1 or 2) and soilless; formulated to suit a wide range of plants and to provide sufficient nutrients not to check growth. General-purpose formulations are suitable for plug plants, bedding, young vegetables, and house plants.
Tree and shrub	Loam-based (John Innes potting compost no. 3) and soilless, formulated to support large vigorous plants, with a higher level of nutrients than potting compost; gives stability and retains moisture more effectively than soilless composts.
Alpine	Loam-based and gritty, formulated to provide the free-draining conditions; a mixture of equal parts John Innes potting compost no. 2, grit and peat, or peat substitute, should suit most rock plants.
Ericaceous	Loam-based or soilless; lime-free compost for rhododendrons and o.her plants intolerant of lime; a high content of fibrous, organic material is beneficial.

A portable potting bench enables repotting and propagation to be carried out in a house, shed, or garden. One made of plastic is easy to keep clean and should be washed thoroughly after each use, as good hygiene is essential when dealing with seeds and cuttings.

Propagators

Many gardeners go through their lives without having a proper propagator and yet succeed in producing enough plants for their own needs and often a few more besides. They are content to use polythene bags placed over plastic pots. Some build their own propagators, which are little more than four planks of wood nailed together to make a square or rectangle with a sheet of glass or old window frame as a lid. The more sophisticated propagators include heating cables buried in sand to supply bottom heat as an aid to rooting. Another refinement is top heat from cables round the side of the propagator. Heated propagating trays, with or without covers, are widely available in various sizes and levels of sophistication; some models are designed to fit on a windowsill and hold several small seed trays. Stand propagators in a warm and light position but not in direct sunlight; heated models will, of course, need a nearby electricity supply. Always clean propagators scrupulously after use.

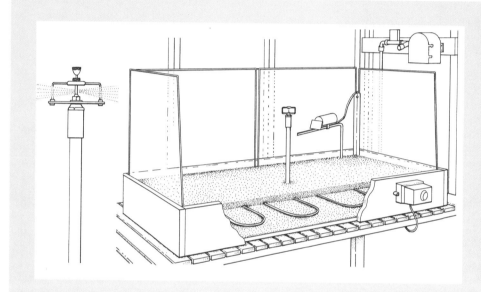

MIST PROPAGATION

A mist unit provides fine sprays of water above cuttings, which stay turgid as they are constantly covered in a fine film of water. Such units are suitable for greenhouses with electricity as they are used in conjunction with soil-warming cables controlled by a rod thermostat. A cut-off switch, responsive to light, moisture or time, controls the water supply. There is no need for a cover.

Home-made propagators

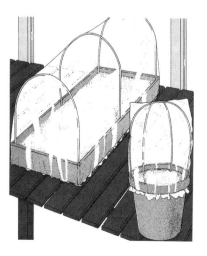

A seed tray or pot can be converted into a propagator, using polythene film or bags. Keep the polythene clear of the cuttings with wire hoops and secure it around the base with a rubber band or string. Pot propagators can also be purchased in various sizes.

Purpose-made propagators

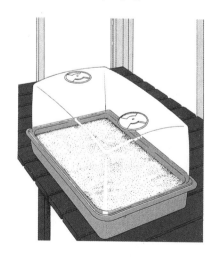

Purpose-made propagators have a domed plastic top over a seed tray or trays. Ventilators are usually fitted and are used to start the hardening off process (see page 47). More sophisticated models incorporate a heating tray with adjustable settings in the base.

Cloches, cold frames, polytunnels

Cloches, cold frames, and polytunnels are all inexpensive means of protecting plants when they are vulnerable to weather conditions. Most have the advantage that they are portable. They are also cheap compared with the cost of a greenhouse.

Cloches and polytunnels

Cloches are a useful aid in most gardens. They can be used either to protect a plant from cold, frost, or from excess wet. They can be used to bring on earlier crops. Strawberries, for example, will crop a week or two earlier if covered with a cloche. At the other end of the season a cloche will allow late trusses of green tomatoes to ripen on the plant if the stem is bent over. Traditional cloches were made of glass, but this type are now expensive. In addition, glass cloches are hazardous to assemble and to take apart, and it is unwise to have glass cloches in gardens where children play. Polythene, polycarbonate, and other forms of plastic have become the norm. Cloches made of these materials are not only cheaper, but safer and easier to store, although they are not quite as effective as glass. Bell jars made of plastic or glass have again become popular and are just the right shape to protect a single plant in a border. Tent-shaped and polythene tunnel-type cloches, or polytunnels, are more functional looking and a practical means of protecting a row of seedling vegetables. To maximize protection close off the end with a pane of glass or sheet of polycarbonate. When the weather warms increase ventilation by spacing out the cloches or, in the case of polytunnels, rolling up the sides. If the polythene will not last another season, cut holes in the sides to allow ventilation. Large walk-in polythene tunnels provide just enough protection to allow you to grow hardy crops over winter. They give more protection than cloches but less than a greenhouse, and are considerably cheaper if less attractive and less permanent.

Fleece

Fleece has all the virtues of cloches but can cover a much larger area if it is tucked into the soil or weighted down with bricks. It will warm the soil, protect seedling crops or cover early salads until they mature, as the material stretches as the plants grow. Carefully secured it can be a barrier to certain pests, including carrot fly. Use it for winter protection, by wrapping lengths round plants, or placing a sheet over wall-trained fruit to protect early blossom from frost.

Cold frames

A frame allows you to grow plants from seeds and cuttings in a protected environment. It may be used for overwintering plants and is useful for hardening off young plants before they are planted out in the garden. There are metal or wooden models, glazed with toughened glass or plastic, or if you have DIY skills you can make your own out of timber or bricks. Double skinned polycarbonate or double glazed lids improve insulation. Some models are light enough to be moved about, particularly useful if you are growing crops like melons each year as it enables rotation (see page 166). These lightweight frames must be anchored securely in the soil. Heavy wooden frames are better on a hard standing with the base covered with grit to ensure good drainage.

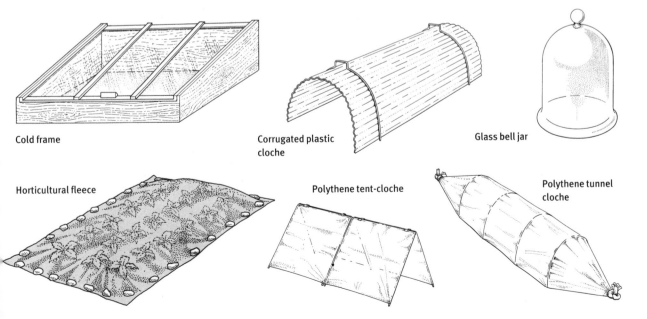

Cold frame

Corrugated plastic cloche

Glass bell jar

Horticultural fleece

Polythene tent-cloche

Polythene tunnel cloche

SOIL MANAGEMENT

Soil has been formed over thousands of years from the breakdown of rocks into mineral particles of sand, silt, and clay. However, this is only its "skeleton", usually making up about half the volume. The rest is made up of air, water, organic matter, plant roots, and the all-important organisms that live in the soil.

A soil type is determined by the different amounts of sand, silt, and clay particles it contains. Those with a fairly equal mixture of these particles are called loams. You can easily identify your soil type by picking up a handful and feeling it. Knead the soil with your fingers – a sandy soil feels gritty, clay is sticky, and silt has a silky feel. Then roll the soil between your palms. Very sandy soil will crumble. If the soil forms a cohesive ball, rub your finger over the surface: a clay-rich soil will shine.

The soil also varies in the amount of calcium, or lime, it contains. Calcium is a vital plant nutrient, but it also controls the availability of other nutrients and affects soil structure. It is important to ascertain the amount of lime in your soil with a pH test.

SOIL STRUCTURE

Soil particles are held together in aggregates or "crumbs", with spaces between. The size of the spaces is important as this defines the soil structure. Large spaces allow drainage so that air can move within the soil, while small spaces hold water. The spaces also allow soil organisms to move about and plant roots to penetrate. The structure can be damaged or destroyed when the soil is compacted by walking, using machinery, flooding, or cultivating in wet or frozen conditions.

ORGANIC MATTER

This is material of living origin. In the garden it usually consists of plant debris, animal manures and the remains of microscopic organisms, insects and small animals. Organic matter is continually being broken down by myriads of soil-dwelling organisms by whose action minerals are released that plants can take up in solution and use as food.

Organic matter has many other benefits. It helps particles of soil to stick together to form crumbs. This crumb structure, as it is known, improves aeration and drainage and is particularly useful in improving heavy clay soils, making them more workable, aerated and more easily penetrated by plant roots. Organic matter also improves light sandy soils because of its ability to retain moisture and nutrients, which would otherwise be washed away. In addition, it is a source of food for soil inhabitants, helping them to thrive and multiply, and in turn release more plant nutrients. Organic matter must be added regularly to maintain soil fertility and structure. It can either be dug in or laid on the surface as a mulch. It is simple to make your own organic matter by recycling garden and kitchen waste in a compost bin, at least one of which should be a part of every garden.

CULTIVATION AND DRAINAGE

Although it is not always necessary, soil is usually dug. It is essential to dig before planting trees and shrubs. It is also a quick way of clearing the ground and exposing pests to their natural predators. On heavy or compacted soils digging helps to improve drainage, but if water lies on the surface regularly you may need to install a drainage system.

Soil types

Soil is the result of organic processes working on inorganic rock. In a ceaseless process, rocks are broken down and creatures colonise the resulting debris. The nature of the parent rock decides much of the character of the resulting soil.

Several factors are responsible for the development of the soil. The most important of these is the climate. Rainwater passing over and through the parent rock breaks it down, and repeated freezing and thawing shatters the rock into smaller particles. Organic matter, such as leaves and dead animals, lodges in this rock waste, allowing bacteria and fungi to break them down. Seeds germinate in the resulting mixture. Once plants are established they will contribute organic material to the soil, so making it capable of supporting other life in the form of more bacteria and fungi, insects, worms, and other animals.

From the gardener's point of view soils are classified according to the amount of sand or clay particles they contain, and according to their acidity or alkalinity. Clay particles are small and tend to adhere to one another making drainage and air penetration poor. Clay soils are sticky when wet and hard when dry.They are slow to warm up but usually rich in nutrients. The addition of organic matter greatly improves clay soils, as it causes the particles to cling together in larger groups, allowing moisture and air to pass through. Lime has a similar effect.

Sandy soils consist of large particles surrounded by air spaces. Water drains through sandy soils quickly and there is plenty of air. It warms quickly in spring but dries out fast and nutrients get washed out. Sandy soils are improved by the addition of plenty of organic material.

Silty soils are intermediate between clay and sandy soils. They are sticky and fairly heavy and can therefore be difficult to cultivate. Although lime does not improve this type of soil, adding organic material increases aeration and helps soil structure.

Loam is the ideal soil for the gardener, containing a mixture of clay, sand and silt particles, plus an adequate supply of organic material and plant nutrients. It is easy to cultivate, retains moisture and nutrients, and yet is well drained. Loam varies and may be classified as light, medium or heavy, depending on the clay-to-sand ratio.

Peaty soils are made up of partially decomposed organic matter, and are often acid and poorly drained. The addition of lime, nutrients, coarse sand, grit or weathered ashes, and constructing drainage systems improves their quality.

Soils naturally accumulate organic matter consisting of plant and animal remains in various stages of decay. Its presence ensures the continued survival of soil organisms essential to soil fertility. Decomposing organic matter also retains moisture, keeps the soil well aerated, and is a source of plant nutrients. On cultivated land organic matter is broken down more quickly than it would if left undisturbed, so supplies must be replenished regularly with well-rotted manure, garden compost or leafmould.

A: Unless cultivated this layer is just organic matter. B: Top-soil incorporating (A) when cultivated. C: Sub-soil of partially broken-down rock. D: Layer of fragmented rock. E: Bedrock or solid parent rock.

SOIL TYPES

Types	Advantages	Disadvantages
Clay	Usually contains a rich supply of plant foods because clay particles have the ability to retain nutrient elements until they are taken up in solution by roots.	Sticky when wet and hard when dry, so difficult and heavy to cultivate. Slow to drain, so prone to waterlogging and slow to warm up in spring.
Silt	Typically alluvial in origin, deep, fertile and with good water-holding capacity.	Silt soil packs down easily, so becomes airless. Sticky and cold when wet and dusty when dry.
Sand	Easy to work. Free-draining, so quick to warm up in spring.	Does not retain moisture. Can be naturally deficient in nutrients as many are easily washed out.

MANAGING YOUR SOIL

Knowing all about your soil enables you to manage it properly, to provide ideal conditions for soil life, and plant roots. This may mean improving drainage if it is poor (see page 40).

You will need to test the soil pH in case the acidity needs adjusting (see page 28).

You will also need to add organic matter and fertilizer, but what type, how and in what quantities? When do you cultivate and how much?

Techniques like mulching (see page 33) and green manuring (see page 165) are also part of good soil management.

CLAY SOIL

pH Check; add lime if necessary. The calcium in limestone can also help to aggregate clay particles, hence improving the soil structure. (On alkaline soils, it is possible to add gypsum for the same effect.)

Drainage The drainage of the top-soil is likely to be poor: Improve soil structure by adding organic matter. Avoid walking on the soil, particularly when it is wet. Use a bed system (see page 162). If the subsoil is clay, you may need a drainage system.

Watering Clay soil retains moisture well; mulch to help prevent drying and cracking in summer.

Cultivation It is particularly important only to cultivate when the soil is just moist, not too wet or too dry. Fork seedbeds in autumn and leave the frost to break up the clods until the structure improves.

Organic matter This is needed to make the soil more workable and improve drainage. Use as a mulch or fork into the top 15cm (6in) of soil. You do not need nutrient-rich organic matter. Leafmould and composted bark are valuable. Do not bury organic matter unless it is very well rotted as there is little air to help decomposition. Green manures are useful to break up the soil.

Nutrients Clay soils are usually rich in nutrients, but a good structure is necessary to allow roots to exploit them.

SILTY SOIL

pH Check; add lime if needed.

Drainage As for clay.

Watering As for clay.

Cultivation This is necessary to remove initial compaction, but avoid over-cultivating as it will destroy the weak structure. Use mulches to protect the surface and to prevent a hard "cap" from forming.

Organic matter This is needed to build up structure and help drainage as for clays. To provide nutrients apply well-rotted manures and compost.

Green manures Use to protect the surface of the soil and build up structure.

Nutrients Silty soils are not as fertile as clays. Check for deficiencies and correct if necessary.

SANDY SOIL

pH Check every year as lime easily leaches out of a sandy soil. Correct if necessary.

Drainage Sandy soils are free-draining and the presence of water may mean that a hard pan needs breaking or a drainage system is necessary.

Watering Add plenty of organic matter to retain moisture and apply a mulch.

Cultivation Avoid turning the soil over if possible as this speeds up the loss of water and organic matter. Mulch the soil to prevent the surface from drying out as it will not re-wet easily.

Organic matter This is needed to hold water and provide plant foods and prevent them being washed out. Use some nutrient-rich well-rotted manure and compost.

Green manures Use bulky green manures to add organic matter, stop nutrients leaching out, and prevent erosion.

Nutrients Sandy soils may lack nutrients, which are easily leached. Check new soils and add fertilizers if necessary.

Soil pH

The pH is a measure of the relative acidity and alkalinity levels. The amount of lime a soil contains governs its acidity. A soil rich in lime or chalk is said to be alkaline. One which lacks lime or chalk is described as acid, or sour. The degree of acidity or alkalinity is measured on the pH scale (see below), which runs from 0 to 14. A soil with a pH of 7.0 is termed neutral; higher readings indicate alkalinity and lower readings acidity. Soils with a pH above 8.5 and below 4.5 are rare. Most plants can be grown satisfactorily in soils with a pH in the range 6.0 to 7.0.

It is possible to reduce soil acidity by adding lime. Ground limestone (calcium carbonate) is the safest and easiest form of lime to apply. Other forms, such as quicklime (calcium oxide) and hydrated or slaked lime (calcium hydroxide), are available but they require careful application to avoid damaging plants in the vicinity. Application rates vary between 250–750 g/sq m (½–1½lb/sq yd), depending on the pH, soil type, and crops.

Apply lime in the autumn or after winter digging so that it is slowly washed in by rain. The best time is in winter when there is frost on the ground and no wind, thus lessening the chance of it blowing about. As a precaution wear safety goggles and gloves when applying lime and seek medical attention immediately in the event of a mishap. Always wash your face and hands after handling lime. Never apply lime at the same time as manure, compost or fertilizers as the lime may react chemically with these substances, releasing ammonia, which can damage plants, and wastes nitrogen. If both are required, apply lime and manure in alternate years. Do not apply lime every year; excess lime is likely to cause nutrient deficiencies.

It is difficult to reduce the pH level of a soil. Adding generous amounts of well-rotted organic matter will help, but where alkalinity is high, make a virtue out of necessity and choose some of the many lime-tolerant plants.

HOW TO TEST THE pH OF YOUR SOIL

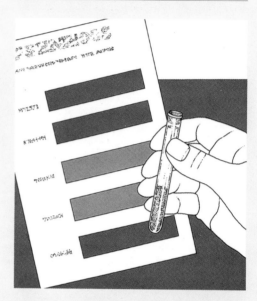

Simple soil-testing kits can be bought which allow a rough check to be made on the soil's pH level. Take small random samples of the soil from different parts of the garden and follow the instructions on the kit. The pH value is indicated by the depth of colour of the solution in the tube. Check the soil regularly, especially if you are attempting to modify the pH, by adding lime for example.

SOIL PH

pH 3	Acid 4	5	Neutral 6	7	Alkaline 8	9
Most plants fail	Acid-loving plants, such as camellias and rhododendrons, thrive.	Most fruit and acid-loving plants thrive.	Most plants thrive.	Tolerable to most plants except acid-loving.	Some plants thrive, such as spinach and clematis.	Most plants fail.
Substances toxic to plants released into the soil	Some plant nutrients washed out of the soil.	Phosphorus becomes less available to plants.	Iron and manganese become less available to plants.	Phosphorus becomes less available to plants.		

Short-term plant nutrients are supplied by fertilizers. Nitrogen (N), phosphorus (P) and potassium, or potash, (K) are the main elements required by plants; calcium and magnesium are also of considerable importance. Sodium, iron, molybdenum, copper, boron, manganese and zinc are essential, but only in small amounts. The main effects of NPK are shown below. Too much of one element may cancel the effects of the other.

Fertilizers may be organic or inorganic. Organic fertilizers are derived from animal or plant remains and include such materials as dried blood, meat and fish meal, and bonemeal. They tend to release their nutrients more slowly than do inorganic fertilizers, such as sulphate of ammonia, superphosphate of lime and sulphate of potash, which are produced by industrial processes.

Fertilizers may be simple or compound. Simple materials supply a major plant food only. For example, sulphate of ammonia supplies nitrogen, whereas compound fertilizers supply a mixture of plant foods. Growmore, for example, is a compound fertilizer which supplies balanced amounts of nitrogen, phosphorus, and potassium. Compound fertilizers are generally used to provide the basic requirements of plants and simple fertilizers, usually nitrogenous ones, are used to top-dress vegetables when the plants need a boost.

Plants usually receive most of their requirements as a base dressing, which is applied during final soil preparation, before they are planted or sown. Top dressings are commonly applied in solid forms around the base of plants. Most fertilizers are formulated as fairly coarse granules which are easy to distribute, but care is needed to ensure that they do not land in the middle of plants. This is likely to cause burning and scorching of the young tissues. Water in top dressing immediately. For ornamental plants, top dressings are likely to be a compound fertilizer rather than a simple one as in the case of vegetables.

ORGANIC FERTILIZERS

Bonemeal	High in phosphate, medium nitrogen
Dried blood	High in nitrogen
Fish blood and bone	High in phosphate, medium nitrogen
Hoof and horn	High in nitrogen
Rock phosphate	High in phosphate; an alternative to bonemeal
Seaweed meal	Low in phosphate medium nitrogen, medium potash
Wood ash	High in potash, low in phosphate and nitrogen

INORGANIC FERTILIZERS

Ammonium nitrate	High in nitrogen
General balanced fertilizer	Equal proportions of nitrogen, phosphate and potash
Liquid tomato and rose feeds	High in potash
Potassium chloride	High in potash
Superphosphate	High in phosphate

IMPORTANT PLANT FOODS

Food	Effects	Deficiency symptoms	Main fertilizers
Nitrogen	Encourages leafy growth. An excess delays flowering and fruiting; and also encourages soft growth which is easily damaged by cold and diseases.	Stunted growth. Pale yellow leaves. Premature ripening, often with improved flavour.	Ammonium nitrate Ammonium sulphate Calcium nitrate Nitrate of soda
Phosphorus	Necessary for good root development. Encourages crop ripening. Useful for strong seedling development.	Poor, stunted growth. Purple colouration of leaves and stems. Poor seedling growth. Fruits ripen very slowly.	Superphosphate (placed close to the roots). Bonemeal
Potassium	Prevents soft growth, makes plants more winter hardy and disease-resistant. Assists fruit development and ripening.	Generally slow growth. High disease incidence. Bronzing of leaves on some crops.	Potassium chloride Sulphate of potash (more liable to cause damage to young plants).

Making compost

One of the most valuable materials for improving soil structure and fertility is well-rotted garden compost. Most garden and kitchen waste can be recycled in a wooden or plastic compost bin. Spread woody materials before adding and mix in grass clippings with drier materials and stable manure. Do not add diseased material, perennial weeds or seeding heads; or cooked meat or fish scraps, or dog or cat litter. Stand the bin on soil and put a layer of twigs at the bottom for aeration.

How to make compost

Collect together as much material as you can. Chop it up with a spade, or use a shredder, then when you add it to the compost bin it will decompose faster.

Air is important for decomposition so turn the heap from time to time. Do not add mowings in bulk as they will turn slimy rather than decompose.

The level of the contents in the bin will drop as the material is broken down. Decomposition is faster in summer when temperatures are high.

Moisture is vital in compost making, so water the contents if it appears dry, or mix in lawn mowings or other succulent leafy waste.

Keep the heap covered with old carpet and a lid. Some bins – wooden or plastic – come in stackable sections, which makes handling compost easier.

PLASTIC BIN

Choose a model that holds 250–300cu litres or measures 1m sq. (3ft sq), and is open at the bottom for good drainage.

Leafmould is an excellent soil conditioner and mulch and is simple to make in a bin 1m sq. (1sq yd). The leaves can be collected every autumn and placed into a container. Do *not* go to the neighbouring woods to collect leaves or existing leafmould, as this will upset the natural cycle and deprive the trees of valuable nutrients. Leaves take a while to break down, but more than one bin will ensure a constant supply. Well-rotted leafmould is a useful soil improver and ingredient in seed and potting composts. Liquid feeds provide nutrients in a form that is readily available to plants. If you have animal manure available, it is easy to make. Manure from sheep is often considered the best, but that from cows, horses or goats is also suitable.

Making leafmould

Hammer four posts into the ground and staple wire netting round them. Fill the container with leaves, pressing them down and watering well if dry. The slow fungal decay process can then begin. As they decay, the leaves will become a dark friable material. They are usually left from one to two years before use.

Wormery

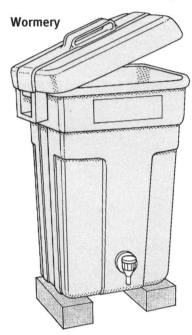

Making your own worm compost is a simple process and not at all smelly. Special compost worms are kept in a container and fed on kitchen waste and other compostable material, which they convert into a high quality compost. A wormery requires very little attention and can be fitted into small gardens. The best time to start a wormery is late spring.

Making liquid feeds

1 Place a bucketful of well-rotted animal or farmyard manure into a hessian sack and tie it securely. Hang the sack from a bar in a barrel or plastic dustbin containing 54.5 litres (14 gal) of water.

2 After two or three weeks the water will have become brown as dissolved nutrients seep out of the bag. Remove the bag from the container. Dilute the liquid with water until it is a pale straw colour before use.

Using liquid feeds

1 Liquid feed can be applied to the soil or used as a foliar feed. It can be watered on the soil direct but it is better to take it down to the roots by sinking a flower pot in the ground next to the plant.

2 A little manure water can be poured directly into the pot from a watering can. Use only when the soil is moist, after a fall of rain, or watering. If applied to dry soil plant roots may be damaged.

Mulching materials

It is essential that the soil is thoroughly moist before you apply a mulch, since rain will only percolate through the mulching material very slowly. Never apply mulches in winter or early spring when the ground is cold or frozen because the mulch acts as an insulation and will prevent the soil from warming up. quickly. However if the mulch is laid on warm, moist soil it will keep it that way and its moderating effect will be beneficial to plant roots and soil life.

USE OF LOOSE MULCHES

Mulch	Example of use	When	Main reason for use
Leafmould	On seedbeds	In autumn before sowing	To improve soil structure
	Around bedding plants, herbs, herbaceous plants	Any time when soil conditions are suitable	To improve soil structure and moisture content, and look attractive
Compost	On vegetable crops with a long growing period	When well-established and still actively growing	To provide nutrients, and keep in moisture
	Around herbaceous plants	In spring	To provide nutrients, keep in moisture, and improve soil structure
Worm compost	Around plants in pots or garden plants that need feeding	Any time when growing strongly	To provide nutrients
Well-rotted manure	Around plants that need a lot of feeding	When making quick growth usually in spring	To provide nutrients, particularly nitrogen
Shredded prunings	Over landscape fabric around trees and shrubs	Whenever soil conditions are suitable	To disguise landscape fabric
	On paths	Any time	To keep the surface clean
Chipped bark	Paths, play areas, woodland	Any time when conditions are suitable	To protect soil surface, control weeds, to provide a soft landing; to keep the surface clean
Composted bark	Around trees and shrubs, especially acid-loving plants	Any time when soil conditions are suitable	To control weeds, conserve moisture, improve soil structure, and look attractive
Straw	Around fruit on the ground	Before fruit forms	To keep fruit clean and keep in moisture
	Between widely spaced shrubs, fruit trees, and bushes	Any time when soil conditions are suitable	To control weeds, keep in moisture, and for winter protection
	On paths	Any time	To keep surface clean
Cocoa shell	Around bedding and herbaceous plants	When in active growth	To provide nutrients, look attractive, and control weeds
Gravel	On paths or drives	Any time	To keep surface clean and well drained; crunching noise provides security
	Rock gardens, trees, shrubs, and herbaceous plants	Any time when soil conditions are suitable	To keep surface clean, improves drainage; looks attractive

Mulching means covering the soil with a layer of material. It can either be biodegradable (leafmould, bark, or garden compost), or non-biodegradable (landscape fabric or gravel). Both types of mulch help to control weeds and to retain soil moisture.

They also protect the soil surface from being pounded by rain and keep plants clean. They insulate the soil keeping it at a more even temperature: warmer in winter and cooler during summer. Mulch when the soil is moist and warm.

Applying mulches

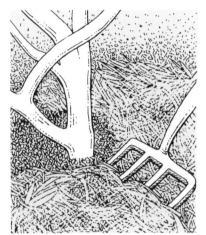

Loose mulches are best spread by hand round small plants and kept clear of the foliage. For fruiting plants, such as strawberries, tuck straw under the leaves to keep the fruit clean and dry.

Mulch round trees and shrubs annually. Spread a biodegradable mulch 5–10cm (2–4in) thick over the root area, but keep it clear of the stems and trunks as it can encourage fungal attack.

Gravel or pea shingle makes an excellent mulch around plants vulnerable to wet and also over heavy clay soils. Spread it 3–4cm (1–1.5in) thick over previously weeded soil and top it up periodically.

Sheet mulches

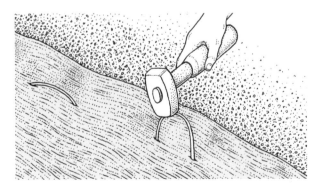

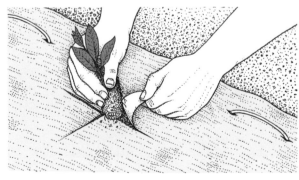

Spread sheet mulches over moist, clean soil and hold in position with staples or lengths of bent wire. Some sheet mulches, such as a geotextile or perforated plastic landscape fabric, allow water to penetrate. Black plastic sheeting is impermeable but ideal for helping to clear ground of weeds (see page 261).

To plant through a sheet mulch cut a cross and dig a planting hole in the soil. Cover sheet mulches with a 2–3cm (1in) layer of bark chips, gravel, or pebbles. This will not only look decorative but also helps to insulate the roots from extreme temperatures. Soil beneath plastic mulches can get very hot in summer.

Single digging

Digging is done for three reasons: to ensure that annual weeds are buried; to introduce manure or compost into the ground; and to aerate the soil. It is best tackled in autumn or early winter, leaving rough soil exposed to be broken down by the winter frosts. By spring, soil that has been well dug should merely need superficial attention, raking or a light forking, in readiness for sowing. Properly carried out, digging should not be an unduly strenuous exercise. Start off gradually and do a little at a time, half an hour on the first day. When the feel of the spade has been gauged, digging efficiently without too much physical effort becomes easier. The choice of tools is important. Choose a spade and fork that suit your height.

Single digging

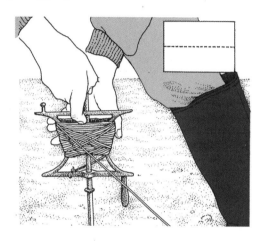

1 In autumn or early winter, once the soil has been cleared of all perennial weeds, divide the piece of ground to be dug down the middle with a garden line.

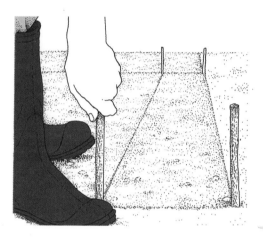

2 Roughly mark a 30cm (12in) wide trench area at the end of one half of the plot, where you want to start. If you are experienced this can usually be done by eye.

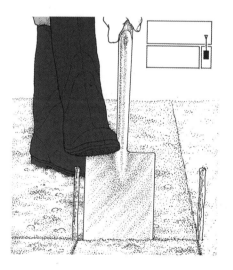

3 Thrust the spade blade vertically into the soil along the line of the trench and again at right angles across the trench to loosen the clod of of earth and allow it to be lifted easily.

ORGANIC MATERIALS TO ADD TO THE SOIL

Chipped bark	Slow to break down and during the process depletes soil of nitrogen. Poor soil conditioner.
Composted bark	Moderately rich in nutrients. Moderate conditioner.
Farmyard manure	Rich in nutrients but often contains weed seed. Good conditioner.
Garden compost	Good nutrient value. Good conditioner.
Leafmould	Good nutrient value. Good conditioner.
Seaweed	Rich in minerals. Good conditioner.

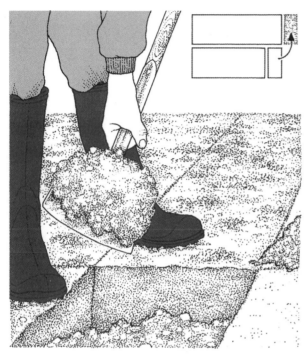

4 Lift the soil and place it in a line at the same end of the plot. It should be placed opposite what will be the last trench to be dug in the other half of the plot.

5 Dig across the half-plot making a trench in the marked area. In heavier conditions, break the surface of the soil on the side of each cut before digging and fork over the trench bottom.

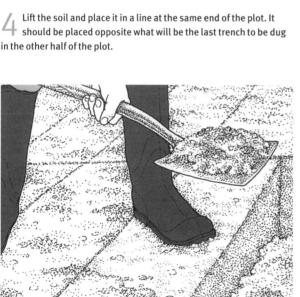

6 Incorporate manure or well-rotted compost, by digging it into the bottom of the trench. Then dig the next trench inverting the soil onto the manured area.

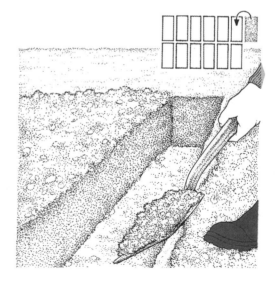

7 Proceed down the first half of the plot one trench at a time, and back down the second half, finishing by putting the line of spare soil into the final trench.

Double digging

Double digging is an extra thorough way of preparing the ground, but is rarely carried out nowadays. However, because it improves drainage, double digging is an especially valuable exercise on heavy soils which may be waterlogged or where a hard "pan", or layer of hard soil, exists. Such a hard pan may develop as a result of single digging over a number of years. Compacted ground is a poor growing medium in any case for any type of plant and double digging may be the answer to break it up. It is also worth double digging soil before establishing a "no-dig" system (see page 39), as it is essential that the soil is deeply cultivated to remove possible problems before you embark on this system of growing.

Start by dividing the plot down the middle and proceed around it in the same manner as for single digging (see page 34). However, in this case take out trenches about 60cm (24in) wide instead of 30cm (12in) as in the case of single digging. As the trenches are wider it is advisable to mark them out with sticks and a garden line in order to keep everything straight and square. Dig the first trench to a spade's depth. Then loosen up the sub-soil at the bottom of the trench with a garden fork. The fork should penetrate a further spit of soil, because the length of the tines is about the same as that of the spade blade. Break up the soil all over the area at the bottom of the trench and not just the area in the middle. If incorporating manure, dig it into the broken-up sub-soil.

Double digging

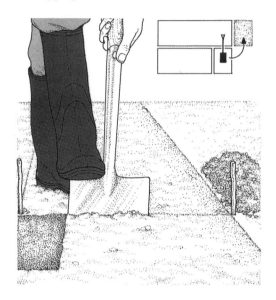

1 In autumn or early winter mark out the first 60cm (24in) trench. Dig it to a spade's depth, placing the soil at the same end of the plot but opposite the return half.

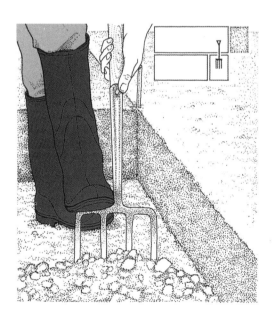

2 Fork the sub-soil to a spit's depth and mix well-rooted garden compost or farmyard manure into the broken soil. Do not mix the sub-soil with the top-soil.

3 Fill the first trench with the top spit of soil removed from the next trench. Fork and manure the sub-soil and repeat down both halves of the plot until complete.

Above: An attractive bed of green manure (*Phacelia tanacetifolia*) ready to be dug in.

Right: Bark chips not only create a cheap informal path but they can eventually be composted.

A mixed bed of annuals and
perennials in spring when the
plants are looking at their freshest.

No-digging methods

In no-dig gardening the soil is never dug except initially, to relieve compaction or break up a hard pan (see page 36). Repeated digging is not only hard work, but it turns up weed seeds, increases moisture loss and may affect soil structure.

To preserve the structure all organic materials are applied to the surface. This encourages the activities of soil organisms. As the soil should not be trodden, no-dig gardening is achieved by adopting a bed system (see page 162).

No-dig seed sowing

1 Before starting to sow, hoe over the area to be sown to remove any weeds and rake aside any coarse remains of the mulch from the previous crop.

2 With a garden line as a guide, use a hoe to draw out a drill: the mulch should have left the surface of the soil fine and crumbly in texture.

3 Water along the drill with a fine spray from a watering can if the soil is dry. Then sow the seeds, taking care to space them out thinly in the row.

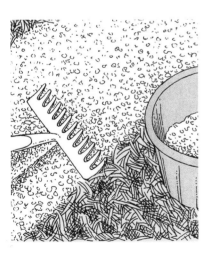

4 Cover the seeds by raking back the soil, or use fine crumbly leafmould or potting compost. Firm the surface lightly with the back of a rake.

NO-DIG PLANTING

If starting a new plot from pasture or weedy ground, clear it by digging thoroughly (see page 36). Once the ground is cleared of weeds, you will need to dig and mulch with rotted manure. Part the mulch before you plant. Dig a hole, keeping the soil removed separate from the mulch. Firm in and water the plant; then even out the surrounding mulch but keep it 5–10cm (2–4in) from the stem to prevent rotting.

Improving drainage

In order for plants to survive the soil must contain both air and water. In poorly drained soil, the roots of plants are restricted to the top few centimetres/inches so they cannot anchor properly or search far for nutrients. The causes of bad drainage may be due to a heavy clay soil, a hard pan in the sub-soil, through which water cannot percolate or a high water table. The water table is the level in the soil below which the ground is saturated. The level of the water table is higher in winter than in summer; normally it is found about 2m (6½ft) below the surface. Where the water table is high, artificial drainage will help move water to a lower level.

Cultivation

To improve the drainage of clay soils dig them deeply (see page 36) and incorporate plenty of grit and organic matter. Hard pans may not be far below the soil surface and can also be broken up by deep cultivation. If they are too hard for piercing with a fork they can be penetrated with a steel bar, which should be hammered through the impermeable layer at intervals. Where these measures do not work or the water table is high, artificial drainage should be considered.

Artificial drainage

Ditches are the cheapest way of draining land. They should be dug 1–1.2m (3–4ft) deep on sloping land, so water is carried to a receiving ditch at the bottom of the slope linked in turn to a soakaway or stream. Ditches can be left open as long as they are cleaned out annually or used to accommodate a covered, land-drain system, as shown on page 41. In small gardens or for small-scale drainage problems a rubble-filled pit or French drain should help. Lining drainage pits with a geotextile membrane allows water to seep in but prevents them from silting up with particles of soil.

Land drains

Originally land-drain systems were built of lengths of clay pipe, called tiles. Now it is more usual to use perforated corrugated plastic. This material is easily cut to length and can be bent round slight curves. The pipes are laid in trenches excavated in herringbone fashion across sloping land, with the main pipe leading to a soakaway situated at the lowest level. The trenches should be dug 60–90cm (2–3ft) deep and about 30cm (12in) wide. The distance between side branches depends on the soil type: on clay soil space them about 4.5m (15ft) apart; on loam space them 7.5m (25ft) apart; and about 12m (40ft) apart on light sandy soil.

Retaining walls

Waterlogging may also occur behind retaining walls. These may also retain a reservoir of water behind them if no provision is made for drainage. To provide weep holes leave one vertical joint unmortared every 1.5m (5ft) along the wall in every second or third course of bricks or stones. Backfill the base of the wall with rubble and install a drainage gully in front if the wall abuts a path or patio, to carry off the water that seeps through to a drain or soakaway.

Ditch

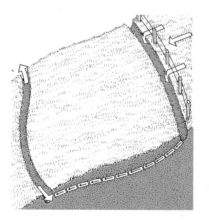

If the land slopes, dig a ditch across the top of the plot to intercept water from higher ground. Connect it, by ditches or land drains, to another ditch at the bottom of the slope.

Rubble

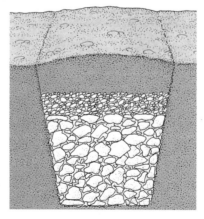

Line a 60–90cm (2–3ft) trench with a geotextile membrane and half fill with broken bricks or rubble. Cap with a layer of gravel and excess geotextile. Replace the top-soil.

Soakaway

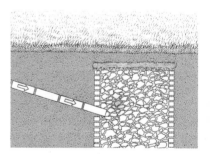

A soakaway must be constructed if there is no suitable watercourse for a drainage system to run to. Dig a hole up to 1.8m (6ft) deep and across. Lead the pipe into it. Line the hole with a geotextile membrane or unmortared bricks and fill it with rubble . Top with a geotextile membrane or upturned turves and cover with top-soil.

Installing a land-drain system

> **CAUTION**
>
> Do not be tempted to fill the trenches merely by returning the excavated earth. Otherwise soil will enter the pipes and slowly block them with sediment.

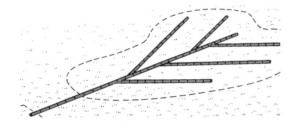

1 First mark out the drainage pattern in a herringbone pattern, using sand or spray paint. The number of side branches is mainly determined by the size of the site.

2 Dig out the trenches and clear off loose debris. Check the fall using a 2m (6½ft) plank and spirit level. Where trenches meet their bases must be at the same level.

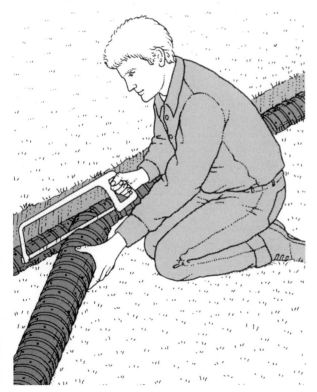

3 First lay the central pipe, which must lead to a soakaway. Then cut the plastic branch pipes at an angle so they fit roughly against the main pipe.

4 Cover the pipes with gravel and a layer of fine plastic mesh to prevent the land-drain system silting up. Finally fill in the trenches with top-soil and replace the turf.

GROWING FLOWERS

This chapter is devoted to the annuals, biennials, herbaceous perennials, and bulbs that are grown for their flowers, which together bring colour to the garden throughout the year.

TYPES OF FLOWERING PLANT

The shortest-lived plants are annuals, which germinate, flower and die all within one growing season. Biennials live a little longer, forming leaves in their first year and flowering in their second year, after which they, too, die. Herbaceous perennials, once they are established, flower regularly for years and often form large clumps. There are a few evergreens like bergenias, some epimediums and hellebores, but most retreat underground for winter, emerging once the weather warms in spring.

Bulbous plants are also perennial and produce some of the most spectacular flowers of all plants. Their above-ground phase is often brief but they continue their development underground fuelled by a food supply stored in swollen leaves, leaf bases or stems, described respectively as bulbs, corms, or tubers or rhizomes.

RAISING NEW PLANTS

Growing flowering plants from seed is the simplest and cheapest method of propagation, but it does require cleanliness and attention to detail for quality results. Hardy annuals are the easiest flowering plants to raise from seed as they can be sown *in situ*. The other groups of plants covered in this chapter are better sown in pots, seed trays or modular trays, and raised under cover. Half-hardy annuals and bedding plants require warmth to germinate and benefit from the protection of a heated propagator. Among these are many tender perennials grown as annuals and discarded after one season, such as lobelias and petunias. These plants need high temperatures to germinate, and growing them from seed takes time and space. This is not a problem if you have a greenhouse, but without one it is easier to buy plug plants or cartons of seedlings.

Plugs are young plants available by mail order from seed companies and nurseries, or direct from garden centres. You buy exactly the number you need and grow on the young plants yourself. Seedlings in cartons are rather more trouble as you have to prick them out as well as grow them on. The best containers to use for this operation are modular trays, as each plant can be inserted in an individual compartment. This means less root disturbance when repotting.

Bulbs raised from seed take several years to flower. Usually they also form clumps of offsets that can be lifted and separated. Herbaceous perennials multiply in a similar way and can be divided into pieces. This not only provides many small plants but also rejuvenates the clump and improves the soil by adding organic matter.

WHEN TO SOW

Annuals and perennials are usually sown in spring and detailed instructions are given on the seed packet. Hardy annuals may also be sown in autumn for an early display. You can collect your own seeds and store them in a cool dry place over winter or transplant self-sown seedlings. A few plants, like umbellifers and ranunculus must have their seed sown as soon as it is ripe.

Growing flowers – annuals

Annuals can be used in their own right as bedding or in containers, or used in mixed borders, sometimes to fill unexpected gaps. There are two main ways of acquiring annuals, the first is to buy them as young plants from garden centres or nurseries, and the second to grow them from seed yourself. The first way is easier, especially if you have neither the space nor the facilities for growing them. However it is more expensive and your choice is more limited than the range offered by most seed catalogues. Many gardeners also prefer to grow their own.

It is always important to plan annual schemes in advance. Draw plans of your bedding schemes so that you can work out plant quantities. It is always a good thing to allow for a number of spare plants to replace any losses or cater for any sudden extra needs.

The raising of annuals is not difficult. In most cases no special equipment is required, just a sheet of glass or a polythene bag to cover the pot until the seedlings emerge. These can be placed in a warm room on a windowsill as long as they are out of direct sunlight. Some annuals need warmth for germination and it is easier to grow these in a heated propagator, but again this is not essential. Seeds in pots can be kept in a warm airing cupboard until they have germinated and then moved into the light as soon as they start to emerge. An ideal arrangement is to have a heated propagator within a greenhouse and a cold frame that can be used for hardening plants off.

A pot 8–13cm (3–5in) will produce enough seedlings for most uses. Modular trays are useful as the seedlings suffer less root disturbance as pricking out is unnecessary. A tray will produce an excess of plants taking up much space and compost.

Starting annuals from seed

1 Mix small dust-like seeds, like begonia, with some dry, fine sand to make it easier to spread the seeds evenly.

2 Scatter the seeds so that they are spread thinly and evenly over the whole surface of the compost.

3 Sieve just enough fine compost over the seeds to cover them with a level and even layer.

4 It is important to label the container immediately with the name of the plant and the date of sowing.

5 Water the container with a fine-rosed watering can. Add fungicide to the water to prevent damping off.

6 Cover the container with a pane of glass. Stand, out of the sun, in a warm position at about 21°C (70°F).

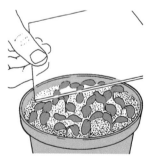

7 Remove the glass as soon as the seedlings start to appear. Place the container in a well-lit place.

8 Prick out the seedlings into individual pots or into trays as soon as they are large enough to handle.

As soon as seedlings can be handled, transplant them into a more suitable compost and give them enough space for unrestricted development. Do this while the seedlings are very small to minimise the amount of damage to the roots. If you wait until the seedlings are drawn and spindly and their roots entangled, they are unlikely to develop into strong plants and the chances of failure and disease increase. After pricking out return the seedlings to a warm protected environment to re-establish. When they are growing strongly wean them on to cooler conditions and pot them up individually when the leaves of adjacent plants touch. Seedlings raised in modular trays should be thinned to the strongest in each compartment.

Growing from seedlings

 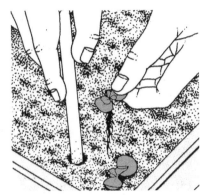 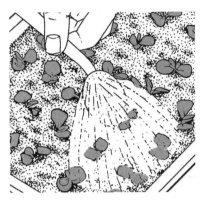

1 Give the side of the tray or pot a sharp tap to loosen the compost. Use a dibber or plant label to ease out a clump of seedlings. Work from the edge of the tray inwards.

2 Gently tease out individual seedlings. Lift each seedling by a leaf. Make a hole, deep enough to take the roots, in fresh compost in a clean tray, or a modular tray.

3 Place the seedling in the hole, then firm back the compost with the dibber. When the tray is full, water and place in a propagator to grow on. When the leaves touch pot up the seedlings.

SOWING TIMES FOR HALF-HARDY ANNUALS

Name	Height	Colour	Sow undercover	Comments
Ageratum	20cm (8in)	blues, pink, white	Early spring	Suitable for edging
Antirrhinum	60–90cm (2–3ft)	wide colour range	Mid winter	Good for cutting
Begonia semperflorens	20cm (8in)	pink, red, white,	Mid winter	Tolerates shade
Brachyscome (Swan River daisy)	30cm (12in)	blue, white, pink	Late wint.–early spr.	
Dahlia (bedding)	45cm (18in)	pink, yellow, orange, white	Late wint.–early spr.	
Gazania	25cm (10in)	yellow, orange, russet	Late wint.–mid spr.	Flowers only open in sun
Impatiens (Busy Lizzie)	20–45cm (8–18in)	pinks, mauves, oranges, white, and bicolours	Mid–late winter	Tolerates shade
Lobelia	15cm (6in) or more	blues, white, purple	Early spring	Tolerates some shade
Mesembryanthemum	10cm (4in)	range of vibrant colours	Early spring	Full sun essential
Nemesia	20–25cm (8–10in)	wide colour range	Early spring	For containers or bedding
Nicotiana (Tobacco plant)	50–75cm (20–30in)	green, yellow, white, red, pink	Early–mid spring	Suitable for shade
Petunia	30cm (12in) or more	range of colours and bicolours	Late wint.–mid spr.	For containers or bedding
Salvia	30–45cm (12–18in)	scarlet, blue	Late wint.–early spr.	For containers or bedding
Tagetes (African and French marigolds)	15–45cm (6–18in)	yellow, orange, russet	Early spring (African) Early–mid spring (French)	For containers or bedding

Potting and potting on

Potting, repotting, and potting on are some of the most frequent tasks that gardeners growing their own plants face. While they are not difficult, the basic techniques should be mastered, for if plants are not potted properly, no amount of subsequent care will make them grow to their full potential. Potting is the initial transfer of a seedling, rooted cutting, or bought-in plant to a pot or other container. Potting on is its transfer to a larger pot as it grows. Repotting is movement to a new pot of the same size as the old one, and renewing some of the compost around the rootball. As an alternative to conventional pots or trays, seedlings can be sown in or transferred to modular trays. Further movement or root disturbance is then unnecessary.

Potting

1 Place broken crocks or small stones to cover the drainage hole in clay pots; this is unnecessary for plastic pots. The seedlings to be potted should be watered an hour or two beforehand.

2 Hold the seedling, by one of its lower leaves, over the pot at the correct planting height and pour moistened compost around the roots in a circular motion so that the pot is evenly filled.

3 Tap the pot on the bench to evenly distribute the compost and to settle it around the plant. Further gently firm down the compost with the finger tips to exclude air pockets around the roots.

4 Place the potted seedlings in a position with good light, but out of direct sunlight, preferably in a greenhouse or cold frame. Water them using a fine rose to settle the compost around the roots.

Potting on

1 Water the plants to be potted on. Select a pot one size larger than the one that you are currently using. Cover the bottom of clay pots with crocks or small stones in order to keep the drainage hole open.

2 Place a hand over the top of the pot with the stem between the fingers. Turn the pot upside down and tap it gently on a surface such as a bench or table so that the rootball slides out of the pot and is held firmly by the hand.

3 Place a little compost in the pot and sit the rootball on it, adjusting the level so that the top of the rootball is just below the rim of the pot. Fill in with fresh compost, firm gently and tap the pot to remove any air gaps.

PEAT PELLETS

Peat pellets allow seedlings to grow and be transplanted without root disturbance. The plants should be potted on or planted out as soon as the roots emerge. The netting will decompose in the soil.

After seedlings have been pricked out they have to be weaned to a stage at which they can be planted out and survive cool temperatures, fluctuating water conditions and the effects of wind without their growth rate being affected. The same treatment is also necessary for young plug plants and plants raised from cuttings. This process of acclimatising plants to outdoor conditions is generally referred to as hardening-off.

Most seedlings will have been germinated in a protected environment during the early part of the year to produce a plant of sufficient size to be planted out as soon as the danger of frost has passed. Because so many seedlings are produced in the early part of the year, and they are not hardy, in most gardens there is a premium on any space that provides sufficient protection, plants tend to be grown at a high density.

Problems can occur when plants are crowded together. The plants tend to grow tall and spindly as they compete for light and there is an increased likelihood of fungal diseases affecting the stems and leaves. The various plants have different watering needs so more day-to-day care and attention are needed, which is, of course, time consuming.

Once the pricked-out seedlings have re-established, move them to a cooler environment. For this purpose there is no real substitute for a cold frame (see page 23), which should be kept firmly closed. Over the course of a few weeks increasingly air the frame during the day by raising the light, or glass cover, until the frame is open throughout the day: indeed the light may be completely removed during the day if the weather is warm. At the same time start to leave the frame open at night, at first just

a crack but then increasingly wide. However, close the lid if temperatures drop quickly or heavy rain is forecast. Eventually the lid can be removed completely once the young plants have been thoroughly hardened-off and ready to plant out in their growing positions.

Frosts as severe as -4°C (25°F) are sufficient to penetrate a cold frame, so, if this level of cold is expected, provide extra insulation to protect half-hardy plants. The best and most easily manageable insulation should be light yet thick; heavyweight fleece, coir matting, old sacks and similar materials are all useful and effective.

Feeding and watering

Regularly check the seedlings in the frame to ensure that they are not drying out excessively. They should not, however, receive too much water. If anything it is better to err on the side of dryness rather than risk waterlogging. Under these cooler conditions wet composts are increasingly susceptible to fungal root rots. Similarly, the close density of plants produces conditions under which leaf diseases may occur.

Another aspect of seedling management is the necessity for feeding. Many pricked-out seedlings will spend several weeks in the potting compost before being finally transplanted, and will need additional feeding. Thus the seedlings should be regularly fed using a liquid fertilizer (see page 29) as recommended by the manufacturer. Avoid over feeding as this will produce very vigorous plants whose growth will be checked on transplanting; it will also increase the risk of disease in the cold frame.

Hardening-off

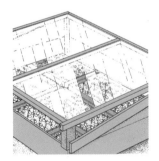

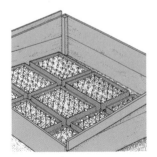

1 All plants raised or kept under glass must be hardened-off before they can be planted in the open. Once the air temperature rises in spring place the trays or individual pots of young seedlings or cuttings in a cold frame.

2 During the first week, as long as the weather permits, leave the light half open during the day to let the outside air circulate through the plants. However the light should be shut at night and during wet, windy, or cold weather.

3 During the second week gradually leave the lights open a little more each night – as long as the weather is not frosty. Towards the end of the second week remove the lights completely except in windy weather.

4 In the third week after the covers are left off completely, the plants can be moved outside the frame and left unprotected. At this stage they have been fully hardened off and can be planted out in their permanent position.

Planting out

Annuals can either be purchased or grown by the gardener from seed (see page 44). The plants should be strong growing, healthy and not overcrowded or drawn in their containers. If purchased by mail order, they are likely to arrive as "plugs" (small plants). Pot them up to establish them before they are planted in the open ground. It is important not to plant out tender annuals until the threat of frost has passed. If they have been kept under glass they must be hardened off properly before planting out.

Beds for planting can be prepared in the autumn after the previous season's annuals have been removed. At that stage remove any weeds and add well-rotted organic material to the soil. In spring, rake over the bed and remove any weeds that have appeared. Plant the annuals as shown below.

As the growing season progresses remove spent flowers to keep the display tidy and to promote further flowering. Later in the summer some annuals may have grown straggly. Cut back some of the looser stems to improve their appearance. Water during dry spells, but there should be no need to feed. As always, remove any weeds as they appear rather than waiting until they flower. In autumn remove the spent plants and either prepare the beds for next year or plant spring-flowering bedding.

Planting out

1 Before planting out ensure that the annuals have been thoroughly hardened-off. A few hours before planting out water them thoroughly with a fine-rosed watering can.

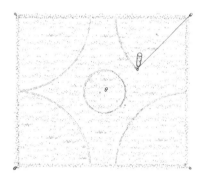

2 If the annuals are to be planted out in a bedding scheme, mark out the areas for each type of plant. A bottle filled with dry sand, which is allowed to trickle out, makes an efficient marker.

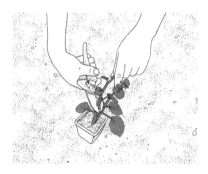

3 Many plants will grow long and straggly if their main shoots are allowed to grow on unimpeded. Check each plant and cut back any long growths so that they bush out with new lateral basal growths.

4 If the plants are in individual pots place them on the bed and stand back to check that the spacing and layout are correct. Avoid leaving plants that are not in pots lying on the surface as they will dry out.

5 Plants that are in strips should be gently teased apart. Avoid tearing the roots as much as possible. Do not buy plants that have outgrown their strips and have a dense tangled mass of roots.

6 Dig a hole with a trowel and plant. For most plants the top of the rootball should be just below the surface of the soil. Firm down with your hands and water with a fine-rosed watering can.

Hardy annuals may be sown directly outdoors. They look best growing in a series of interlocking irregular drifts. Draw a plan of the planting scheme on paper first. Roughly grade the annuals according to height with short plants at the front and the tallest at the back. Colouring in the bays also helps the plan. Before you sow prepare the soil (see page 34). Rake the surface level, leave for a week or two, and clear off any weeds that have germinated. Then mark out your design in the soil with a stick before you define the bays more clearly with flour or a trickle of sand. Draw out shallow drills within each bay; the drills should run at different angles in adjacent bays. Sow seed thinly, one type per bay, cover and label.

Direct sowing

 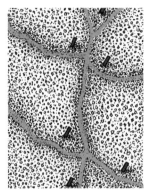  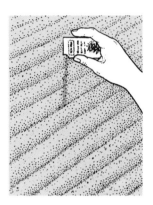

1 Mark out bays with a stick. Once you are satisfied with your design use sand to define the bays more clearly.

2 Draw out shallow drills within each bay. Sow the seeds thinly, one type per bay. Cover the seeds and mark with a label.

3 Once the seedlings have germinated thin the rows as necessary. By sowing in drills it is easy to see and remove weeds.

4 You can also broadcast the seed thinly over the entire bay. This works well for annuals that dislike disturbance, such as poppies.

HARDY ANNUALS FOR DIRECT SOWING

Name	Season of interest	Colour	Height	Comments
Agrostemma (Corncockle)	Summer	Bright pink	to 1m (3ft)	Sow *in situ*
Briza (Quaking grass)	Summer	Cream flowerheads	45–60cm (18–24in)	Seedheads dry well
Calendula (Pot marigold)	Summer	Yellow, orange	40–60cm (16–24in)	
Centaurea (Cornflower)	Summer	Blue	30–75cm (12–30in)	
Clarkia	Summer	Pink, mauve, red, white	45cm (18in)	Sow *in situ*
Consolida (Larkspur)	Summer	Blue, white, pink	1m (3ft)	Good for cutting
Cosmos	Summer	Pink, mauve, red, white	50cm (20in)	Good for cutting
Convolvulus tricolor	Summer	Blue, white and yellow	20–30cm (8–12in)	Attracts pollinating insects
Eschscholzia (California poppy)	Summer	Orange, yellow, cream	30cm (12in)	
Gypsophila elegans	Summer	White	60cm (24in)	Good for cutting and drying
Helianthus annuus (Sunflower)	Summer	Yellow or orange daisies	to 3m (10ft)	Birds enjoy the seedheads
Limnanthes (Poached-egg flower)	Summer	Yellow and white	15cm (6in)	Attracts pollinating insects
Nemophila maculata (Five-spot)	Summer	White with blue markings	25cm (10in)	Good for edging; sow *in situ*
Nigella (Love-in-a-mist)	Summer	Blue, white	40cm (16in)	Decorative seedheads
Papaver (Poppy)	Summer	Red and many other colours	15–60cm (6–24in)	Sow *in situ*; seedheads
Scabiosa stellata (Scabious)	Summer	Blue, pink, cream	30–45cm (12–18in)	Seedheads dry well

Planting perennials

Perennial plants are likely to be in the ground for several years, some for many years. It is therefore very important that the ground should be thoroughly prepared. Dig it in the autumn, clearing it of any old plants and perennial weeds. Add plenty of well-rotted organic material as you dig as this will help preserve moisture down by the plant's roots where it is needed, as well as providing nutrients. In the spring rake over the bed removing any perennial weeds that have reappeared.

Planting according to a prepared plan can start in the spring or earlier if the soil is not wet or frozen and the weather is fair. If the soil is still wet and time is limited, work from a wooden plank so that the soil is not compacted. Larger perennials may need holes dug with a spade, but the smaller ones can be planted using a trowel. Once you have finshed planting, mulch the surrounding soil (see pages 32–33).

Despite working to a plan there are always going to be a few plants that when they mature and start flowering are in the wrong place. These can be moved in the autumn or spring to a new position. Some plants never settle down and look unhappy. Sometimes this is because the rootball is too congested but with other plants you will find that just moving them a small distance away seems to solve the problem.

Planting perennials

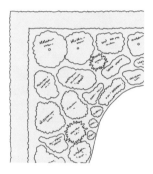

1 Before planting draw up a detailed plan of the border. This will not only help with the layout but also ensure that you obtain all the plants required before planting starts.

2 Water all the plants thoroughly several hours before you plan to start planting. Once they have drained you can move them to the site in readiness.

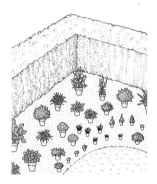

3 Position the plants, still in their pots, according to the plan. Stand back and check spacings, trying to visualise them in flower. Make any adjustments that are necessary.

4 Remove plants from their pots by placing the palm of one hand over the top of the pot with the stems between your fingers. Invert and tap the pot and the plant should slip out.

5 Starting at the back of the border, put the plants in their intended position. Dig a hole in the soil slightly bigger than the rootball of the plant with a trowel or spade.

6 Adjust the height of the plant by adding or taking out more soil from the base of the hole so that the top of the rootball is level with the surface of the soil. Spread the roots out.

7 Fill in the space around the plant using spare soil from the hole. Make certain that there are no air pockets. Gently but firmly press down the soil round the plant with your hands.

8 After planting is completed, water all the plants. Rake or prick over the bed using a fork to remove any foot marks and depressions; then apply a mulch.

While many herbaceous plants are low or strong enough to support themselves, others need some form of staking. This can be a time consuming exercise and so some gardeners try to avoid having to do it. There are several ways of avoiding this task, but using only sturdy plants that do not need support, and planting close together so that the plants support each other, are the two most common methods.

However, such restrictions limit the range of plants that can be used, and most gardeners find that they must do at least some staking. The main problem is wind, and planting a windbreak will do a great deal to improve the situation in most gardens. Strong draughts between buildings are another problem and the positioning of the bed and windbreaks of some kind may alleviate the situation. A further problem is rain. Heavy showers can beat the plants to the ground, and even a light shower can fill the flowerhead of a double peony, for example, with water and pull it over.

The secret of staking plants is to do it early when the growth is still quite short. This not only allows the plant to grow through and over the support, thus hiding it, but also to get support at an early stage. Strapping up a plant that has already flopped over very rarely works as it never looks natural. Try to keep all supports unobtrusive and hidden so that they do not detract from the attractiveness of the plants.

Herbaceous plant supports

Push pea sticks around the plant and bend their tops over to form a supporting grid through which the plant grows.

A metal hoop works the same way. The hoop should be at about half the plant's eventual height and raised with growth.

A series of linked metal stakes can be erected around and through the plant in a variety of configurations.

A sheet of square-mesh wire netting tied to stakes can be suspended over large areas of plants.

SUPPORTING WITH STAKES

Single stemmed and top heavy plants, such as large headed chrysanthemums, should be supported with canes. Each stem should have its own cane, tying two to a cane looks ugly as well as crowding the plant too much. In ornamental borders place the cane behind the stem to reduce its visual impact. This is not so important in reserve or nursery beds. Try to avoid pushing the cane through the roots. Tie the stem to the cane with soft string, raffia, or plant ties. Check ties regularly and tie in the top of the stem as it grows. You can also buy proprietary supports for individual stems.

Routine care of perennials

Planting a border and then leaving the plants to look after themselves is a recipe for disaster. It is important to undertake a regular maintenance programme in spring and autumn. Watering, weeding, and deadheading must be done when necessary.

Watering, weeding, and deadheading

Watering may be necessary in periods of drought and is essential for young plants until they are established. Weed regularly. Because perennials grow undisturbed for a number of years the chance of perennial weeds establishing themselves is greater, so it is important to remove them while they are young and before they get a chance to seed. Pernicious weeds like bindweed and couch grass need to be rooted out otherwise they will smother and weaken border plants.

Dead flower heads should be removed regularly. There are several reasons for doing this. Deadheading keeps the border looking neat. It will also prolong the display by encouraging more flowers and vigorous foliage by channelling the plant's energy into strengthening the root system, rather than into seed production. However, there are exceptions to this rule, if you want to collect seed for example. Also some plants have attractive seedheads that stand long into winter giving interest in the border at an uneventful time of the gardening year.

In spring

The first job is to tidy up the border removing all plant debris and winter protection. Cut back ornamental grasses and other plants left to stand over winter. Most perennials need lifting and dividing every three or four years to rejuvenate them. To do this dig up mature plants and discard the older inner pieces, and replant the younger outer pieces (see pages 58–59) in soil enriched with organic matter. Apply a balanced fertilizer around established plants (see page 29) and once the soil has warmed up and is thoroughly moist spread a mulch; this will reduce the need for watering in summer and will also suppress weeds (see pages 32–33). Stake plants early (see page 51) around and between the plants.

In autumn

This is the time to tidy up the border before winter, removing plant debris and weeds. Plants can be cut back once their display is over, but for those of borderline hardiness it is better to leave top growth to protect the crown over winter. In milder areas plants can be lifted and transplanted, but where hard winters are normal it is better to leave this until spring (see page 53).

PLANTS WITH ATTRACTIVE SEEDHEADS

Acanthus	*Foeniculum* (Fennel)
Achillea (Yarrow)	Ornamental grasses
Astilbe	(*Miscanthus*, *Stipa*)
Dipsacus (Teasel)	*Rudbeckia*
Echinacea	*Sedum spectabile* cultivars
Eryngium	

Deadheading

Some perennials are best cut down to the ground after flowering as this will promote fresh bushy growth and possibly a second flowering.

Other less vigorous perennials and annuals will not regenerate in the same season if cut back hard, so remove only the spent flowers at a leaf joint.

Some perennials and annuals throw up flowering stems direct from the ground, usually from a rosettes of leaves. Cut these stems out completely.

It is important that bulbs build up energy for the following year, so remove all flower heads before they seed, as this will use up the bulb's food resources.

Without some attention border plants will gradually become old and flower less well; the more vigorous plants will begin to grow into and through other plants. There are two main ways of maintaining a border: first by a regular programme of maintenance as described on page 52, with bursts in spring and autumn; second by digging out the border completely every few years, and cleaning and replenishing the soil with organic matter (see pages 29–32) before replanting. This is a major operation and unless you have space for the lifted plants it could be easier to divide the border in half and do the job over two years.

Renovating a border

1 After moving the plants to a temporary bed, clear the ground of weeds.

2 In late summer dig the border over and add plenty of well-rotted organic matter.

3 In mid autumn replant the border. Space the plants correctly and water them in.

4 In the early spring hoe off any weeds, and apply a compound fertilizer and mulch.

HARDY HERBACEOUS PERENNIALS

Name	Height	Flowers	Comments
Acanthus (Bear's breeches)	to 1.2m (4ft)	Mauve and white; summer	Handsome foliage; faded flower heads attractive
Alchemilla (Lady's mantle)	50cm (20in)	Yellow-green; summer	Good ground cover and edging
Aster (Michaelmas daisies)	30cm–1.8m (1–6ft)	Purples, pinks, white; summer/autumn	Attracts bees and butterflies; good for cutting
Coreopsis	60–75cm (2–2½ft)	Yellow, pink; summer	Good for cutting
Delphinium	60cm–2m (2–7ft)	Blue, white, pink; summer	Stake tall plants
Doronicum	45–60cm (1½–2ft)	Yellow; spring	
Echinops (Globe thistle)	1–1.5m (3–5ft)	Blue, white; summer/autumn	Flowers cut and dry well; tolerates poor, dry soil
Gaillardia	30–60cm (1–2ft)	Red and yellow; summer/autumn	Good for cutting; require well-drained soil
Geranium (Cranesbill)	25–60cm (10–24in)	Pink, purple, white; summer	Good for ground cover; clip over after flowering
Helenium (Sneezeweed)	60cm–1.5m (2–5ft)	Orange, yellow, rust; summer/autumn	Support tall plants
Hosta (Plantain lily)	60cm–1m (2–3ft)	Mauve; summer	Grown for blue, green, or variegated leaves
Iris (bearded)	15cm–1.2m (6in–4ft)	Many colours; late spring/summer	Divide after flowering
Kniphofia (Red hot poker)	60cm–1.2m (2–4ft)	Red, orange, yellow; summer	Protect over winter in cold areas
Lupinus (Lupin)	60cm–1m (2–3ft)	Many colours and bicolours; summer	Stake tall plants
Paeonia (Peony)	60cm (2ft)	Red, pink, white; early summer	Support plants
Papaver (Oriental poppy)	60cm–1m (2–3ft)	Red, white, pink, apricot; early summer	Support plants
Phlox	60cm–1m (2–3ft)	Pink, red, white, mauve; summer	Support tall plants; shade tolerant
Rudbeckia (Coneflower)	60cm–1.2m (2–4ft)	Yellow; summer/autumn	Stake tall plants
Solidago (Golden rod)	75cm–1.2m (2½–4ft)	Yellow; summer/autumn	Remove flower heads to prevent self-seeding
Stachys (Lamb's ears)	30–40cm (12–16in)	Pink	Grown for velvety silver leaves
Veronica (Speedwell)	20cm–1.2m (8in–4ft)	Blue, pink, white	Stake tall plants

Collecting and drying seedheads

Not many gardeners collect their own seed but there are several good reasons for doing so. It enables you to increase your own stock of plants, both for your own use and for giving away or selling. You may well have plants that are not commonly available and collecting seed helps to give other gardeners the opportunity to acquire them. One of the most exciting reasons for collecting seeds from your own open-pollinated plants is that there is always a possibility that they will produce a new variety of note. As a general rule seedheads are picked as they become ripe but before the seeds are dispersed.

Collecting and drying seedheads

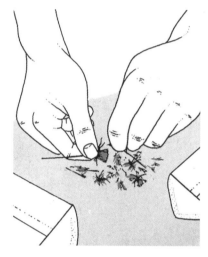

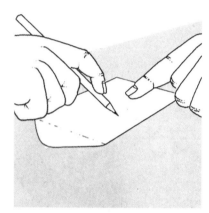

1 Collect small seedheads when nearly dry. Place in an open paper bag and leave to dry further.

2 Open the dried seedheads. Remove all the bigger pieces of detritus and then separate the seed from the chaff.

3 Place the dried seed into linen bags or paper envelopes. Label clearly and store in a dry, cool place.

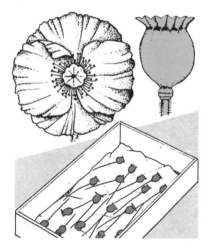

Spread fleshy capsules on paper in a tray or box. Leave them to dry until they burst open and the seed can be extracted.

Bunch other types of flowers together by the stems before hanging them to dry with their heads enclosed in a paper bag.

PERENNIALS FROM SEED

Seed from species usually breed true, but seed collected from most hybrids and cultivars will not breed true and their offspring may well be a disappointment. Try raising seed from:

Aquilegia
Campanula
Coreopsis
Doronicum
Erigeron
Eryngium
Geranium
Helleborus (sow fresh)
Meconopsis (sow fresh)
Thalictrum
Veronica

Right: The pasque flower (*Pulsatilla vulgaris*) grows well in an open site, such as a rock garden.

Below: The common sage (*Salvia officinalis*) is not only a useful culinary herb but is also attractive when in flower.

Below: Used for both culinary and medicinal purposes, angelica (*Angelica archangelica*) is a statuesque herb that needs plenty of space.

Above: Chinese chives (*Allium tuberosum*) illuminate a potager in late summer. All parts are edible.

Raising herbaceous perennials from seed is a useful way of producing a quantity of plants, but there is no guarantee that the offspring will be identical to their parent. Some species as well as cultivars can be very variable. If you want to be certain that you are getting identical plants, then divide the clumps (see pages 58–59) or take cuttings (see pages 60, 124–25). However slight variation often does not matter, and seed is a convenient way of growing extra plants.

Raising perennials from seed

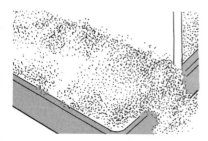

1 Heap a good quality seed compost into either a tray or a pot. Firm gently, then strike off level with the rim.

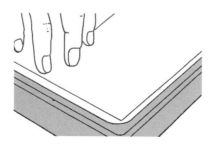

2 Firm compost to within 5–10mm (¼–½in) of the rim using a presser board or the flat bottom of a clean tray.

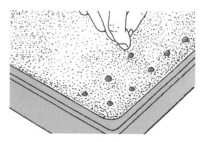

3 Sow large seeds individually a regular distance apart. Scatter smaller seed from the hand or packet evenly and thinly.

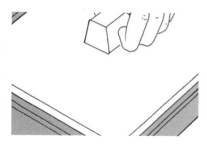

4 Firm the seeds gently into the compost with a presser board or the clean bottom of another tray or pot.

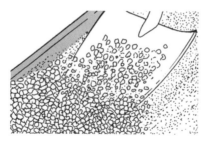

5 Cover the seeds with a layer of grit vermiculite or sieve a layer of compost about the thickness of the seed over them.

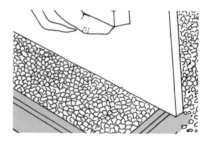

6 Level off the top of the grit by striking it off with the presser. Very gently firm down compost, if used, with the presser.

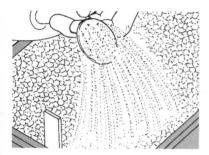

7 Label with the name of the plant and the date. Water with a fine-rose watering can and place on a well-drained surface.

8 Apply fungicide to the seedlings at regular intervals to prevent them damping off. Do not over-soak the compost.

9 Prick out the seedlings at the two to six leaf stage into individual pots. Hold the seedling by a leaf.

Dividing perennials with fibrous crowns

Dividing a plant is the usual way to propagate a large number of herbaceous perennials, and it is also the method used to rejuvenate existing plants that have been in the ground for some time. Division is a comparatively easy method of propagation. The only variable feature is the time of the year at which division is carried out.

As a general rule, the most opportune time to divide such plants is directly after flowering, as this is when the new vegetative shoots are being produced and the new root system is developing. However if this is in the dryness and heat of the summer, such plants should only be divided and the divisions put into pots if their environment can be controlled. For division and direct replanting it is best to wait until the spring, just as the plants are coming into growth. If you want to divide and replant after flowering it is important to do this during dull, preferably damp, weather. Keep the plants well watered until they have become established. If the weather turns very hot and sunny screen the plants until they are well established.

Division of fibrous crowns

1 Lift the plant that is to be divided with a garden fork, loosening the soil around it to prevent roots tearing.

2 Shake as much loose soil from around the roots as possible. This may be difficult in heavy soils.

3 If plants are infested with perennial weeds wash off any remaining soil in a bucket of water and separate.

4 If dividing during the growing season, reduce the height of the taller stems to minimise water loss.

5 Many clumps will divide easily into smaller pieces, by teasing them apart with the fingers into individual plantlets.

6 Some are more difficult and will need to be cut into individual portions, each with a growing point.

7 Vigorous outer portions can be replanted directly into the soil as long as the weather is not too hot or dry.

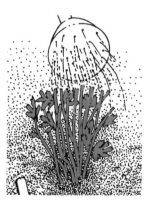

8 Water the plants in well. Unless the weather is wet, continue to water until plants are well established.

Some plants with fibrous-rooted crowns: *Achillea, Alchemilla, Aster, Aubrieta, Caltha, Campanula, Chrysanthemum, Doronicum, Erigeron, Gentiana* (some), *Geranium, Helenium, Hemerocallis, Lythrum, Mimulus, Monarda, Polemonium, Prunella, Pyrethrum, Rudbeckia, Scabiosa, Tiarella, Trollius, Veronica.*

Dividing perennials with fleshy crowns

Perennials with fleshy crowns frequently have roots that are more entangled and individual crowns that are joined together. These will be difficult to pull apart with the fingers, but can easily be divided by using a sharp knife. It is better to wash off all soil so that you can see what you are doing. Plants are best potted and grown on before replanting. Plants with runners are very easy to propagate – it is just a matter of severing the runner and digging up the new plant when it has rooted.

Dividing fleshy crowns

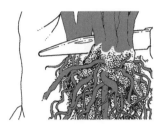

1 Lift the plant in the spring before it has got into active growth, when the soil is workable and beginning to warm up.

2 Wash the crown well, removing all the soil. If it will not easily pull apart, cut between individual crowns.

3 Dust the cut surfaces with a fungicide and replant into individual pots. Plant out when they have become established.

Propagating by runners

1 Runners are more or less horizontal stems that spread out from the main plant. Either at their tips or at points along the runners new plants will be formed. These can be dug up and replanted elsewhere.

2 To make it easier to transplant plants formed on runners, perhaps for giving away, they can root directly into a pot. Fill a 9cm (3½in) pot with a good quality potting loam-based compost, such as John Innes no. 1.

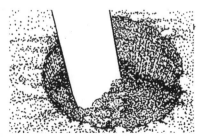

3 Dig a hole near a plantlet that is just beginning to develop. Place the pot of compost in the hole.

4 Position the plantlet over the centre of pot of compost and pin the runner with a piece of bent wire.

5 When they have rooted the runners can be severed and the plant, still in its pot, removed and replanted elsewhere.

Some plants with fleshy crowns: *Hosta, Sedum spectabile , Yucca.*
Some plants that produce runners: *Ajuga reptans, Fragaria* (Strawberry), *Geum reptans*, Grasses (some), *Saxifraga sarmentosa.*

Perennial root cuttings

Tap and thick-rooted plants are often difficult to increase by division or from stem cuttings. One way to increase plants is to take root cuttings. This is usually done in the early to mid winter while the plants are dormant. Enough for most purposes (up to

about seven) can be fitted vertically into a 9cm (3½in) pot of cutting compost and covered with a thin layer of grit. The pots are then placed into a cold frame until shoots appear above the compost when they can be potted up.

Root cuttings

1 Lift the plant in its dormant season. Remove any loose soil from around the roots, and any remaining top growth from the previous season.

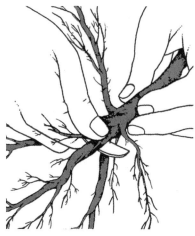

2 Wash off any remaining soil from its roots in a bucket of water. Then cut off a few thick young roots close to the crown and set them aside.

3 Return the plant to its usual position in the garden, planting at the same depth it was before being removed.

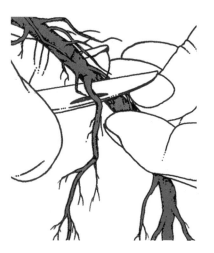

4 With a knife cut off cleanly any fibrous lateral (side) roots that appear on the main root, if necessary. Try not to damage the root in the process.

5 Make a right-angled cut at the end where it was severed from the parent plant. This flat cut will indicate that it is the top of the cutting.

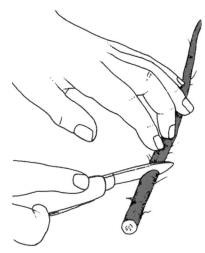

6 About 5cm (2in) below cut across the root at an angle. The cutting is then inserted upright (flat cut at the top) in a pot of cutting compost.

Hardy perennials: *Acanthus, Anchusa, Anemone x hybrida, Eryngium, Limonium, Papaver, Phlox, Romneya, Verbascum.*
Alpine plants: *Anchusa, Erodium, Geranium, Primula denticulata, Pulsatilla.*

A rhizome is a stem that grows laterally either just on or below the soil surface. In many cases it stores food. There are two types of rhizome found among perennials. The continuously extending ones, such as mint, are easily divided by digging up the new plants as they appear from the underground rhizome. The thicker ones, such as irises, that extend through lateral buds need more care. The best time to divide these is immediately after flowering. Replant at the same depth as the original plants.

Division of bearded iris

1 Divide the rhizomes of crowded clumps as soon as all the flowers have faded when the old root system dies back.

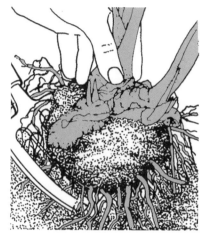

2 Lift the clumps with a fork being careful not to damage the rhizomes. Loosen and remove as much of the soil as you can from the roots and rhizome.

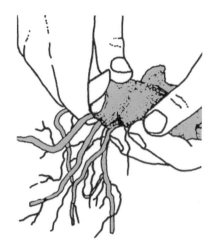

3 Cut away and discard any old rhizome from the current season's growth with a knife. All cuts should be clean and dusted with fungicide.

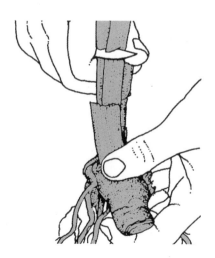

4 Shorten back the leaf blades with a clean cut to form a fan about 10cm (4in) long, and then cut back the roots to about 5–8cm (2–3in).

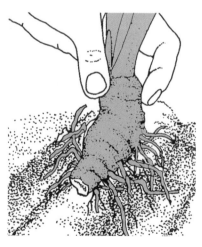

5 Replant each rhizome at the same depth as before, so that the top half remains exposed while its roots are buried in the soil.

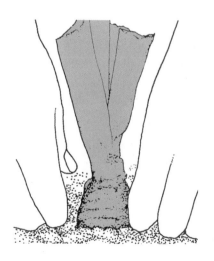

6 Gently firm back the soil over the roots, leaving the bulk of the rhizome exposed to the sun. Resettle the soil by watering, and clearly label the plant.

Some plants that produce rhizomes: *Canna*, *Convallaria majalis*, Ferns (some), *Iris* (bearded), *Mentha* (mint), *Polygonatum*, *Zantedeschia*.

Dividing tuberous-rooted perennials

Some herbaceous perennials, such as dahlias, die back to crowns of buds each dormant season, and their roots are modified to store food. These specialised swollen roots are described as tuberous roots. Just before the growing season, divide the tuberous roots into portions, each with at least one crown bud. Protect all cut surfaces with a dusting of sulphur. Place the divisions in a warm (21°C/70°F), airy place for two days to seal the surface, and then pot up in John Innes no. 1.

Dividing dahlia tubers

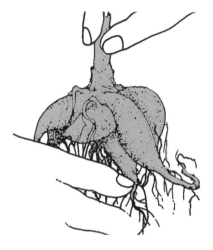

1 Carefully lift a plant at the end of the growing season. Cut off the stem leaving about 5cm (2in). Remove all soil and clean the crowns thoroughly.

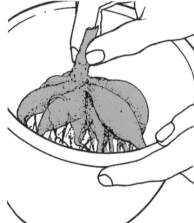

2 Dust the entire crowns, including the crevices, with a fungicidal powder to protect them. Place them onto a few sheets of old newspaper.

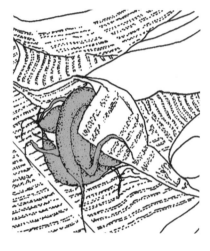

3 Either cover with slightly moist compost or loosely wrap in newspaper. Store in a tray in a dry, cool, frost-free place until the buds begin to swell.

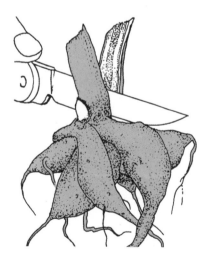

4 Just before the growing season starts divide the tuberous roots into portions with a knife; each portion should have at least one swollen crown bud.

5 Dust all the cut surfaces with a fungicide and place divisions in a warm, dry, airy place for a few days while the cut surfaces seal themselves.

6 After two or three days the cut surfaces will have formed a corky layer. At this stage pot up the divisions into individual pots.

Some plants that produce tubers: *Cosmos atrosanguineus, Dahlia, Nymphaea* (water lilies).

Bulb is a term commonly used to describe plants that develop underground storage organs. These include true bulbs, like daffodils, and corms, which include crocuses and gladiolus. Other storage organs formed by perennial plants are rhizomes (see page 61), and tubers (see page 62). Rhizomatous and tuberous plants are sometimes grouped under bulbs.

Superficially bulbs and corms look similar, but their structure differs considerably. Bulbs are modified stems with fleshy, scale-like leaves. Some bulbs, daffodils and tulips, for example, are covered with a papery membrane, or tunic, while lilies and fritillaries lack this membrane and are described as naked because the fleshy leaves are exposed. Because they lack the protective tunic naked bulbs need to be handled with great care. Corms are generally shorter and broader than bulbs and hold their food store in a swollen stem. They have a covering of papery scales that protect lateral buds.

Buying bulbs and corms

Always buy bulbs and corms from a reputable grower specialising in these plants. Most of these operate a mail order service, and it is in their interest to sell good quality, disease-free bulbs that have been grown commercially, and not collected in the wild. If you buy bulbs loose from a garden centre or nursery select only the largest, firmest, and plumpest bulbs. The covering membrane should be intact and there should be no sign of disease or sprouting. It is a false economy to buy very small, soft or shrivelled bulbs as they will rarely do well and frequently do not produce any flowers.

Planting bulbs and corms

Mail order suppliers will send you bulbs at the right time for planting. In general spring-flowering bulbs are planted in early autumn; summer-flowering bulbs in early spring; and autumn-flowering bulbs in early summer. More details are given in the chart on page 65.

Bulbs are easy to plant and can be grown in borders or in containers, or they can be "naturalized" in grass or woodland. In the garden plant bulbs individually with a bulb planter or narrow-bladed trowel at the correct depth (see page 65) – for most bulbs this is two to three times their height.

Groups of bulbs can be planted in borders among shrubs and other perennials, as shown below. The surrounding plants will mask the dying foliage, which although unsightly should be left to die down naturally. Mark where the bulbs are so you don't dig them by accident or pierce them with a fork.

Bulbs planted in formal spring bedding schemes should be lifted once the display is over to make way for summer displays. Heel the bulbs in so the leaves can die down naturally, and then lift and store (see page 66).

Plant narcissus bulbs in containers in two staggered layers so the flowering period is lengthened. For instant colour bulbs can be planted in perforated baskets, like those used for aquatic plants, or plastic troughs, drilled with extra drainage holes, and plunged into the border soil or a container such as a window box. When the display is over the basket is lifted and moved to an out-of-the-way place in the garden so the bulbs can die down out of sight.

Planting bulbs outdoors

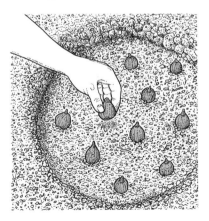

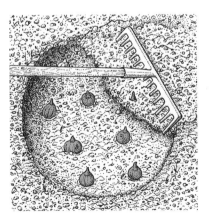

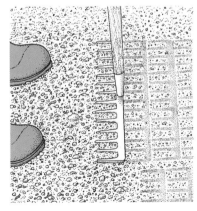

1 Bulbs can be planted individually with a trowel or by drawing back the earth over a larger area. Unless in precise bedding schemes, bulbs look better in groups.

2 Bulbs are usually planted at a depth equal to two or three times their height and spaced twice their width apart. Cover the bulbs with soil, ensuring they stay upright.

3 Once the bulbs have been covered over, gently tamp down the soil with the back of the rake and then rake it over. Water the area thoroughly.

Naturalising bulbs

Bulbs naturalised in grass or woodland can be left undisturbed for years. Each bulb will increase to form a clump so don't plant the bulbs too closely together initially. Before you plant make sure the soil is thoroughly moist and free from perennial weeds. In lawns this means spot weeding or digging out any dandelions or plantains. Cut the grass, too, as planting large quantities of bulbs is a back breaking task. To make the job easier use a long-handled bulb planter, which is far less effort to insert than a short-handled version. Naturalised bulbs do not have to be spring flowering. Remember the autumn-flowering crocuses and colchicums. Plant these in gaps left among the daffodils, crocuses, and snowdrops.

Naturalising small bulbs in turf

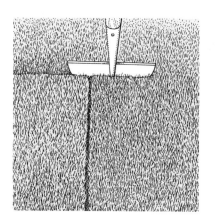

1 Use a sharp border spade or half-moon edging tool to cut an H-shape in the turf. Cut deep down to get below the roots of the grass.

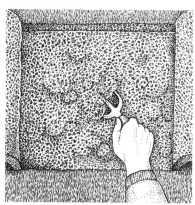

2 Peel back the turf and fork over the soil. Use a border fork as the soil will be compacted. Scatter the bulbs thinly and randomly over the soil surface.

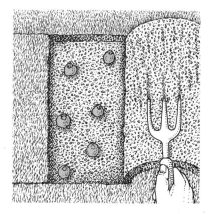

3 Press the bulbs lightly into the soil. Roll back the two flaps of turf and firm gently into place. Avoid applying weedkiller over naturalised bulbs.

Naturalising large bulbs

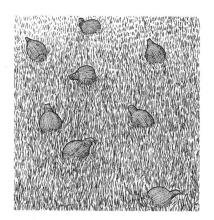

1 Planting bulbs in a natural-looking distribution can be difficult. However try gently scattering the bulbs on the ground, and plant them where they fall.

2 A trowel can be used to plant bulbs but a special bulb-planter is easier. Press it into the soil with a twisting motion. When you lift it out, a plug of soil comes as well.

3 Place the bulb in the bottom of the hole. Remove the plug of soil from the bulb-planter and re-insert it into the hole, covering over the bulb.

PLANTING DEPTHS

As a general rule bulbs and corms are planted at
approximately two or three times their own depth.
However, some bulbs, like nerines, do better if their tip,
or nose, is at or just below soil level. At the other extreme
tulips are planted deeply, at about four times their depth.
Crocuses and bluebells are examples of bulbous plants
that are capable of pulling themselves down to the depth
they prefer by means of special contractile roots.

The chart shown here gives an indication of the
various depths needed for the different types.
The letters given beside the name of each bulb
refer to the planting depth chart.

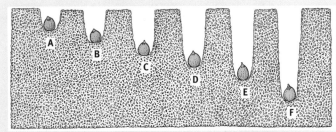

Anemone A–B	Galanthus A–B	Muscari B
Chionodoxa B	Gladiolus D	Narcissus C–E
Colchicum E	Gladiolus, species B–C	Narcissus, miniatures A–B
Crocus A–B	Hyacinth C	Scilla A–B
Eranthis A	Iris A	Tulipa C–D
Erythronium B	Lilium B–F	

BULBS FOR THE GARDEN

Name	Colour	Flowers	Plant	Comments
Allium	Mauve, pink, white, green, yellow	Late spring–mid summer	Early–mid spring	
Camassia	Blue, white, pink	Early–mid summer	Early–mid spring	
Cardiocrinum (Giant lily)	White	Mid–late summer	Early–mid spring	Moist shade; plant so tip is just proud of soil
Chionodoxa (Glory of the snow)	Blue	Early spring	Early–mid autumn	
Colchicum	Mauve, pink	Early–mid autumn	Early summer	Leaves appear in spring
Crinum	Pink, white	Late summer–early aut.	Late spr.–early summer	Plant in sheltered sunny place so tip is just proud of soil; leave clumps undisturbed
Crocosmia (Montbretia)	Orange, yellow, red	Early summer–early aut.	Early–mid spring	
Crocus (spring flowering)	Mauve, white, yellow	Late winter–early spring	Early–mid autumn	
Crocus (autumn flowering)	Mauve	Early–mid autumn	Early summer	Leaves appear after flowering
Erythronium (Dog's-tooth violet)	Pink, white, yellow	Early–mid spring	Early–mid autumn	Moist shade
Fritillaria (Fritillaries)	White, yellow, purple, blue, pink	Early–mid summer	Early–mid autumn	
Galanthus (Snowdrops)	White	Early–late winter	Early–mid autumn	Divide clumps after flowering
Gladiolus	Many colours	Mid summer–early aut.	Early–mid spring	Lift before frost and store indoors over winter
Hyacinthoides (Bluebells)	Blue, white, pink	Mid–late spring	Early–mid autumn	Moist shade; self seeds
Hyacinthus (Hyacinth)	Blue, pink, white, yellow, apricot	Mid spring	Early autumn	
Iris (Reticulata type)	Mauve, purple	Mid–late winter	Early autumn	Plant in alkaline soil
Lilium (Lilies)	Many colours	Mid summer–early aut.	Mid–late winter	Most prefer acid soil
Muscari (Grape hyacinth)	Blue, white	Early–mid spring	Early–mid autumn	Self seeds
Narcissus (Daffodils)	Yellow, white	Mid winter–mid spring	Late summer–early aut.	
Nectaroscordum siculum	Green and purple	Late spring–early summer	Mid autumn	Moist shade; self seeds
Nerine	Pink, white	Early autumn	Late spring	Plant in sheltered sunny position; leave clumps undisturbed
Scilla (Squill)	Blue, violet, white, purple, pink	Early–mid spring	Early–mid autumn	Self seeds
Tulipa (Tulips)	Many colours and colour combinations	Early–mid spring	Mid-late atumn	Bedding cultivars can be discarded after flowering

Dividing bulbs

The most common way of increasing a stock of bulbs is to lift a clump and divide it. Even if you do not want extra bulbs it is still important to lift clumps up every few years and divide them, as clumps that are left undisturbed for years become overcrowded and their flowering declines dramatically. The best time to divide many bulbs is in the dormant period, but some, such as snowdrops, are better divided once the leaves begin to turn pale green or yellow. Dividing them earlier can prove detrimental.

Splitting bulb clumps

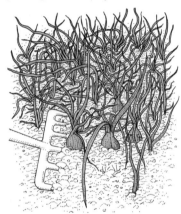

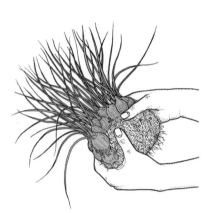

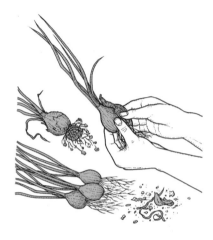

1 Lift clumps of bulbs to be divided with a fork. Put the fork into the soil well clear of the bulbs, dig under them and lift. If you go too close to the clump the tines of the fork may pierce some of them.

2 The bulbs will often come out of the soil in a solid clump. Gently shake some of the soil off the roots and then gently but firmly pull away the bulbs one at a time.

3 Remove any loose dead material from around the bulb. If the leaves have died back, remove them. Check the bulbs and discard any that are damaged or diseased before replanting.

Storing bulbs

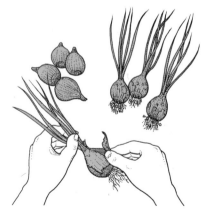

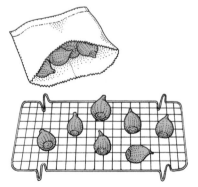

1 Lift bulbs once their foliage has begun to turn yellow and die back. If the foliage is still green (for example, tulip bulbs used in spring bedding), replant them elsewhere until it dies back.

2 Clean the lifted bulbs, removing any loose membranes and other dead material. Cut or pull off the remains of the leaves and clean off any soil from the roots. Discard any damaged or diseased bulbs.

3 Place the bulbs on a rack, with plenty of space around each, and let them dry off for a day or so. Dust them with a fungicide and place them in paper bags or envelopes in a dry, cool but frost-free place.

Some bulbs, notably lilies, develop tiny bulbs called bulbils, where the leaf joins the stem. These can be removed after the flowers fade and used for propagation purposes. Below ground many bulbs and corms develop offsets and this is the main means of propagation for gardeners. These tiny offsets can be grown on for two to three years until they reach flowering size.

Propagating from bulbils

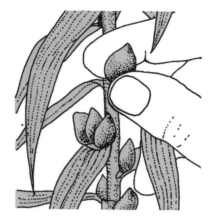

1 Several lilies, including *Lilium lancifolium*, naturally develop bulbils. Others, like the Madonna lily (*Lilium candidum*), can be induced to form bulbils if the flowers are removed at an early stage, as shown.

2 The bulbils are similar to small bulbs. They develop in the leaf axils, where the leaves join the stem. Pick them off as they mature in late summer. They should flower in two years.

3 Place the bulbils 3cm (1in) apart in a pot filled with gritty compost and press them into the surface. Cover with 1.5–2cm (½–¾in) of compost. Label and place the pot in a cold frame until autumn the following year. Then transplant into open ground.

Propagating from offsets

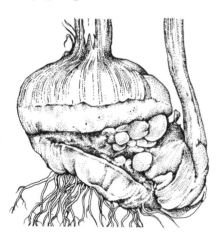

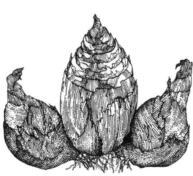

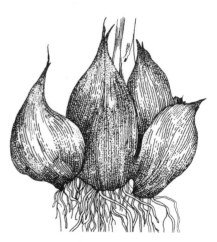

Offsets are produced between the new corm and the old. Collect them when the corm is lifted and store over winter in a dry frost-proof place. In spring plant them in rows to grow to flowering size.

Many bulbs propagate naturally by producing offsets. Daffodils produce offsets during the growing season. Dig up the bulbs and detach the offsets from the mother bulb and replant.

With bulbous irises and tulips the original bulb is replaced after flowering by a cluster of small bulbs and, usually, a new, large flowering bulb. In autumn separate the clusters and plant bulbs individually.

Scaling lily bulbs

To increase a particular lily rapidly artificial techniques are used as the plant's natural rate of increase is too slow. Each bulb is made up from a number of fleshy scales (modified leaf bases) and the technique is known as bulb scaling. Always use fresh, plump bulb scales as older damaged scales will not develop.

Bulb scaling

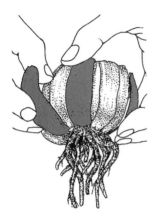

1 Gently remove a bulb scale leaf from the bulb by gently but firmly easing it outwards until it breaks free. Alternatively it can be cut as close as possible to the basal plate with a knife or a scalpel.

2 Snap or cut off a few more healthy, plump scale leaves from the outside of the bulb. The bulb will suffer and may take a while to regain strength if you remove too many scales.

3 Bulb scales rot easily. Place them in a bag with sulphur dust which will help to protect them from fungal attack. Close the bag tightly and shake it vigorously to coat the scales with the powder.

4 Carefully mix the sulphur-coated scales with four times their volume of damp vermiculite or a mixture of damp peat and grit. Place the mixture in a clear polythene bag.

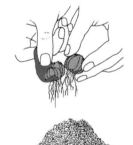

5 Place a label in the bag showing the name and variety of the bulb. Blow into it to fill it with air, secure tightly and place in a warm area such as an airing cupboard.

6 Check the bag regularly for any growth and remove the bulb scale from the polythene bag as soon as the tiny bulbs appear on the broken basal surfaces.

7 Remove the developed bulb scales from their bag and plant those with small bulbs in gritty compost so the tips are visible. Place in a warm, light position.

8 In summer, once the bulblets have produced a few leaves above the compost they are mature enough to be hardened-off. Continue to grow them on in the same pot.

9 Once the foliage has died back, dig up the remains of the bulb scale and separate the new bulbs. Pot them up separately in fresh compost and grow them on.

Bulbs can also be grown from seed as well as by separation of offsets. Raising bulbs from seed is simple but patience is required, as bulbs will not reach flowering size for several years. It is a good way of acquiring bulbous plants that are not generally available, as seed is often offered by various specialist societies. Some specialist bulb merchants also sell seed – this is a good way of increasing your own stock.

Growing bulbs from seeds

1 A pan (also known as a half pot) or a conventional pot are the best containers for growing bulb seed. If a large quantity is to be sown use two pans or a deep tray. Fill with a good quality seed compost and lightly press it down, smoothing off the surface.

2 Sow the seeds thinly across the surface of the compost, moving them apart with a label if they fall too close together. Larger seeds, such as those of lilies, can be placed on the surface by hand, but again make certain that they are evenly spaced.

3 Cover the seed and the compost with a thin layer, up to 1.5cm (½in) deep, of washed grit or fine gravel. This will help to keep the seed in place as well as conserve moisture. Watering is also easier as the surface of the compost does not form a hard layer.

4 Once the seed is sown and covered, it can be watered. Use a watering can with a fine rose. Alternatively, the pan or pot can be watered from below by standing it in a shallow tray of water which comes part way up the pot.

GROWING ORNAMENTAL TREES, SHRUBS, ROSES, AND CLIMBERS

Trees and shrubs are excellent for bringing balance and harmony to the garden in contrast to surrounding buildings. They help to screen the garden, filter wind and noise, obscure unsightly outlooks, and bring privacy. They are also attractive features in their own right.

There is a huge range of trees and shrubs available and as they are permanent, expensive and cannot be moved about at will you should choose them with care. They originate from all over the world, often from countries where the climate is very different. Because of this you should be aware of your local climate and soil conditions as these have a bearing on which trees and shrubs will thrive in your garden. Before you buy you should check that the tree, shrub or hedge you are choosing will thrive in these conditions; also find out whether they are hardy or not as this is a key to their survival. Fortunately, the majority of trees and shrubs on sale in garden centres and nurseries are hardy, and most will thrive in reasonable garden soils, provided they are well drained. These are the sort of reliable plants that should be your first choice.

HARDINESS

A plant's hardiness depends mainly upon its resistance to frost and upon its adaptation to the cycle of seasons prevailing. The length of the growing season is of particular importance and is defined as the number of days in the year when the temperature rises above $6°C/43°F$, the temperature at which grass begins to grow. In the subtropics the growing season is almost continuous, so unless you live in a particularly mild sheltered area with reliably frost-free winters you will probably be

disappointed if you try to grow plants from these regions. It is not just frost that can be a problem. Shrubs from dry regions will suffer in wet conditions, particularly wet winters, while many evergreens suffer if exposed to chilling winds or periods of drought in summer. Subarctic and alpine plants may not thrive in moist, temperate gardens because they are used to short growing seasons and prolonged periods of dormancy.

OBTAINING PLANTS

Although you can grow some trees and shrubs from seeds, this is a slow process and most are propagated from cuttings or by layering. In fact many cultivars can only be multiplied by such methods. A few trees and most roses are grafted or budded. These are specialist techniques, widely used by commercial growers, but rarely attempted by home gardeners.

Specialist tree and shrub nurseries are most likely to have a range of ornamental species. Look for small, vigorous plants which usually establish much better and more quickly than older, larger specimens; they are also less expensive and may not require staking.

MAINTENANCE

Until trees and hedges are established, keep the area around them free from weeds and grass, and water in dry spells; mulch plants that lack vigour with compost in spring. Trim hedges regularly. Pruning trees is usually limited to removing diseased or damaged branches. Tree ties must be checked regularly and loosened if they are getting tight, otherwise the tree will suffer and could die.

Trees and shrubs in the garden

Trees and shrubs form the backbone of any garden; they are the permanent structure. In a herbaceous border most of the plants die back in winter leaving nothing but a flat surface with the previous season's foliage. In a mixed border, which includes shrubs, even though the leaves may fall the bare bones of the plants still provide shapes, silhouettes, coloured and textured bark, and other features that create interest during the winter months. They also create the framework throughout the other seasons as plants come and go.

From a practical point of view, many trees and shrubs have an advantage over other plants as they need relatively little maintenance. Most trees, evergreen shrubs, and some deciduous shrubs need very little attention other than the removal of any dead, damaged or diseased wood. On the other hand, for those who want to include a wider selection of shrubs, it is necessary to give them some attention. At first pruning may seem confusing as different types of shrubs and climbers need different methods of control. However, once the basic techniques have been mastered, pruning is not difficult to carry out correctly.

Trees and shrubs can be categorised according to their shapes, the more common of which are illustrated below. Choose the preferred or appropriate shapes and forms of the trees and shrubs first, then consult a nursery catalogue to find which have the particular characteristics, which are the right size, and which suit the site and soil in your garden.

The basic shapes and forms of evergreen trees and shrubs are permanent throughout the year but the mass of an evergreen is ever-present and may lack the sense of season of deciduous types. There are also qualities other than overall shape that might influence choice. Some trees, such as the corkscrew hazel, *Corylus avellana* 'Contorta', are grown especially for their winter appearance. Flower colour is short-lived in most trees and shrubs, with notable exceptions such

as roses, and should be only one and not the main reason for choosing that particular plant. Think as well about the plant's leaf tints, bark colour, and fruits. Consider also the adjacent trees and bushes, how they will complement each other, and how they will look in a group at any time of year.

Where trees and shrubs are chosen to perform a particular function, such as hedging, check that they are suitable for the purpose. Here, as in other aspects of garden design, function needs to take priority over form. For example, those trees and shrubs planted primarily for wind screening should not just be tough. If they also have close, supple branches and small leaves they not only filter the wind efficiently but also yield a certain amount so that the plant is not damaged.

A narrow, upright tree has strong vertical emphasis.

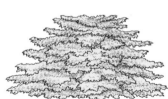

A layered tree whose many tiers leads the eye horizontally.

A low, open-centred bush with a spray effect.

A weeping shape is dramatic and potentially romantic.

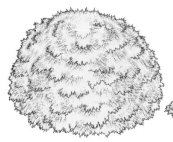

A dome has a solid, fixed feeling about it.

A spreading weeping shape is well anchored to the ground.

A spreading fan shape has a liveliness about it.

An open bowl shape has an uplifting quality about it.

An indication of the contribution that climbers – here, ivy, Virginia creeper, and hop – can make to the garden scene.

Right: A beautiful scene with an understorey of *Ceanothus* setting off the white trunks of two silver birches.

Below: The bright red berries and purple-tinged leaves of the shrub *Gaultheria procumbens* show how attractive ground-cover can be.

Buying trees and shrubs should be thought about very carefully. This is partly because of the cost. Trees and shrubs, particularly the former, are likely to be expensive, so buying the wrong one could be a costly mistake. The other reason is that trees and shrubs are likely to be in the same place in the garden for many years, and the wrong plant in a particular position may be a constant source of irritation. To add to these problems an unsuitable tree in a town garden might be difficult to remove once it has grown to a certain height without getting planning permission, which may not be forthcoming. It is, therefore, best to work out exactly what you want, first considering the various factors laid out on page 72.

It is important to remember that shrubs and trees will produce additional growth annually, and sometimes ultimately grow to a great height. It is not always possible to visualise this when you see them growing in small pots in a garden centre. To a certain extent many can be kept under control by pruning, but some may become distorted and out of character if they are pruned hard.

Container-grown plants

When buying a tree or shrub, always examine it closely before purchase. Avoid plants that have obviously been in the pot for a long time, and are rootbound or have rooted into the standing ground. Other plants that have been too long in pots may have had their leading branches removed to keep them within bounds in their pot. Avoid any that show signs of damage or disease.

Unless you are purchasing a flowering shrub or rose from a reliable source, see it in bloom to check it is the colour you require, as labelling on cheaper plants is often inaccurate. However, this is not always possible as the plant may not flower until it is several years old, so, even though it may be a bit more expensive, it is better to buy from a reputable nursery which will also guarantee a healthy, well-grown plant.

Traditionally trees and shrubs were bought and planted between late autumn and early spring. This is still the best advice, but with most now being container grown it is possible to buy and plant them at any time of the year as long as the weather is not too extreme and they are properly cared for after planting.

Bare-root and rootballed plants

Bare-rooted trees and shrubs are only available from late autumn to early spring. As they need to be planted immediately try to prepare the planting hole beforehand. If you obtain them at a time when the weather or soil is not suitable for planting, by mail order for example, remove the packing and heel them into a spare piece of ground until conditions improve. Rootballed evergreens are sold at the same times of year. If you cannot plant them straight away, heel them in (see page 180) but do not remove the wrapping.

THREE WAYS OF BUYING TREES AND SHRUBS

A pot grown shrub. These have usually spent their entire lives in pots, although sometimes they are barerooted plants that have been potted up for sale. Make certain that they are not rootbound.

A rootballed shrub. This has been grown in the open ground and then dug up with the soil still intact and then wrapped in hessian. These should only be available for planting between late autumn and spring.

A bare-rooted shrub. This has been dug up during its dormant period and the soil shaken from the roots. The plants most commonly sold in this form are roses. Plant in soil as soon as possible.

Planting trees

Trees are best planted between late autumn and early spring, at some point when the weather is not too cold or wet and the soil is in a workable condition. Since a tree is likely to be in position for many years prepare the ground thoroughly. When choosing the position, take into account the ultimate height and spread of the tree, which will shade the ground and if too close to a building may obscure windows. The roots also spread widely, remove moisture and nutrients from nearby beds and borders, and in some types of tree, undermine the foundations of buildings, walls, patios, and paths.

Container-grown tree

1 Thoroughly prepare the ground where the tree is to be positioned. Dig out an area much larger than the present dimension of the root spread. Add plenty of organic material to the soil in the bottom of the hole, as well as to the spare soil for infill.

2 Hammer the supporting stake into the hole just off centre. It is put in at this stage because if it is knocked in after the tree has been planted it might accidentally hit a root and damage it. Use a treated post that will last a number of years.

3 Plant the tree next to the supporting stake. Add or subtract soil in the bottom of the hole so that the top of the rootball is level with the surface of the surrounding soil. Spread out the roots, especially if the tree was bare-rooted when purchased.

4 Fill in the remainder of the hole using the to-soil that was removed when the hole was dug. This can be improved by adding well-rotted organic material to it before backfilling. Do not use sub-soil. Tread the soil lightly to firm in the tree.

5 Once the tree is in position, give the ground a thorough soaking so that the water gets right down to the roots. Mulch the soil around the tree with bark or some other organic mulch to help conserve moisture and keep the weeds at bay.

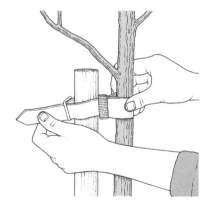

6 Use a tree tie to secure it to the supporting stake. The tie should support the lower part of the tree about 30cm (12in) above the soil, to prevent the rootball moving, leaving the top free to move and strengthen in the wind.

Planting shrubs is, in principle, the same as that for planting trees (see page 76). Again, it is important to remember that the shrub will be there for a long time and so the ground should be thoroughly prepared beforehand. If the shrub is planted in a border, ensure that all perennial weeds are removed first, as it might not be possible to get rid of these later on and their roots can become entangled with those of the shrub. Although container plants can be planted at any time of year if they are kept watered, and sheltered from hot sun and strong winds, the best time is between late autumn and early spring.

A container-grown shrub

1 Make certain that the ground is free from weeds, especially perennial ones, which will cause trouble later on if left. Dig a hole that is larger than the rootball. The depth can be gauged by standing the shrub, still in its pot, in the hole.

2 Since the shrub will be in the ground for a long time the soil should have plenty of well-rotted organic material incorporated into it. Dig some in when the bed is prepared and dig more into the bottom of the hole and into the infill top-soil.

3 Some shrubs, but not all, will need to be cut back on planting (see the section on pruning for details, pages 87–102), cutting above a bud. At the same time remove any dead, damaged or diseased wood that you can find.

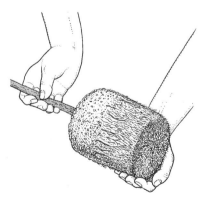

4 It is best not to buy plants that are pot bound, that is if their roots are wound round and round the inside of the pot. If you do, carefully tease out the roots, separating them, and when planting ensure that they are spread out, radiating from the rootball.

5 Place the shrub in the hole so that the top of the rootball is level with the surface of the soil. Backfill the space around the rootball, using the infill top-soil that has had organic material mixed with it. Do not use any sub-soil that has been dug from the hole.

6 Gently firm down the soil with your feet, being careful not to compact it too much. Mound a ring of soil around the plant to act as a reservoir and fill it with water. This ensures water reaches the roots of the shrub. Apply a 5–8cm (2–3in) mulch around the shrub.

Transplanting

Move deciduous trees and shrubs between mid autumn and early spring, evergreens in mid autumn or early to mid spring. Choose a time when the weather is not too cold or wet. Always insert strong plastic or sacking under the rootball and never lift the plant by its neck or branches. If necessary bring the sheeting round the rootball and tie it to a horizontal pole so that two people can lift it.

Transplanting a young tree or shrub

1 Tie in any spreading branches with soft string to protect the plant while it is being moved. Wrap the branches of smaller shrubs in hessian.

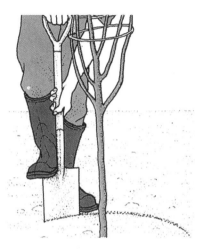

2 Make vertical slits in the soil with a spade to encircle the plant. The slits need to be 30–60cm (1–2ft) away from the stem and the depth of the spade blade.

3 Take out a trench a spade's width wide and a spade blade's deep, starting from the outside of the slit. Cut through any roots that protrude into the trench.

4 Thrust the spade under the rootball at a 45° angle, severing the roots. When it will move, roll the rootball from one side to the other, sliding a plastic sheet under it.

5 Dig a hole at the new site at least 30cm (12in) wider all round than the rootball. Add rotted compost or manure and a slow-release fertilizer and fork over the base.

6 Drive in a stake, if necessary. Place the plant in the hole so that it is at the same level as before. Backfill the hole, firm the soil, water and mulch. Tie the tree to the stake.

Erect supports for climbers before planting as this may be difficult to do once growth is underway. Prepare the ground thoroughly before planting. As with all container-grown plants, climbers can be planted at any time as long as they are kept well watered, and protected from strong sun and drying winds, but the best time is between late autumn and early spring.

Planting a climber by a wall

1 A few hours before planting, water the climber thoroughly so that the rootball is uniformly moist, and allow to drain.

2 Dig a hole that is about twice the size of the rootball of the plant, and at least 45cm (18in) away from the wall or fence.

3 If the ground has not already been prepared, fork in plenty of well-rotted organic material to the base of the hole.

4 Adjust the hole depth so the top of the rootball is level with soil surface. Plant the climber at a slight angle to the wall.

5 Slope canes from the plant to the supports. Use these as temporary supports to train the shoots up the wall.

6 Water the soil around the plant thoroughly and then mulch the area with organic matter.

Training a climber up a support

1 Climbers can be supported by horizontal wires set about 45cm (18in) apart. Tie in growth with string or plant ties.

2 Self-clinging plants can be simply guided between a plastic mesh fixed to a wall.

3 Another alternative is to use wooden trellis, which can either be free-standing or fixed to a wall or fence.

Protecting young trees

Trees are long-term investments and it is important to protect them in their early years from wind damage and animals.

Staking

Newly planted trees can support themselves as soon as their roots are established. Until that time, usually two or three years, they are best staked, particularly in windy places.

In the past trees used to be given tall stakes to support them. Now the practice is to support the lower third, about 30–60cm (1–2ft) above the ground. This prevents the rootball from moving about and severing new roots spreading into the surrounding soil, but allows the slender trunk to flex in the wind, strengthening it. Holding the whole trunk rigid for several years may cause it to snap in high wind as it has not developed any flexibility. For bare-root trees the stake is driven in vertically before the tree is positioned. This can be done for container-grown trees, or you can position the rootball in the hole first and then drive in the stake at an angle of 45° into the side of the planting hole.

There are still a few occasions when a tall stake is required. The most usual situation is to support shrubs and climbers trained as standards, such as wisteria, fuchsias and roses. In these cases the stems seldom become strong enough to support the head and need supporting throughout the life of the plant.

Wind protection

Young trees, especially evergreens in winter, are vulnerable to drying winds and they may need some protection. Individually they can be protected by wrapping hessian, fleece, or plastic sheeting around four stakes.

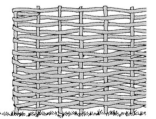

A temporary shelter can be provided by erecting a woven panel screen of fine-mesh netting. This allows the wind to filter through, reducing its speed. A solid barrier may cause turbulence, which can cause worse damage than the wind.

Whether the stake is short or tall it should be sturdy, at least twice the diameter of the trunk, and treated with a plant-safe preservative. Using a block of scrap wood to protect the top, drive the stake at least one-third of its length into the ground on the windward side, or so that the end faces the prevailing wind if the stake is at an angle. Attach the tree to the stake with a tree tie fitted with a spacer. The idea is to hold the tree firm without chafing the bark and the tie must be adjusted as the trunk thickens, so it is not constricted.

Protecting against wind and animals

Various designs of tree guards are available but all protect the young soft bark from grazing deer and rabbits, and from scratching cats. The damage these animals cause is capable of killing a young tree or, at least, stunting its growth.

Newly planted trees, particularly evergreens, should be screened from drying winds in exposed sites, otherwise they may become desiccated, which causes their foliage to wilt and turn brown.

PROTECTING TREE STEMS AND NEWLY-PLANTED SHRUBS

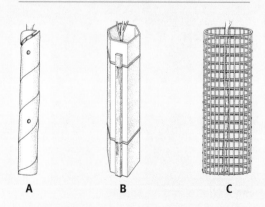

A   B   C

A. This trunk protector consists of a spiral of plastic that is wrapped round the young tree. It should be removed before the trunk gets too large, but should open without constricting the trunk if needed.

B. This is a shelter for saplings and young shrubs. It is translucent so light can enter. It is usually slipped over the whole tree, and it acts as a mini-greenhouse until the seedling tree grows out of it.

C. This is a steel or plastic mesh tree guard. These are used once the trees are more mature and a higher more robust form of protection is needed against larger animals, such as horses and deer. Steel is more durable.

When choosing a hedge make sure it suits your purposes. Evergreens lend themselves to formal clipping, they give privacy, and act as a buffer against the noise and dirt of the street. They also provide a calm backdrop to other garden plants. Thorny hedges are natural obstacles against animals and human intruders. Boundary hedges of deciduous plants protect the garden from the wind better than evergreens (see pages 220–221), while mixed hedges of native plants offer a haven to wildlife. Hedges can also be planted within the garden to divide it into sections, and dwarf hedges make neat edges for beds.

Hedges can be formal or informal. Formal hedges require regular clipping to maintain their shape, often two or three times a year. A powered hedge trimmer makes this job easier than using shears. Always trim hedges from the bottom up, taper the sides so the base is wider than the top, and use a string line as a guide when trimming the top. It is easier to cut at arm height or below than overhead, so for tall hedges work from a standing board supported by two step ladders.

A much wider range of shrubs can be used for informal hedges. Allow them to grow freely and only trim them to keep them within bounds. Prune them, if necessary, after flowering to prevent them from becoming overgrown and straggly. This can be done with shears, but large-leaved plants are better pruned with secateurs as mutilated leaves will turn brown and unsightly.

Hedges will rob the soil and neighbouring plants of nutrients unless you feed and mulch the plants and the hedge regularly.

PLANTING AND AFTERCARE

The best time to plant a hedge is between mid autumn and early spring. Small young plants, around 30–45cm (12–18in) high, are cheaper and usually establish more quickly than larger, more mature specimens.

Where hedges of 90cm (3ft) or a greater thickness are required, stagger the plants in a double row. Set the rows 30–50cm (12–20in) apart, against garden lines stretched along the trench.

After planting use secateurs to cut out any damaged stems. Prune back deciduous hedges by about one third, and hawthorn and privet to 15cm (6in) (see also the chart on page 83). The leading shoots of evergreens and conifers should not be pruned until they reach the required height. After ensuring the soil is moist apply a 8cm (3in) deep mulch of organic matter (see pages 32–33).

During the early years, water young hedges frequently in dry weather, and in winter refirm the soil round plants after frost. In spring, once the soil begins to warm up, apply a balanced fertilizer and mulch with organic matter (see page 32). Do this annually to keep the hedge growing strongly and to discourage its roots from spreading in search of food.

Planting and aftercare

1 Excavate a trench about 60–90cm (2–3ft) wide and 30cm (12in) deep along the line where the proposed hedge is to be planted.

2 Fork over the bottom of the trench, adding well-rotted organic material as well as a compound fertilizer at 110g per sq m (4oz per sq yd).

3 Carefully check each of the bare-rooted hedging plants and trim back any broken or damaged roots with a pair of secateurs or a sharp knife.

4 Spread out the roots of each plant, place them in the trench, adding soil if necessary to get the right depth, and replace the soil, firming it well.

Trimming hedges

Many deciduous and evergreen shrubs respond to clipping by producing dense compact growth, suitable for formal hedging. Clipping the hedge is only a form of pruning. Normally hand or electric shears are used for clipping hedges, but broadleaved evergreens should be cut with secateurs as shears will cut leaves in half, giving an ugly finish to the hedge.

The first year

1 Plant the hedge between mid autumn and early spring. After planting cut back deciduous plants to 15cm (6in).

2 In early to mid-summer trim back all the laterals lightly to encourage further side shoots.

The second year

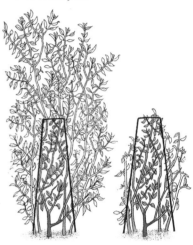

3 In late winter to early spring reduce the previous season's main growths by half. Then trim laterals to 8–10cm (3–4in).

Third and subsequent years

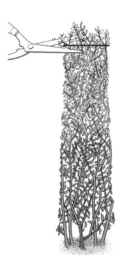

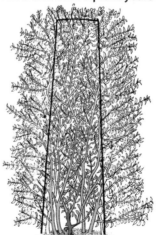

4 During the summer trim back at regular intervals all the laterals to maintain the tapered shape.

5 In the autumn trim back the uneven leading shoots to a uniform height. Continue until the final height is reached.

6 In summer trim back the top and sides to maintain the height and shape. Use taut string guides to ensure a straight cut.

RENOVATING AN OLD HEDGE

A few hedge species, such as hornbeam, respond well to drastic pruning if they have been neglected. Cut back one side of the hedge, then cut back the other side the following year. Mulch and fertilize the base of the hedge.

HEDGING PLANTS AND TRIMMING TIMES

Name	Planting distance	Initial pruning*	Features	Formal/ informal	Growth rate**
Aucuba japonica (Spotted laurel)	60cm (24in)	Group 3. Use secateurs	Evergreen	F/I	5
Berberis darwinii	45cm (18in)	Group 1	Evergreen, flowers, thorns	F/I	6
Berberis x stenophylla	45cm (18in)	Group 1	Evergreen, flowers, thorns	F/I	5
Buxus sempervirens (Box)	30cm (12in)	Group 1	Evergreen	F	8
Carpinus betulus (Hornbeam)	45cm (18in)	Group 2	Dead leaves held over winter	F	6
Chamaecyparis lawsoniana and cultivars (Lawson cypress)	60cm (24in)	Group 3	Evergreen	F	5
Corylus maxima 'Purpurea' (Purple hazel)	60cm (24in)	Use secateurs	Purple deciduous foliage	F	3
Cotoneaster simonsii	45cm (18in)	Use secateurs	Deciduous, flowers, fruits	F/I	5
Crataegus monogyna (Hawthorn, quick, May)	30cm (12in)	Group 1	Flowers, fruits, thorns	F	7
x *Cupressocyparis leylandii* (Leyland cypress)	30cm (12in)	Group 3	Evergreen	F	3
Escallonia rubra var. *macrantha*	45cm (18in)	Use secateurs	Evergreen, flowers	F/I	4
Fagus sylvatica (Beech)	45cm (18in)	Group 2	Dead leaves held over winter	F	5
Forsythia x *intermedia* 'Spectabilis'	30cm (12in)	Use secateurs or shears	Deciduous flowers	F/I	4
Fuchsia magellanica	45cm (18in)	Use secateurs	Flowers	I	5
Ilex aquifolium and cultivars (Holly)	45cm (18in)	Group 3	Evergreen, fruits, spines	F	8
Lavandula angustifolia and cultivars (Lavender)	45cm (18in)	Shears	Evergreen, flowers	I	only 60cm (24in)
Ligustrum ovalifolium (Privet)	30cm (12in)	Group 1. Trim 3–4 times/year	Evergreen	F	4
Lonicera nitida	45cm (18in)	Group 1. Trim 3–4 times/year	Evergreen	F	5
Olearia x *haastii* (New Zealand daisy bush)	30cm (12in)	Group 3. Use secateurs	Evergreen, flowers	I	7
Poncirus trifoliata	60cm (24in)	Group 3	Deciduous fruits, spines	F/I	
Prunus laurocerasus (Cherry laurel)	30cm (12in)	Group 3	Evergreen, flowers, fruits	F/I	3
Rhododendron (Compact cultivars)	60cm (24in)	Use secateurs	Evergreen, flowers	I	5
Rosa rubiginosa (Sweet briar)	60cm (24in)	Use secateurs	Deciduous flowers, thorns	I	3
Rosa rugosa	60cm (24in)	Use secateurs	Deciduous flowers, thorns	I	5
Tamarix gallica (Tamarisk)	45cm (18in)	Group 1. Use secateurs	Deciduous flowers	I	4
Taxus baccata (Yew)	45cm (18in)	Group 3	Evergreen	F	8
Thuja plicata 'Atrovirens' (Western red cedar)	45cm (18in)	Group 3	Evergreen	F	5
Ulex europaeus (Common gorse)	60cm (24in)	Group 3. Use secatuers	Evergreen, flowers, thorns	I	6
Viburnum tinus (Laurustinus)	60cm (24in)	Group 3	Evergreen, flowers	F/I	5

Initial pruning*
Group 1: Cut each plant back to 15cm (6in). Group 2: Cut main leading shoot and longer side shoots by one-third. Group 3: Cut back untidy side shoots; do not prune leading shoot.
Growth rate** approximate number of years to reach 1.5m (5ft).

Pruning feathered trees

The feathered tree is the most natural form of deciduous tree, with a single main stem well furnished with laterals, almost to the base. This is the typical growth pattern for silver birches, rowans, alders, and many other common trees. Early training is simple. The most important point to ensure is that the prominent leader remains dominant and that a forked or double leader is not allowed to develop. Similarly, any basal stems that grow and may rival the leader should be removed as soon as possible, unless a multi-stemmed tree is required. A feathered tree will branch naturally and roughly symmetrically on its own,

and only if a lateral is badly placed or likely to unbalance the overall shape is any pruning needed. Any lateral that is poorly placed should be cut out in mid to late autumn. The first few lateral branches are usually small and do not develop well, but thereafter the laterals increase in size and vigour, keeping pace with the leader. As the tree develops the smaller near-basal laterals are removed leaving a short, clear stem. A feathered tree can readily be trained as a standard with a central leader by cutting back the laterals flush with the stem each autumn until the required height is reached.

Feathered tree: The first year

1 Plant during the autumn or winter. Tie on planting and continue to tie in the leader as it develops during mid spring to mid summer.

2 By mid to late autumn lateral shoots will have developed. Any shoots that have appeared at the base of the tree should be removed.

The second year

3 Mid spring to mid summer. In the second year, continue to tie in the leading shoot as it develops. No pruning is required at this time of year.

4 In mid to late autumn carefully remove any weak laterals at the base flush with the main stem. Cut out dead, damaged or diseased wood.

The third year

Fourth and subsequent years

5 During spring and early summer, further extension growth of the leader will occur. Cut out any lateral that is trying to compete with the leader.

6 In mid or late autumn, cut out any badly placed or weak laterals or sub-laterals that spoil the symmetry and the balance of the young tree.

7 In mid or late autumn cut out a few of the lowest laterals if a clear trunk is required. Repeat in the following years until the desired height of clear stem is reached.

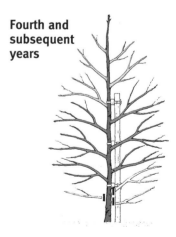

Pruning standard trees

The standard tree is the commonest form used for ornamental trees. The main stem is clear of branches for the first 1.8m (6ft) from ground level, so that the trunk can be clearly seen. The formation of the crown of the tree will differ depending on the natural growth of the plant and the kind of tree that is required. There are two forms of standard tree. In the central-leader standard (below left) the structure is the same as a feathered tree (see page 84) but with the lowest branches 1.8m (6ft) from the ground. The other type is the branch-head standard (below right). With this the lowest branches are again 1.8m (6ft) from the ground, but this time there is no central leader. Instead a branched but balanced head is formed, either naturally or by artificial training. This growth habit is really only suitable for small trees such as ornamental cherries and crab apples. It is not recommended for large trees. Oaks, elms and a number of other trees sometimes form branched heads naturally, but mechanically this kind of branch formation is less sound than the central-leader growth habit.

CENTRAL-LEADER STANDARD

Tie the vigorous extension leader of a young seedling or rooted cutting to a bamboo cane. Usually but not invariably, lateral shoots grow from lower down the stem. All laterals produced during the first year are cut back by one-half their length when they reach 23–30cm (9–12in). A few of the upper laterals produced later in the season may be left unpruned. Cut back the pruned laterals flush with the stem in late autumn or early winter. The training process is repeated each year until the desired length of clear trunk has been produced.

Training a branched-headed standard

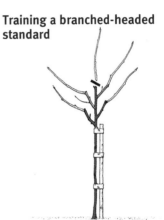

1   During mid or late autumn of the third year cut back the leader to a strong bud or lateral, 30–45cm (12–18in) above the length of clear stem required.

2   From mid spring to mid summer of the fourth year an increasing number of laterals and sub-laterals develop. No further pruning is required at this stage.

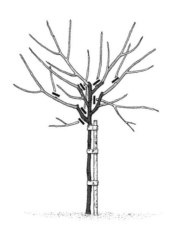

3   In that autumn a framework of 3–5 laterals are formed by removing wrongly placed stems. Remove any upright shoots which may form a new leader.

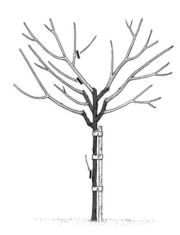

4   In the autumn of the fifth and subsequent years cut out any young branches that threaten the open symmetry. Remove any feathers from the clean stem.

Pruning trees

Although many gardeners will prune roses and shrubs regularly each season, few consider it necessary to train or prune the trees they grow. Training and pruning during the early years of a tree's life, however, are essential to obtain shapely, well-furnished specimens. Usually nurseries can be relied upon to produce well-trained young trees that have been correctly dealt with from propagation stage. In most cases only relatively minor pruning is required to continue to produce an attractive tree with a symmetrical, well-balanced crown. The aim is to obtain a plant with evenly spaced branches that form a strong framework. Crossing or misplaced branches should be cut out wherever possible at this early stage, but care must be taken not to spoil the natural habit of the tree (see page 84).

The weight of the branches in the mature tree is considerable and it is essential that the stems and main branch system are able to support them. Good early training cuts down the risk of wind or storm damage in later years. Once the trees are well established the need for more than cosmetic pruning is minimal, and any pruning is mainly restricted to removing dead, damaged or diseased wood. Occasionally a branch may be removed to allow more light into the canopy, but inevitably the natural habit and growth of trees affects the ways in which they can be trained and pruned. It cannot be emphasised too strongly that the individual growth characteristics of a tree can be spoilt by rigorous training and over enthusiastic pruning.

Most gardeners will not find it practical, nor necessary, to do more than cut out the occasional branch once the tree has reached any size. Any major pruning or thinning of the crown of the tree is best dealt with by a professional tree surgeon with the appropriate knowledge, experience and equipment to carry out the task safely and correctly. Avoid "jobbers" who may profess to be tree surgeons. They may be cheaper but are liable to mutilate trees and may leave them in a more dangerous condition than before they started pruning.

Removing small branch

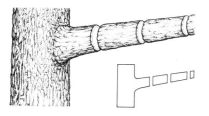

Cut the branch into convenient lengths, at the points shown, to reduce weight. Remove the final stub of 30–45cm (12–18in) flush with the collar, the swollen area at the branch base.

Removing medium branch

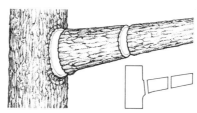

First reduce the length of the branch. Make the final cut to sever the stub from above. Take care to cut flush with but not into the branch collar.

Removing heavy branch

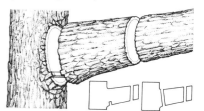

Again reduce the branch gradually to lessen the weight. Undercut the stub slightly, close to the trunk to prevent the bark being torn. Cut the stub from above flush with the collar.

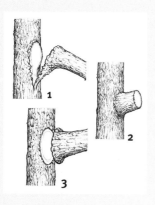

INCORRECT PROCEDURE

1. Unless it is undercut the weight of the branch will tear the bark of the trunk, providing an entry point for disease.
2. An ugly stub of branch left behind will almost certainly die back and will become an entry point for disease.
3. A dangerously large and vulnerable wound results from a cut made too close to the trunk. Because the branch collar has been cut into healing by callus formation will be inhibited.

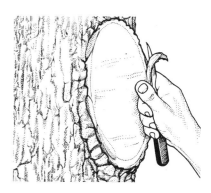

To finish off pare round the edge of the cut surface with a sharp knife to remove the jagged surface left by the saw. Wound paint is no longer applied to cut surfaces.

A commonly held but incorrect belief is that all shrubs should be pruned, and pruned hard, each year. The other extreme of leaving the shrub entirely unpruned is to be preferred. Many deciduous and most evergreen shrubs will grow satisfactorily and give adequate flower without being pruned, provided the plant has ample room and the soil is reasonably fertile. There, are however, several groups of shrubs where correct pruning is beneficial in producing regular and abundant flowers together with healthy vigorous growth and foliage. When pruning a shrub, try to obtain the optimum decorative effect. The technique will vary from shrub to shrub and with the effect required. Some shrubs may be pruned in different ways to obtain a different effect. For example, one may be left unpruned to obtain strong growth and flowers, or cut back hard to provide larger leaves than normal. Pruning should, with many shrubs, encourage the production of new basal or near basal growth.

Principles of pruning shrubs

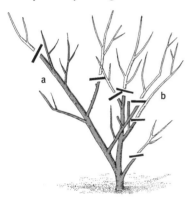

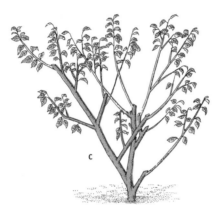

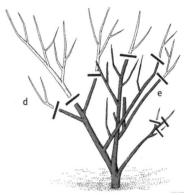

1 Unevenly growing shrubs need pruning to restore their shape. Strong shoots (a) should be lightly pruned while weak wood (b) should be cut back hard.

2 This will help to rebalance the shape as the strong shoots (c) will only put on moderate growth while the weaker ones, will put on stronger growth.

3 On the other hand you should not cut back the strong growth hard (d) and leave the weak wood virtually unpruned (e) so that the overall height is the same.

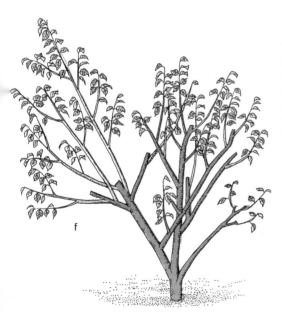

4 This will result in further strong growths being produced from the hard-pruned side (f) but not from the unpruned growth, so accentuating rather than correcting the lack of balance in the shape of the shrub.

PRUNING CUTS

All pruning cuts should be made as shown. Incorrect cuts can result in die-back and disease. Cut at an angle just above an outward-pointing bud or shoot, or straight across above a strong pair of buds so that the resulting shoots will be well placed in relation to the other new growths.

Pruning shrubs

Reversion

Occasionally branches of shrubs with variegated foliage may revert to the original green-leaved form of the species concerned. If this occurs it is most important to remove completely the non-variegated branches as soon as they are seen. They are frequently more vigorous than the variegated shoots and, if allowed, will gradually take over and become dominant. Eventually the shrub will almost revert to its green-leaved form.

Removing suckers

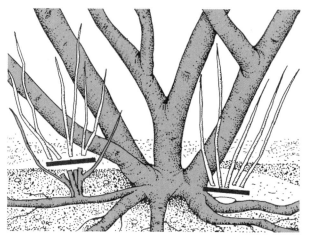

Although most shrubs are propagated vegetatively from cuttings and grow on their own roots, a few are still budded or grafted on to rootstocks. Suckers may occasionally grow from the rootstock and should be removed as soon as they are seen. Trace the suckers back to their point of origin, and carefully cut them off flush with a knife or pull them off by hand so that dormant buds at the base of each sucker are removed at the same time.

Early training

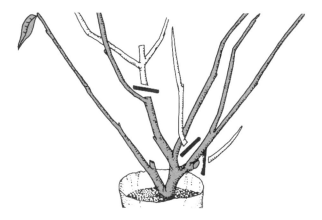

1 Most shrubs produce a number of vigorous basal shoots during the first year or two after planting. These shoots will form the basic framework of the shrub and it is important to make sure that they are evenly spaced. Often the shoots are too close to each other or are crossing so that, if left, they will spoil the balance and overall symmetry of the shrub.

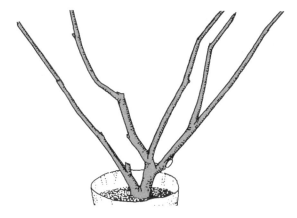

2 If the shoots are ill-placed or surplus, cut them out. It is particularly important to do this with shrubs that do not usually renew their growth from basal replacement shoots when older. It is desirable in many shrubs to keep the centre open to allow the free circulation of air. This avoids stagnant conditions, which favour the spread of diseases.

Pruning deciduous shrubs: Group 1

Group 1 of deciduous shrubs consists of a considerable number of shrubs that do not regularly produce vigorous replacement growths from the base or lower branches of the plant. Their extension growth is produced on the perimeter of a permanent framework of older branches. The growth habit, therefore, may be likened to the crown of an oak tree without its trunk. Once established they require the minimum of pruning, but it is important to build up a good basic framework in the early years.

The first year

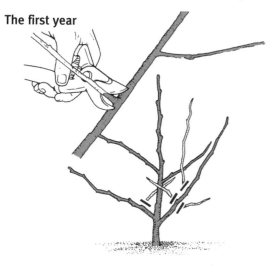

1 *Magnolia stellata* at the time of planting, some time between late autumn and mid spring. Remove any weak or crossing branches. Create a balanced framework by removing any unruly growths.

The second year

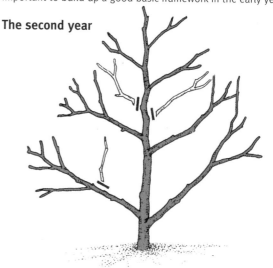

2 From early to mid spring cut out any badly spaced extension growth and laterals that have been produced during the previous, first, growing season. If they are well-spaced they can be left alone.

The third and subsequent years

3 By the following early to mid spring only a minimum of pruning is now required. Allow the plant to develop its natural habit, but always removed any dead, diseased or damaged wood.

4 By mid spring of the third year the basic shape of the bush, seen here in flower, has been formed and little pruning will be required from now on, except to remove any dead, diseased or damaged wood.

Group 1 includes: *Acer japonicum* (Japanese maple), *A. palmatum* (Japanese maple), *Amelanchier, Buddleja globosa, Clethra, Colutea, Cornus florida, C. kousa, Corylopsis, Cotinus* (or as Group 4, see page 97), *Cotoneaster* (deciduous species), *Daphne* (deciduous species), *Euonymus* (deciduous species), *Fothergilla, Hamamelis, Hibiscus syriacus, Magnolia* (deciduous species and hybrids), *Syringa* (Lilac), *Viburnum* (deciduous species and hybrids).

Pruning deciduous shrubs: Group 2

Group 2 includes those shrubs that flower on shoots produced during the previous growing season. The flowers are formed either on short laterals produced from this one-year-old wood or directly from the one-year-old branches. Many spring and early summer-flowering shrubs belong to this group. They need renewal pruning to maintain them at a reasonable height and to ensure a regular supply of strong young shoots each season from low down on the plant.

The first year

1 A young *Deutzia* at the time of planting, at some point when the weather is suitable between autumn and early spring. Cut out all the weak and any crossing growth, and tip back all the main shoots to a strong pair of buds, or to an outward-facing bud if the buds are alternate on the stems. Apply a mulch of organic matter (see page 32) to the soil around the base of the plant.

2 By mid to late autumn a few strong basal growths and many laterals from the main branches will have developed during the first season. Cut out any weak or misplaced shoots to maintain a symmetrical framework. Mulch well in spring.

The second year

3 In early and mid summer flowers are produced from short laterals along many of the upper shoots which grew during the previous season. As the flowers fade strong shoots are produced from the base of the plant and low down on the main stems.

4 In mid summer, straight after flowering, cut back the stems that have flowered to vigorous young growths developing lower down on the main stems. Remove any weak growth. Make sure that the overall balance and symmetry of the shrub is maintained.

5 By late autumn the vigorous young shoots have grown considerably and produced laterals on which the following season's blooms will be borne. Mulch well with organic material round the base of the shrub.

The third and subsequent years

6 In mid summer, straight after flowering, cut back the stems that have flowered to vigorous young growths developing lower down. Remove any weak growth. If the main stems are becoming crowded, cut to the base one quarter to one fifth of the old growths.

Group 2 includes: *Buddleja alternifolia*, *Cytisus scoparius* and hybrids, *Deutzia*, *Dipelta*, *Forsythia*, *Hydrangea macrophylla*, *Kerria*, *Kolkwitzia*, *Neillia*, *Philadelphus*, *Ribes sanguineum*, *Spiraea x arguta*, *S. thunbergii*, *Stephanandra*, *Tamarix* (spring flowering), *Weigela*.

In a small garden colour variations
can come from mixing flowers,
herbs and vegetables in containers.

Right: Terracotta pots are attractive with or without plants.

Far right: Winter and early spring can be brightened by planting containers with bulbs and other early-flowering plants.

Below: Troughs make ideal containers for small plants that might well be swamped in a border.

Pruning deciduous shrubs: Group 2

Also in group 2 are shrubs like *Kerria* that produce almost all of their new growth from ground level. They flower on one-year-old wood. Immediately after flowering cut the flowered shoots to the ground or to a vigorous young side shoot. If left much of this growth would die back naturally. Do not prune hydrangeas hard in the spring, just take out a number of old shoots.

Kerria: The first year

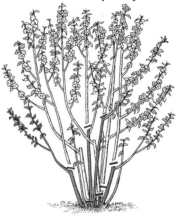

Second and subsequent years

1 This is a young *Kerria* at the time of planting, at some point in autumn or early spring. Cut out any thin, weak growth but leave the more vigorous stems and their laterals as these may possibly flower later this first season.

2 In late spring, at some point soon after flowering, cut out the flowered shoots right to their base or, with very strong stems, to points low down where vigorous young shoots are forming. It helps to mulch the plant well (see page 32).

3 As before, in late spring, after flowering, cut out the flowered shoots to the base or, with very strong stems, to points low down where vigorous young shoots are forming. Basal growths develop. Mulch the plant well to preserve moisture.

Hydrangea

1 Mid spring. Cut out one third to one quarter of the older, exhausted shoots at the base. Cut out any weak thin shoots still remaining. Cut back the old flower heads to a strong pair of buds.

2 Early autumn. The upper growth buds on the pruned shoots have grown and the strongest have produced flower heads. New vigorous basal shoots have developed but will not flower until next season.

BROOMS

Early-mid summer. In second and subsequent years, after flowering, cut back the flowered wood by two thirds to vigorous young growths developing near the base of last season's wood.

Pruning deciduous shrubs: Group 3

Group 3 includes those deciduous shrubs that bear their flowers on the current year's growth. When pruned back hard in early spring they produce vigorous shoots, which flower in summer or early autumn. If left to their own devices they soon develop into unkempt, twig-filled bushes, which gradually deteriorate in the quality and quantity of flower produced. The group also includes a few deciduous shrubs, such as *Prunus triloba*, that flower early in the year on the previous season's wood.

The first year

1 This is a deciduous ceanothus. At some time in early to early mid spring cut out any damaged or very weak growths. Tip back the main shoots by 3–5cm (1–2in) to strong outward-facing buds. Cut out entirely any badly placed shoots.

2 In late summer or early autumn the plant should appear like this. Strong shoots have grown from upper buds on last season's growths and these will flower during the late summer.

The second year

Third and subsequent years

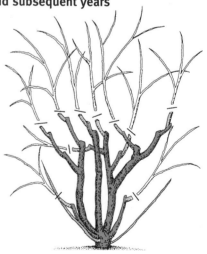

3 At some time between early spring to early mid spring cut back all last season's growths by one-half to strong outward-pointing buds. Remove entirely any weak, straggly or damaged shoots. Apply a mulch round the base of the shrub.

4 Early to early mid spring. Cut back all last season's shoots to within one or two buds of the previous season's growth. The basic framework of woody stems is formed. Always apply an annual mulch around the base of the shrub (see page 32).

Group 3 includes: *Buddleja davidii, Caryopteris, Ceanothus* (deciduous), *Ceratostigma, Fuchsia* (hardy), *Hydrangea paniculata, Perovskia, Prunus glandulosa, P. triloba, Romneya, Spiraea* x *bumalda, S. douglasii, S. japonica.*

Group 3 of the deciduous shrubs also includes such plants as *Perovskia* (Russian sage), *Leycesteria formosa,* the hardy fuchsias, and *Ceratostigma.* These may not develop a woody framework and are cut almost back to ground level each year. Most of these plants, as well as some like *Cestrum parqui,* can be left to grow naturally if they have not been frosted during the winter, but they soon become very tall and flower almost out of

sight. If left unpruned they will flower earlier and often longer, but a better overall result is achieved if they are cut back to almost ground level in the spring. If the old wood of such plants as the fuchsias and cestrum becomes frosted, they will need cutting back.

It is important to feed and mulch shrubs pruned in this way to ensure that adequate healthy growth is produced each season.

Perovskia: The first year

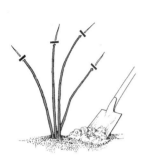

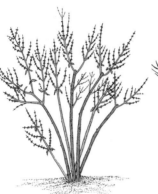

1 At some time between early to mid spring *Perovskia* can be planted. Cut back any weak, thin tips by a few in/cm to a pair of strong buds. Add a good mulch around its base.

2 By mid autumn the basal shoots will have developed and last year's shoots will have produced new lateral growths. The grey-coloured stems remain active in the winter.

The second year

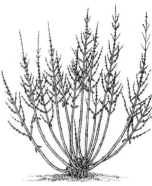

3 At some point in the early to mid spring cut back all the stems almost to ground level. Make the cuts just above pairs of strong buds.

4 By early autumn the strong growths have developed to a height of 60–90cm (2–3ft). Laterals have been produced towards the top of each shoot, which have produced flowers.

Third and subsequent years

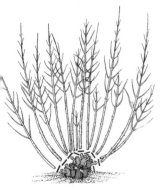

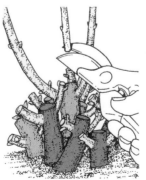

5 Each summer strong flowering growths will develop to a height of 60–90cm (2–3ft). During the following early or mid spring cut all these back to almost ground level.

6 Each stem should be cut back to the lowest pair of strong buds. Cut just above the buds, taking care not to leave any snags that will die back during the year.

CREATING A FRAMEWORK

If taller plants of *Perovskia* (Russian sage) are required they can be grown on a framework of woody shoots. Early training and the subsequent pruning is exactly as explained in the techniques shown on page 94. Instead of cutting back to the ground in the spring of the second year, the main stems are cut back by one half to a strong pair of buds. Any weak growth is also removed. This structure then forms the permanent framework, and subsequent pruning involves cutting back to this rather than right back to the ground.

Pruning deciduous shrubs: Group 3

Group 3 also includes vigorous shrubs, such as *Buddleja davidii* (Butterfly bush), that will grow 2–3m (7–10ft) in a year and are generally cut back hard annually. To maintain those shrubs with a low basal framework all the shoots should be cut back to just above ground level initially. If taller plants are required then the basic framework is allowed to grow to the required height before annual pruning takes place, to keep it cut close to this height. Every spring cut back the previous year's growth to one or two pairs of buds from the framework. The bush grows back at an astonishing speed and is ready to flower freely again in summer. Feed and mulch after pruning to ensure continuing strong healthy growth.

Buddleja davidii: The first year

1 Plant *Buddleja davidii* in early or early mid spring. Cut back all main shoots by one-half to three-quarters to a pair of strong, swelling buds. Cut out all weak wood. Mulch well.

2 By mid and late summer, long wand-like growths have been produced from the pruned branches and also from the base. These will flower near the tips in late summer.

The second year

3 In early to early mid spring cut back new shoots hard to within one or two pairs of buds of the previous year's growth. Cut back any basal or near basal growths.

4 By mid autumn the plant has flowered on terminal shoots and upper laterals of the current season's shoots. In windy gardens cut these back by a third to reduce wind-rock.

The third year

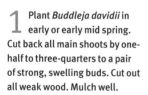

5 In early to early mid spring cut back new shoots hard to one or two pairs of buds of the previous year's growth. Any basal shoots can be used to fill the framework if necessary.

6 By late summer the *Buddleja* will have filled out again and should be now a well-shaped, vigorous bush. Trim back all stems in mid autumn by a third to reduce wind rock.

Fourth and subsequent years

7 Continue each year in early spring to carry out normal pruning by cutting back all the main stems to one or two pairs of buds of the previous year's growth.

8 When the framework becomes very woody and congested remove one or two of the stumps, especially badly placed ones. Train new shoots to replace them.

Group 4 includes shrubs that are pruned hard – coppiced or pollarded – in early spring each year so that the maximum decorative effect is obtained from their foliage or bark of their stems in the winter. The technique is very similar to that described for Group 3. Most of the shrubs listed here would flower on wood produced the previous year, but pruned by this method do not bloom at all. With appropriate feeding the leaves of shrubs grown for foliage, will be two or three times larger than normal.

Cotinus coggygria: The first year

The second year

1 Early spring. *Cotinus coggygria* Rubrifolius Group at planting. Cut back main growths to 30–45cm (12–18in) to create the basal framework. Cut out any weak basal growths.

2 Mid to late summer. Vigorous unbranched shoots have developed during the summer each carrying larger and more handsome foliage than that of an unpruned bush.

3 Cut back hard the previous season's growth to above a bud within 3–5cm (1–2in) of the framework. If a higher framework is needed cut back these growths to the appropriate height.

4 Mid to late summer. The established plant with a strong basic, woody framework and numerous vigorous growths, each producing large colourful foliage.

Cornus alba: The first year

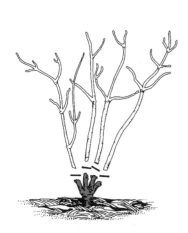

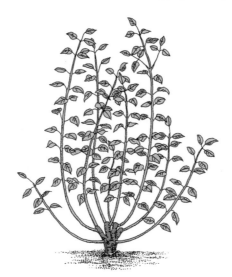

The second year

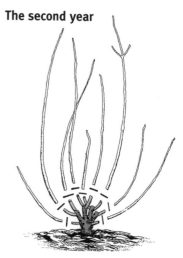

1 Plant between early to early mid spring and cut back hard all the main shoots to within a few in/cm of the base. Cut out any weak basal growths. Mulch well.

2 By mid autumn vigorous, whippy shoots, usually unbranched, will have grown. Once the leaves have fallen the stems form an attractive feature throughout the winter.

3 During the early spring cut back hard all main shoots to within a few in/cm of the base. Cut out any weak basal growths.

Group 4 includes: *Cornus alba, C. stolonifera, Salix* (many species), *Cotinus coggygria, Corylus maxima* 'Purpurea', *Sambucus* (golden- and purple-leaved cultivars).

Pruning shrubs for special effects

Shrubs can be pruned hard in early spring each year so that the maximum decorative effect is obtained from their foliage or winter stems. It is also a means of limiting the size of some trees and shrubs that would otherwise grow very large, and is a useful technique to employ in small gardens. The technique is known as coppicing, when trees or shrubs are routinely cut down to the ground, or pollarding, when young growths are cut back to a permanent stem or trunk (see pages 97–98).

Many shrubs with beautifully coloured bark react well to this drastic pruning, producing vigorous, unbranched new growth with more pronounced colour than unpruned specimens. Plants grown for foliage effect produce much larger leaves than normal. When this drastic pruning is carried out every year the shrubs will suffer loss of vigour. It is therefore important to feed with a balanced fertilizer after pruning and to apply a mulch (see page 34).

White-stemmed brambles *(Rubus cockburnianus, R. thibetanus)* sucker from the base to produce annual replacement shoots like the related raspberry. Pruning consists of cutting all growths down to the ground in spring. If the previous season's growths remain they will flower in summer, but they are not particularly decorative, so remove them before active growths starts. The plant's energy is then diverted into producing vigorous new canes. Where growth is poor, one or two of the previous year's shoots may be left; this helps to stimulate a new supply of vigorous canes during summer. In autumn the leaves fall but the glistening white stems remain attractive throughout the winter.

DECORATIVE LEAVES

Acer negundo 'Flamingo'
Ailanthus altissima
Catalpa bignonioides 'Aurea'
Corylus maxima 'Purpurea'
Cotinus coggygria 'Royal Purple'
Eucalyptus gunnii
Eucalyptus pauciflora subsp. *niphophila*
Paulownia tomentosa
Rhus typhina 'Dissecta'
Sambucus nigra 'Guincho Purple'
Sambucus nigra f. *laciniata*
Sambucus racemosa 'Plumosa Aurea'

COLOURFUL STEMS

Cornus alba 'Kesselringii' (purple-black)
Cornus alba 'Sibirica' (red)
Cornus sanguinea (orange)
Cornus stolonifera 'Flaviramea' (yellow-green)
Rubus cockburnianus (white)
Rubus thibetanus (white)
Salix alba var. *vitellina* (yellow-orange)
Salix alba var. *vitellina* 'Chermesina' (red)

White-stemmed brambles

During early and mid spring cut out all of the stems close to ground level. Gloves may be needed with these thorny species of brambles to avoid being scratched. After pruning mulch the soil well around the plants with organic matter.

POLLARDING

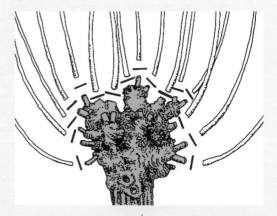

If required, many willows and some *Cornus* can be allowed to develop a single woody stem or stems to the required height, and then pruned back in the same way. This method of pruning is usually known as pollarding.

In spite of the gardener's good intentions, many vigorous shrubs, such as *Philadelphus* and *Syringa* (lilacs), either become too large for their positions or become overgrown through neglect. One course of action is to dig them up and start again with young shrubs. This may be the best course in some circumstances, although it will not always be necessary. Many shrubs have remarkable powers of recovery and with drastic pruning can be rejuvenated in a short time.

Syringa: The first year

1 This old lilac, seen here in winter, has become very bare at the base and only bears flowers at the top of the plant. It can be improved by severe pruning.

2 Between late autumn and late winter, cut back all strong stems to within 30–60cm (1–2ft) of the ground. Cut out entirely any remaining weak growths. Mulch and feed well.

The second year

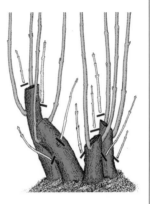

3 During the spring and summer strong shoots have developed. In mid autumn cut back these shoots, leaving two or three of the strongest and best placed on each stump.

Twiggy shrubs: The first year

1 This is an old *Deutzia* that has become full of twiggy growth. Between late autumn and late winter, when the plant is dormant, all twiggy growth should be cut to the base.

2 At the same time cut out about a half of the very old stems to within about 8cm (3in) of the ground. Add a mulch of well-rotted compost or manure to the soil around the plant.

The second year

3 From early to mid summer the plant will flower sparsely from the remaining laterals. New vigorous basal and near basal shoots will develop.

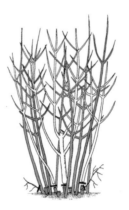

4 During the second winter, between late autumn and late winter, cut out the remaining old stems. At the same time cut out any new weak growths. Mulch the soil well.

Third and subsequent years

5 In the following early to mid summer flowers will appear on the previous year's laterals. New shoots are produced from the base. Prune as normal in subsequent years.

Pruning evergreen shrubs: Group 5

Group 5 of the shrubs includes the evergreens, most of which are naturally bushy and reasonably compact. Provided sufficient room is available they should be allowed to develop with only minor pruning. This usually amounts to no more than the removal of spent flowers, wayward shoots, and any branches that affect the overall symmetry of the shrub if allowed to remain.

Dead, diseased, damaged and any misplaced shoots can be removed at any time of the year, while winter-damaged growth is best cut back in late spring, just as the growth buds are beginning to swell. This gives the maximum period for new shoots to ripen before winter sets in. Pruning earlier in the year renders the plant liable to both wind and frost damage, while any summer and autumn pruning will produce growth that is too soft. This will almost certainly be killed during the following winter.

RHODODENDRONS

Unless seed is required, deadheading should be carried out immediately after the flowers fade and before seed pods form. Carefully snap off the spent flower truss taking care not to damage the growth buds, which are immediately below.

Training

A young camellia in mid to late spring displaying a well-developed leader. Cut back the uppermost vigorous lateral slightly. If it is left unpruned an unbalanced growth may result.

1 A young camellia in late spring with a spindly leader and only a few laterals. Prune back the weak leader to a strong bud to stimulate vigorous lateral growth, thereby developing a better balanced plant.

2 By early to mid summer the lateral growths should have developed. The uppermost new lateral is trained vertically so that it becomes the replacement leader.

Unpruned lavenders develop into woody, gnarled shrubs with bare lower stems sparsely topped by grey foliage. It is not worth while trying to rejuvenate misshapen or unkempt plants as they seldom produce satisfactory young growth if you cut back into old wood. It is far better to replace them with young plants, which should be pruned hard in mid spring to establish a low bushy habit. Do not prune immediately after flowering as is sometimes recommended as this only stimulates late young growth. *Erica arborea* (Tree heather) and its relatives do not require regular pruning. The removal of awkwardly placed or wayward branches is, however, occasionally necessary. This should be done in mid spring. Most summer- and autumn-flowering heathers benefit from regular trimming in early spring. If left unpruned they usually become leggy with shorter, less attractive flower heads. Remove old flower heads in the autumn. Winter-flowering heathers are naturally compact or spreading in habit and when they have finished flowering can be lightly trimmed to remove their old flower heads. No further pruning is required.

Lavandula: The first year

1 Mid spring. Young lavender at 23cm (9in) tall. Prune hard to remove straggly shoots and encourage new growth.

2 Early autumn. Vigorous bushy growth is produced during spring and summer along with a few flower spikes.

Second and subsequent years

3 Mid spring. Clip over the bush removing all old flower spikes and 3cm (1in) of the previous season's growth.

4 Early autumn. Old plant after flowering showing the form that should be created by regular pruning.

Erica

1 Early to early mid spring. Trim back the previous season's flowerheads to a point just below the lowest flowers on the spike. Take care to follow the natural shape of the plant.

2 Late summer to early autumn. *Calluna vulgaris* in flower; a compact plant with long flower spikes. Do not trim old flower heads, except for coloured-leaved cultivars, as they are attractive throughout winter.

Renovating evergreen shrubs

Evergreen shrubs will often become too large and outgrow their position. In many cases this is because it is not the normal practice to prune them regularly other than to remove dead or damaged branches. Many, but not all, will respond to a drastic pruning which in essence starts the shrub again. Vigorous growers such as laurel will cope with this. If in doubt renovate the plant over two or more seasons, removing a proportion of the branches each year. Scrap old lavender and rosemary and start afresh.

The first year

1 The winter appearance of an old laurel which has grown too straggly and too large for its position in the garden, and is in urgent need of renovation.

2 During late spring cut back all strong stems to within 30–60cm (1–2ft) of ground level. Cut out entirely any weak, damaged or dead growths.

The second year

3 At the same time, cut out the remains of any branch which is badly placed and may spoil the overall balance. Apply an organic mulch to the soil around the plant.

4 Late spring. Strong shoots have now developed. Cut out surplus new shoots leaving one, two or three of the strongest and best placed on each stump.

Most people grow at least a few roses in their garden or against the walls of their house, but to many gardeners the correct way to prune roses remains a complicated and mysterious process.

Roses in the wild produce strong new shoots from near the base of the plant each season. In subsequent years the secondary, or lateral, growth from these shoots becomes progressively weaker. When strong new shoots appear, the food taken in by the roots is directed to this new growth and the original shoots are gradually starved out. Eventually the old shoots die and remain as dead wood before falling to the ground. The purpose of pruning is to short-circuit nature by cutting away the old worn-out shoots and so encourage vigorous, disease-free, new growth and the optimum number of flowers for the rose concerned.

Pruning is a simple operation, but as roses range in size from miniatures, which are less that 30cm (1ft), to vigorous climbers, which may reach more than 10m (over 30ft), they require a variety of pruning techniques to keep them healthy, free-flowering and within bounds.

There are certain general principles that apply to pruning all roses, and these are illustrated below. It is not only how you prune that is important but also the tools you use. Always use sharp secateurs and a knife, as a ragged cut from using blunt tools may cause the shoot to die back. The cut must not be more than 6mm (¼ in) above a bud and must slope gently away from it. If you cut too high the snag will die back, but a cut too low may damage the bud or allow disease to enter the wound. A cut in the wrong direction allows moisture to gather by the bud.

Cut back into healthy wood. If the pith is brown or discoloured cut back the shoot until healthy white pith is reached. Cut out completely any dead and diseased stems, and weak spindly growth, even if it means cutting to ground level. Where two branches cross, cut one back to prevent them rubbing against each other or on their supports. Keep all branches well-spaced to allow free air flow through the plant and to allow light to reach the leaves. This lessens the likelihood of diseases such as black spot, rust, and mildew.

When you have finished, burn or otherwise dispose of prunings to reduce the chance of spreading disease.

Principles of pruning

Rose "eyes" or growth buds are located in the axils of the leaves. If the leaf has fallen they can be seen just above a leaf-scar.

Cut to an outward-pointing eye to encourage an open-centred habit. Roses of a spreading habit are sometimes pruned with some branches cut to an inward-facing bud.

Vigorous modern roses may often produce two or three shoots from one eye after pruning. As soon as possible reduce these to a single shoot by pinching or cutting out the other young growth.

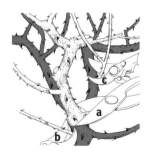

Cut out completely any dead and diseased wood (a) and any weak or spindly growth (b). Cut out one branch where two cross (c).

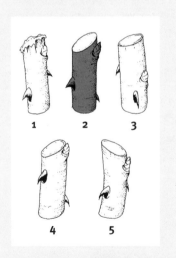

THE CORRECT CUT

1. A ragged cut – incorrect
2. The correct cut, just above a bud
3. Cut too high – incorrect
4. Too close to a bud – incorrect
5. Slopes in the wrong direction – incorrect

Pruning roses

You may not know to which group the roses in your garden belong. If you are not sure how to deal with them, confine your pruning to the principles outlined on page 103. In the following summer you can see from the way they flower to which group they belong and prune accordingly.

Suckers

Most roses are budded on a rootstock of a wild rose species. During the growing season shoots may arise from below the budding point. These are suckers and they should be removed as soon as they are seen, otherwise they will weaken and eventually dominate the cultivar. Trace the sucker back to the root and pull it off at the point of origin. Never cut it off at ground level; this only encourages basal buds to produce more suckers. With standard roses the suckers arise on the main stem and must be pulled off, or pared away with a sharp knife.

Standard roses

These are created by budding a desirable cultivar on a tall stem, varying in height from 75cm to 1.5m (2½–5ft). The "head" is most usually a Hybrid Tea or Floribunda. Pruning a standard Hybrid Tea involves cutting back strong shoots to three to five buds or 15cm (6in). With Floribundas cut back one-year-old growth to six to eight buds or 25cm (10in), and two-year-old shoots to three to six buds or 15cm (6in). Weeping standards are usually formed from ramblers with flexible stems belonging to Group 1 (see page 114). Prune them in late summer or early autumn by cutting out the two-year-old shoots that have flowered and leave the vigorous young shoots to flower the following season.

Standard roses need support throughout their lives. Use a tall stake that ends just below the graft point, and attach the rose by means of plastic tree ties.

Pruning with hedgetrimmers

Pruning trials on bush roses have compared the traditional system of precise cuts with other methods, including shearing plants back to about 60cm (2ft) with a hedgetrimmer. Despite the jagged cuts and non-removal of dead wood the roses have bloomed as well as the traditionally pruned bushes. Alternatively, shear back the roses as described but then remove any dead wood. This results in improved flowering. However, trials have not been running long enough to assess the possible detrimental effects of this rough and ready treatment in the long term.

BLIND SHOOTS

Some Hybrid Tea, Floribunda, and climbing roses produce a few shoots that are "blind" and do not flower. These blind shoots should be cut hard back as soon as they are seen, to encourage vigorous growth from buds lower down on the shoot; otherwise the flowering potential of the plant is diminished.

Deadheading

Correctly cut Hybrid Tea

Cut back to a strong outward facing shoot or eye below the flower head.

Incorrectly cut Hybrid Tea

The stems are cut too long on this plant and as a result it will be weakened.

Correctly cut Floribunda

Remove the whole truss by cutting back to the first strong outward-pointing eye or shoot.

Incorrectly cut Floribunda

The individual flowers in each of the trusses have been cut, leaving weak stems.

Pruning Hybrid Teas and Hybrid Perpetuals

Hybrid Teas and Hybrid Perpetuals are both pruned to encourage the production of strong basal growths to form an open-centred, cup-shaped plant with an evenly spaced framework of shoots. They both flower on new (current) season's growth and most benefit from a moderate to fairly severe annual pruning. This keeps plants bushy and ensures a constant supply of strong young shoots. Very vigorous roses should only be pruned lightly as severe pruning stimulates robust but often flowerless shoots.

Hybrid Teas, Hybrid Perpetuals: The first year

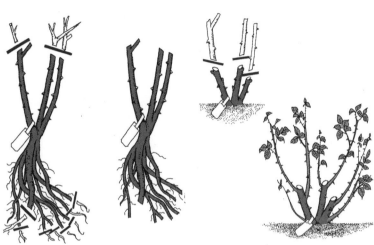

1 Autumn. Bare-rooted, open-ground bush as received. Cut back main shoots slightly if not already done. Prune any long, coarse or damaged roots before planting.

2 Late winter or early spring. Cut back each shoot to 15cm (6in) from ground level to encourage strong basal growth. By early summer new shoots will have grown.

3 Early to mid autumn. At the end of the first season's growth, tip back flowered stems and cut out any soft, unripe shoots. The main pruning is left until the spring.

Second and subsequent years

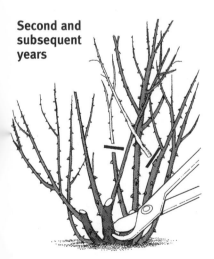

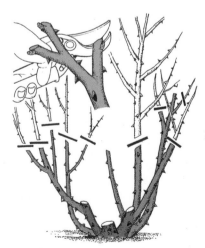

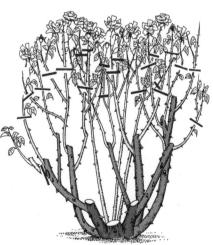

4 Late winter to early spring. Moderately prune by cutting out the dead or diseased wood. Cut out any weak, crossing or inward-growing stems.

5 At the same time, cut back strong stems to 4–6 buds or 23cm (9in), and less vigorous stems and remaining laterals to 2–4 buds or 15cm (6in).

6 Early to mid autumn. At the end of the season's growth, tip back flowered stems and cut any soft, unripe shoots. As the plant gets older cut 1 or 2 stems from the base.

Hybrid Teas include: Blessings, Fragrant Cloud ('Tanellis'), Ingrid Bergman ('Poulman'), Just Joey, Remember Me ('Cocdestin').
Hybrid Perpetuals include: Baron Girod de l'Ain, Frau Karl Druschki, Hugh Dickson, Paul Neyron, Roger Lambelin.

Pruning Floribundas

Floribunda roses are more vigorous than most Hybrid Teas and Hybrid Perpetuals, and produce a succession of large clusters of moderate-sized flowers. It is sometimes difficult to prune Floribundas to obtain the optimum number of blooms. Severe annual pruning, as used for Hybrid Teas and Hybrid Perpetuals, can weaken Floribundas within a few years, while light pruning creates large bushes filled with weak, spindly growth. Moderate pruning of each shoot to 6–8 buds or 30–45cm (12–18in) in

length is often recommended and proves reasonably successful, particularly in windy areas. It does not, however, always produce the almost continuous summer display which can be achieved, and some of the older wood may die away without replacement basal shoots forming. A combination of light pruning of some shoots to produce early flowers, and harder pruning of other shoots to encourage renewal of basal growths and provide later flowers, has proved the most satisfactory method.

Floribundas: The first year

The second year

1   Autumn. Open-ground bush as received. Cut back main shoots slightly if not already done. Prune long, coarse or damaged roots before planting.

2   From late winter to early spring begin to cut back all healthy growths to 15–23cm (6–9in) from the base. Remove any weak shoots.

3   Mid autumn. Growth at the end of the first season. Tip back main growths and cut out any soft, unripe shoots which will be lost in the winter.

4   In late winter prune back one-year-old basal shoots by a third. Reduce older wood to 15–23cm (6–9in) and any laterals by 10–15cm (4–6in).

Third and subsequent years

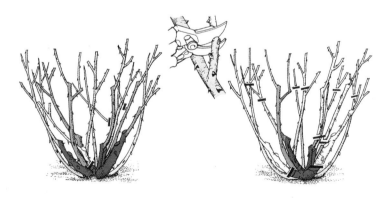

5   Mid autumn. Growth at the end of the second season. Tip back main growths and cut out any soft unripe shoots which will be lost in winter.

6   Late winter to early spring. Cut out dead or diseased wood. Cut out weak and crossing stems. Also cut out inward-growing growth.

7   At the same time, prune back all main one-year-old basal shoots by a third and their laterals to 2–3 buds. Prune older wood to 3–5 buds.

Floribundas include: 'Arthur Bell', Escapade ('Harpade'), 'Fragrant Delight', Iceberg ('Korbin'), Mountbatten ('Harmantelle'), 'The Queen Elizabeth', and many others.

Pruning Miniatures, Patios and Dwarf Floribunda Roses

Miniature roses are a popular group of low-growing roses that reach 30–60cm (1–2ft) in height. The flowers are similar in shape to those of Hybrid Teas and Floribundas, and are produced on the current season's growth. Pruning Miniature roses is basically similar to that recommended for Hybrid Teas and Hybrid Perpetuals, although it is best not to cut back newly planted Miniatures too severely. Very strong, vigorous shoots are occasionally produced which alter the overall symmetry of the plant. It is best to remove these entirely when pruning in early spring so that balanced growth can be maintained.

If a miniature rose continually produces vigorous shoots which unbalance the plant, it is best treated as a Floribunda for pruning purposes (see page 106). A number of so-called miniatures are of this kind, and are sometimes known as "Patio" roses.

Patio roses are also grouped with Miniatures and Dwarf Floribunda roses. Low, bushy, usually repeat-flowering roses, they seldom exceed 60–90cm (2–3ft) in height, and produce a large amount of rather twiggy, thin growth that needs to be pruned annually.

Miniatures: The first year

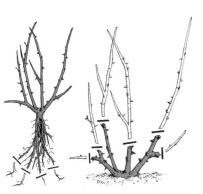

Second and subsequent years

1 Late winter to early spring. Bare-rooted bush as received from the nursery. Trim roots. Cut back strong shoots to 3–5 buds. Remove weak growth.

2 Early to mid summer. Vigorous shoots forming at base. Flowers are produced in clusters on thinner, twiggy growth. Summer prune to maintain flower production.

3 Late winter to early spring. Cut out any dead, diseased or weak shoots entirely. Prune well-spaced, stronger growths to 3–4 buds or 10–15cm (4–6in).

Patio and dwarf Floribundas: The first year

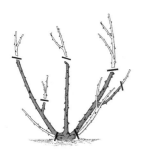

The second year

Third and subsequent years

1 Late winter to early spring. Trim roots before planting. Cut back strong shoots by one third, and remove completely any dead, diseased or weak wood.

2 Early summer to early autumn. The bush is now in flower, with new growth. Faded flowers are pruned to maintain a succession of blooms.

3 Late winter to early spring. Cut back strong stems by one third and maintain an open-centred bush by cutting out old, weak, diseased and dead wood.

4 Late winter to early spring. Tip back strong stems by one third. Remove twiggy growth and maintain an open-centred bush by cutting out old wood.

Miniatures, Patio and dwarf Floribundas include: Anna Ford ('Harpiccolo'), Gentle Touch ('Diclulu'), Harvest Fayre ('Dicnorth'), Orange Sunblaze ('Meijikatar'), Robin Redbreast ('Interrob'), Sweet Magic ('Dicmagic').

Pruning species and shrub roses: Group 1

Group 1 roses require minimal pruning. It includes species roses (excluding climbers), and their close hybrids; *Rosa pimpinellifolia* and *R. rugosa,* and their hybrids; Gallica and Hybrid Musk roses.

Most of these roses are fairly dense and bushy, and flower on lateral shoots of older wood. In the first year little pruning is needed other than removing any thin, weak or damaged shoots.

Group 1: The second year

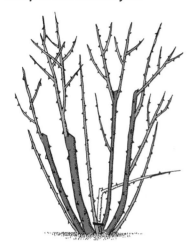

1 Early spring. Tip back all vigorous shoots. Cut to the base any badly placed shoots. Basal shoots have developed.

2 Early to late summer. Flowers produced on laterals of old wood; now the basal shoots are developing. No pruning required.

3 Early autumn. Summer prune. After flowering cut out thin, weak growth and any dead and diseased wood.

Third and subsequent years

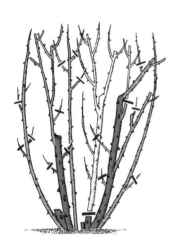

4 Late winter to early spring. Tip back all vigorous shoots and laterals if required. Cut out one or two older main shoots that have flowered sparsely.

5 During late summer the plant is flowering on laterals of old wood. New basal shoots will develop. No pruning required.

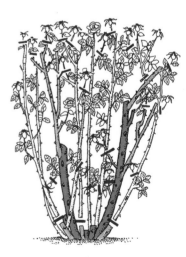

6 Early autumn. Summer prune flowered laterals. After flowering cut out thin and weak growth. Cut out any dead and diseased wood.

Group 1 includes: 'Charles de Mills', 'Fru Dagmar Hastrup', 'Frülingsgold', *R. gallica* 'Versicolor', 'Pink Grootendorst', 'Stanwell Perpetual'.

In the informality of a cottage garden, twiggy brushwood is the most suitable support for tall plants.

Right: The effect of the bright red foliage of *Photinia* x *fraseri* 'Red Robin' can be heightened by minor pruning in early spring.

Below: Hard pruning of the willow *Salix alba* ensures that the young stems appear at their most attractive every winter.

Pruning species and shrub roses: Group 2

Group 2 of species and shrub roses consists of roses that flower mainly on short lateral and sub-lateral shoots produced from second-year or older wood. This includes "old roses" such as Albas, Centifolias, Moss roses, and most Damasks. A large number of non-repeating, modern shrub roses are also included. First year roses are treated as Group 1 (see page 108).

Group 2: The second year

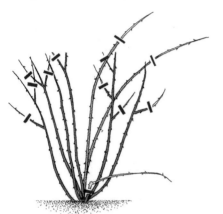

1 Late winter to early spring. Cut back long, new basal growths by up to one-third. Cut back laterals on flowered shoots to 2–3 buds or 10–15cm (4–6in). Cut out any badly placed shoots.

2 During the summer months the plant will flower on cut-back laterals of old wood. New shoots will develop from the base of the plant. Summer prune flowered laterals.

3 At some point in the autumn tip back extra-long growths to minimise any wind-rock, especially if the plant is in an exposed position. No other pruning is required.

Third and subsequent years

4 Late winter to early spring. Cut back long new basal growths by up to one-third. Cut back laterals on flowered shoots to 2–4 buds or 10–15cm (4–6in). Cut out any badly placed shoots.

5 In the summer months the plant will flower on cut-back laterals of old wood. New shoots will develop from the base of the plant. Summer prune flowered laterals.

6 At some time during the autumn tip back extra-long growths to minimise wind-rock of plants in exposed positions. No other pruning is required.

Group 2 includes: 'Céleste', 'Fantin Latour', 'Félicité Parmentier', 'Fritz Nobis', 'Königin von Danemark', 'William Lobb'.

Pruning species and shrub roses: Group 3

Group 3 can be regarded as a minor variant of Group 2, but are repeat flowering, and includes most of the China roses and some modern shrub roses. Many Bourbons come into this group. Certain robust Hybrid Teas and Hybrid Perpetuals can be included in this group and treated as shrubs for borders. First-year plants in this group are as those in Group 1 (see page 108).

Group 3: The second year

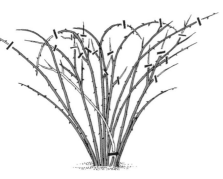

1 In the late winter and early spring cut back very long new basal or near-basal, one-year shoots by up to one-third. Take care to maintain the arching habit of the plant. Cut back laterals on shoots which have flowered last season to 2–3 buds or 8–15cm (3–6in). Cut out weak or badly placed shoots.

2 In early to mid summer the plant will flower on laterals from the previous season's wood. Basal and near-basal shoots are developing. Summer prune flowered laterals as the flowers fade. Mulch the soil around the base of the plant well after watering to preserve moisture and keep the weeds under control.

3 During late summer and early autumn flowers are being produced on laterals from the current season's growth. Twiggy sub-laterals have developed from summer-pruned growth.

Third and subsequent years

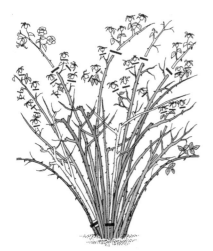

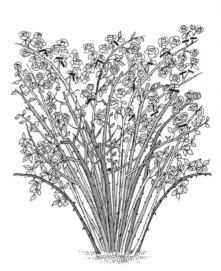

4 At some point during mid autumn tip back any extra-long growths to minimise wind-rock, especially for those plants in exposed positions. No other pruning is required at this time of year.

5 Late winter to early spring. Cut back very long, basal or near-basal one-year-old shoots by up to a third. Maintain the arching habit. Cut back laterals on shoots that flowered last season.

6 During early to mid summer the plant is in flower on laterals produced from previous season's wood. Basal and near-basal shoots are developing on the plant. Summer prune dead flowers as they fade.

Group 3 includes: Gertrude Jekyll ('Ausbord'), Graham Thomas ('Ausmas'), 'Honorine de Brabant', 'Louise Odier', 'Madame Isaac Pereire', 'Marchesa Boccella', Peace ('Madame A. Meilland'), 'Zephirine Drouhin'.

Renovating bush roses

Unpruned and neglected bush roses may continue to flower for years, but they are usually a sorry sight. Most roses will stand being cut almost to the ground. For the majority, however, a somewhat gentler approach can be adopted which will give equally good results. Even the most neglected rose will usually have a few vigorous shoots and the first aim is to preserve these.

The first year

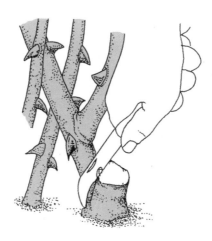

1 Late winter to early spring. Cut out dead and diseased shoots and half of the main stems to the base, leaving those with strong young growth. Cut back laterals to 2–3 buds.

2 At the same time, to prevent infection, pare away any loose bark around the cuts. Apply fertilizer and then mulch with organic matter.

3 Early to mid summer. Flowers are now present on laterals of the remaining older wood. Vigorous young basal shoots are beginning to appear.

Second year

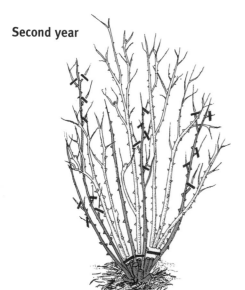

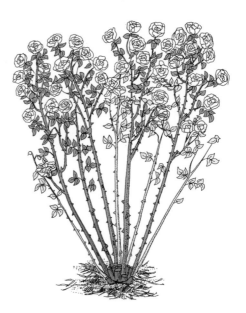

4 Late winter to early spring. Cut out all the remaining old growths to the base. Prune any laterals on new growths to 2–3 buds or 15cm (6in). Repeat procedure described in step 2.

5 Early to mid summer. The bush flowers on one-year-old shoots and new, vigorous shoots fill in the framework of the plant. Continue to prune as the appropriate group.

Pruning climbers and ramblers: Group 1

For convenience, ramblers and climbers have been divided into four groups, but these should not be taken as rigid divisions and some overlap of pruning techniques occur. If sufficient space is available, train new extension shoots of climbers and ramblers as near to the horizontal as possible. Horizontally placed shoots will produce flowering laterals along most of their length, and create a far better display than vertical shoots, which tend to form only a few flowering laterals at the tips.

Group 1 (Ramblers): The first year

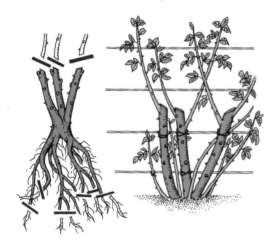

1 Plant as received in autumn with 3–4 shoots about 1.2–1.5m (4–5ft) long. Prune back shoots to 23–38cm (9–15in) and trim any uneven and coarse roots before planting. In spring new shoots begin to develop.

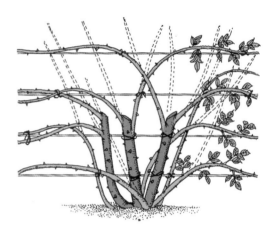

2 From early summer to early autumn strong shoots will have developed from the pruned growth and from the base of the plant. Train them into place along the wires or trellis (see pages 79 and 248).

Second and subsequent years

3 During the early to mid summer months the plant flowers on lateral shoots produced on previous year's growth. Young basal shoots develop; train these more or less horizontally, if possible, and tie them in securely with string or plant ties.

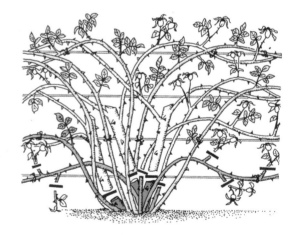

4 During late summer and early autumn cut out the flowered shoots to the base, leaving one or two to fill in the framework if required. Cut back laterals to 2–3 buds or 10–15cm (4–6in). Tie in all new growth.

Group 1 includes: 'Dorothy Perkins', 'Excelsa', 'Albéric Barbier', 'Crimson Showers', 'Paul's Himalayan Musk', 'Rambling Rector', 'Sander's White Rambler', 'Seagull', 'Wedding Day'.

Pruning climbers and ramblers: Group 2

Group 2 climbers include many well-known, vigorous roses, such as 'Albertine' and 'Chaplin's Pink Climber'. They flower once in the summer on the laterals of long shoots produced the previous year. They differ from true ramblers in producing very few basal shoots each season, most of the new growth coming from higher up the stems. The aim of pruning is to remove old wood in proportion to the new.

In the first year newly planted roses in this group are treated in the same way as in Group 1 (see page 114). In the second and subsequent years, pruning of established plants takes place soon after flowering. Cut away completely one or two old growths and train in their place any basal shoots that have started to develop. If no basal shoots are forming cut back one or two old growths to 30–45cm (12–18in) from the base. Cut back old wood, higher up the plant to a point where a vigorous new leading shoot has started to grow. Keep leading shoots at full length and train them as near to the horizontal as possible. Any shorter laterals should be cut back to 2–3 buds or 15cm (6in).

Group 2: The second year

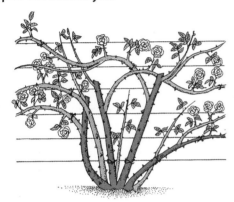

1 In early to mid summer the plant will flower on lateral shoots produced on the previous year's growth. One or two basal growths begin to develop and some leader shoots higher up. Tie in these new growths horizontally on the training wires.

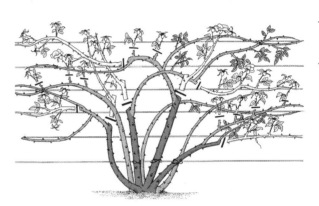

2 Late summer to early autumn. Cut back old growth to main replacement leaders. Cut back flowering laterals to 2–3 buds or 15cm (6in). Train replacement leaders as near to horizontal as possible. Cut back weak leaders to 2–3 buds or 15cm (6in).

Third and subsequent years

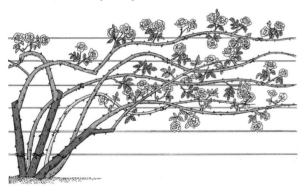

3 During the early to mid summer the flowers are produced along last year's leaders and spurred back laterals. New leaders begin to develop as well as new growth from the base, all of which should be tied in horizontally to the supports.

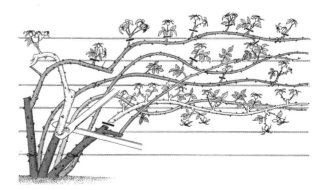

4 During the late summer and early autumn repeat the pruning operation in step 2. Cut back one or two of the older shoots to 30–45cm (12–18in) from the base to encourage replacement basal growth.

Group 2 includes: 'Albertine', 'Blairii Number 2', 'Bobbie James', 'Chaplin's Pink Climber', 'Félicité et Perpétue', 'Veilchenblau'.

Pruning climbers and ramblers: Group 3

Group 3 of climbers and ramblers contains those roses that produce their blooms on current season's growth and includes climbers of Hybrid Tea style and climbing sports of Hybrid Teas and Floribundas. Most of the roses in this group are repeat-flowering. Their long, flexible shoots make them ideal for training against walls, fences, or on pergolas. On planting, roses in this group should not be pruned back, although the roots should be trimmed, and damaged tips and weak growth removed. Pruning should be avoided because many are climbing sports from bush varieties and hard pruning may cause them to revert.

During the first year it is essential to build up a strong, evenly spaced framework of branches, as roses in this group do not really produce vigorous basal growths once established, but develop most of their young shoots higher up on existing main stems. Horizontal or angled training of new leader shoots at an early stage will help to prevent the base of the plant becoming too bare. Apart from maintaining the plant within its allotted space, pruning and training of mature roses in this group is restricted to summer pruning of flowering laterals during the growing season as the flowers fade. With old plants it will occasionally be necessary to cut back weak and exhausted shoots to a few cm/in from the base. This will encourage one or two new, vigorous basal shoots.

Group 3: The first year

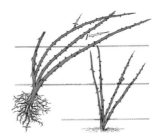

1 At some point either in the autumn or the early spring a plant similar to the above will be bought with 3–4 shoots 1.2–1.5m (4–5ft) long. Trim any uneven damaged or coarse roots. Tip back slightly any unripe or damaged growths. Do not prune except to cut out any weak side shoots. Begin to train shoots against the wires.

2 During the mid to late summer tie in a framework of new shoots on the wires as they develop. Some flowers will be produced at the tips of new growths and on laterals. New shoots will develop and should be tied in as they grow. Summer prune flowering laterals as the flowers go over.

Second and subsequent years

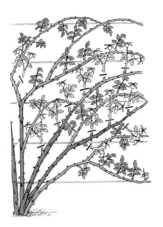

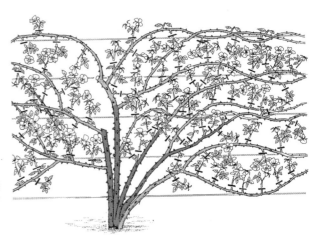

3 At some point when the weather allows from mid autumn to early spring prune back all flowered laterals to 3–4 buds or approximately 15cm (6in). Cut out weak wood and tie in leading shoots. Mulch the soil around the base of the plant.

4 During the mid to late summer flowers will appear at the tips of new growth and laterals. Summer prune flowering laterals as the flowers go over. As the new shoots develop, tie them in regularly to the supporting wires or trellis.

5 At some point when the weather allows from mid autumn to early spring prune back flowered laterals to 3–4 buds or approximately 15cm (6in). Cut out completely any weak and diseased wood. Tie in leading shoots from the main stems of the framework onto the supporting wires or trellising. On older plants it may be occasionally necessary to prune out old and exhausted main stems right back to within a few cm/in of the base. This will encourage new vigorous, basal shoots thereby revitalising the plant for the forthcoming seasons.

Group 3 includes: 'Climbing Iceberg', 'Climbing Lady Hillingdon', Compassion, 'Gloire de Dijon', 'Schoolgirl', 'Swan Lake'.

Pruning climbers and ramblers: Group 4

Group 4 includes pillar roses, which are repeat-flowering and produce their blooms on the current season's wood. They differ from roses in Group 3 in their more moderate, upright growth and seldom exceed 2.5–3m (8–10ft) in height. Their shoots are usually flexible, and they are suitable for growing against pillars, or for training in positions with limited horizontal space.

Group 4: The first year

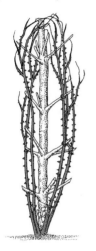

1 A plant in autumn to early spring showing the shoots tied to a vertical support such as a post or pillar.

2 Mid to late summer. Flowers on laterals of the old growth. New growth has formed on last year's stems and from the base.

3 Late autumn. Cut back flowered laterals and some new leaders sufficiently to maintain the symmetry of the plant.

The second year

4 At the same time cut out weak, diseased and dead wood. Tie in the new shoots to the framework.

5 Early to late summer. Prune by removing all fading flower trusses. New growth has developed from older stems and the base.

6 Late autumn. Cut back flowered laterals and some new leaders sufficiently to maintain the plant's shape and symmetry.

Group 4 includes: Aloha', Bantry Bay, Danse de Feu, Dortmund, Dublin Bay ('MacDub'), Golden Showers, Handel ('Macha').

Pruning clematis: Group 1

Group 1 consists of the late-flowering *Clematis*, which includes the species and hybrids that flower in the summer and autumn entirely on new growth produced during the current season. If left unpruned they begin growth in the spring from where they flowered the previous year, and rapidly become bare at the base with flowers at the top only. Pruning is very simple and consists of cutting back the whole of the previous year's growth virtually to ground level in mid to late winter.

Cuts should be immediately above the lowest pair of strong buds. New growth will appear from these points.

Group 1 Late-flowering clematis: The first year

1 Mid to late winter. A newly planted clematis. Cut back to the lowest pair of strong buds. Mulch the plant well around the base.

2 Late spring to early summer. Train in the strong young growths and any new basal growth. Flowers may appear in late summer.

The second year

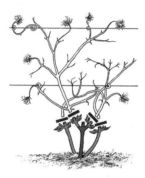

3 Mid to late winter. Cut back all growths to the lowest pair of strong buds on each stem. Mulch the plant well around the base.

GROUP 1 INCLUDES

C. 'Duchess of Albany'
C. 'Ernest Markham'
C. 'Gravetye Beauty'
C. 'Gypsy Queen'
C. 'Hagley Hybrid'
C. 'Jackmanii'
C. orientalis
C. 'Perle D'Azur'
C. 'Star of India'
C. tangutica and hybrids
C. 'Ville de Lyon'
C. viticella and hybrids

Third and subsequent years

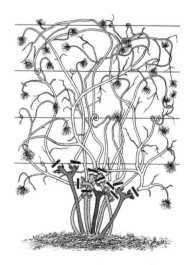

4 Late spring to early summer. Train and tie in all young growths, and any further basal shoots as they develop. Keep the plant watered in dry periods.

5 Flowers are produced, often in abundance, on the current season's growth. Keep the plant well watered in dry periods. Mulching helps.

6 During mid or late winter. Cut back all growths to the lowest pairs of strong buds on each stem. Mulch the soil well around each plant.

Group 2 is the early-flowering category of *Clematis*, and consists mainly of the vigorous spring-flowering species and their hybrids. These flower between late spring and early summer on short shoots from growth produced the previous summer. Examples are *Clematis montana*, *C. alpina* and *C. macropetala*. *C. montana* is very vigorous, and attempts to restrict them on a low fence or wall usually results in a great deal of work. They are best given ample space on a house wall, or trained over a large tree and left unpruned or merely sheared over after flowering to keep them tidy. If they get out of hand, renovate them by cutting the old stems back to within 60–90cm (2–3ft) of the ground level in late winter or early spring.

Initial pruning at planting will encourage vigorous growth that can be gently guided to cover the area available, and to form the basic framework over a two-year period. Once this has been achieved, the pruning of mature plants consists of cutting away all the stems that have borne flowers to within a few cm/in of the main framework immediately after flowering.

This will stimulate vigorous long growths that can be trained or guided in as required, or allowed to cascade naturally, and form a curtain of flowers. This new growth will provide next season's flowering display and therefore must not be winter-pruned.

Group 2 Early-flowering clematis: The first year

1 Mid to late winter. A newly planted clematis with a single main stem. Cut back the stem above the lowest pair of strong buds. Mulch well around the base.

2 In late spring or early summer train in the strong young growths, and any further basal growths that may have developed, to ensure maximum coverage of the supports.

The second year

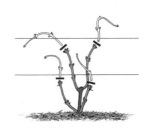 

3 At some point in mid to late winter, cut back all the main growths trained in the previous summer by one-half their length to a pair of strong buds. Mulch well.

4 Mid spring to early summer. Train or guide the new shoots as required. Prune back any laterals that have flowered low down on the plant to one or two pairs of buds from the base.

Third and subsequent years

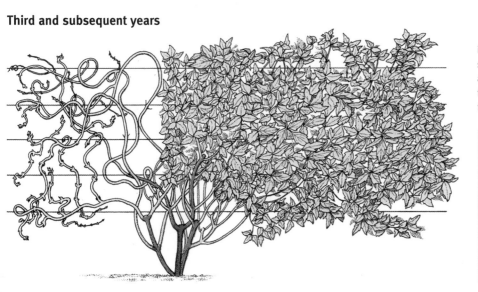

5 Mid summer to early autumn. Train or guide in new growth as required. In subsequent years prune back all growths in June that have flowered to just one or two buds from the framework branches.

GROUP 2 INCLUDES

C. alpina and cultivars
C. cirrhosa
C. macropetala and cultivars
C. montana and cultivars

Pruning clematis: Group 3

Included in Group 3 are all the hybrids that provide large, sumptuous flowers from late spring to mid summer. On stems formed the previous year. While the flowers develop on side shoots from the old wood, new growth is being formed. This produces further crops of medium-sized flowers during the late summer and early autumn. The growth habit of this category of *Clematis* makes them difficult to prune without a great deal of work, and they may be left entirely unpruned or only lightly pruned until they become straggly, when they must be rejuvenated by cutting right back during the winter. Alternatively, they may be treated as early-flowered and pruned hard to the base in mid to late winter, although they will then only flower in late summer.

Group 3 Large-flowered hybrids: The first year

1 Late winter. A newly planted clematis with a single main stem. Cut back the stem to above the lowest pair of strong buds. Mulch the plant well.

2 Between late spring and early summer train in strong young growths and any basal growths which develop. A few flowers may be produced during the late summer.

The second year

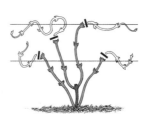

3 In mid to late winter cut back all the main growths trained in the previous summer by one-half to a strong pair of buds. Mulch well around the plant.

4 Early summer to early autumn. Train in the new growths as required. The basic framework has been established. Some flowers will be produced in summer and autumn.

Third and subsequent years

5 Plant will flower on old wood. Immediately after flowering cut one-quarter to one-third of the mature shoots to within 30cm (12in) of the base.

6 In late summer and early autumn the plant flowers on young shoots. Guide and tie into place any new basal shoots that develop from the cut-back stems.

GROUP 3 INCLUDES

C. 'Barbara Dibley'
C. 'Barbara Jackman'
C. 'Belle of Woking'
C. 'Capitaine Thuilleaux'
C. 'Countess of Lovelace'
C. 'Duchess of Edinburgh'
C. 'Edouard Desfossé'
C. 'Elsa Späth'
C. 'Fair Rosamond'
C. 'Fairy Queen'
C. 'Gillian Blades'
C. 'Gladys Picard'
C. 'Guiding Star'
C. 'Henryi'
C. 'Lawsoniana'
C. 'Marie Boisselot'
C. 'Nelly Moser'
C. 'Proteus'
C. 'The President'
C. 'Vyvyan Pennell'
C. 'Walter Pennell'
C. 'William Kennett'

Pruning wisteria

The pruning of *Wisteria* baffles most gardeners as the tremendous vigour of their whip-like summer shoots seems almost impossible to control. It is, however, quite practicable to keep them restrained and trained into a reasonably confined space, although they are capable of clambering 30m (100ft) or more up a tree or along a wall. Successful control demands a good deal of attention from the gardener as pruning needs to be carried out twice during the season to ensure adequate flowers, and to confine the plant's naturally robust growth.

A young *Wisteria* planted in the winter or early spring will normally produce one or two vigorous basal growths that increase rapidly in length. Few or no lateral shoots develop at this stage. If a plant is to be grown in espalier form to cover a wall or fence, the main shoot must be cut or tipped back to 75–90cm (30–36in) from ground level at planting. This stimulates two or three lateral buds to develop, which should be trained into the positions required. Tie in the upper shoot vertically and the other growths at an angle of approximately 45°. If the laterals are trained in a horizontal position initially their growth may be checked. At this stage the branches are flexuous and easily positioned on the support system. The following winter cut back the leading shoot leaving 75–90cm (30–36in) of wood above the uppermost lateral. Bring down the laterals to a horizontal position. Cut back the horizontal leaders of those

laterals by about one-third. This stimulates further lateral growth, and a similar training process is carried out during the subsequent years to form a new vertical leader and further well-spaced horizontal laterals. Train a leader for each pruned back lateral and cut back other laterals to 4–5 leaves of the main framework in late summer to form flowering spurs.

Once the basic framework of branches has been trained to fill the area available any further extension growths, which may reach 3–3.6m (10–12ft) in a season, and lateral growths are pruned back in late summer to within 15cm (6in) (4–6 leaves) of the main branches to form flowering spurs. This summer pruning is followed by further shortening of these spurs in winter to 8–10cm (3–4in), leaving only 2–3 buds on each spur shoot. The following season's flowers are borne on these spurs. In winter the plump flower buds are easily distinguished from the flattened growth buds so the flowering potential is readily observed. A more laborious procedure to provide more flower buds involves pruning back the extension growths to 15cm (6in) at two week intervals during the summer. This stimulates further laterals to form, and constant pinching back produces more congested spurs.

Wisterias can, however, be grown in a number of other ways and trained not only as espaliers but as fans, as low standard shrubs, or semi-informally against walls or fences.

Wisteria: The first year

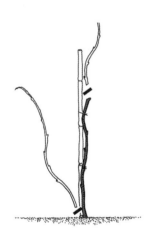

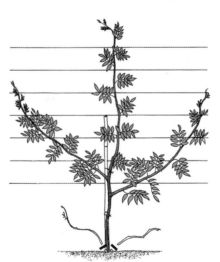

The second year

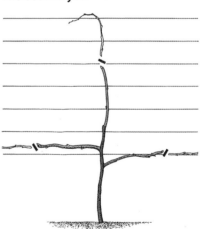

1 This is a young *Wisteria* at the time of planting. At some point when weather allows during winter to early spring, prune or tip back the strongest growth to 75–90cm (30–36in) from ground level. Stake and tie in this main shoot. Remove to the base any surplus shoots present. Mulch the plant well.

2 Early to late summer. Two or three vigorous shoots develop from lateral buds. Train in the uppermost vertically. Tie in other laterals on the support framework at about 45°. Remove any new basal growths. Tie in further extension growth. If sub-laterals are produced, cut them back in late summer to 15–23cm (6–9in).

3 At some point in the early to mid winter months cut back the vertical leader to within 75–90cm (30–36in) of the uppermost lateral. Bring down the laterals that have been trained at 45° to a horizontal position, and cut back their leaders by about one-third. Make certain that they are well tied to their supports. Mulch the soil well.

Pruning wisteria

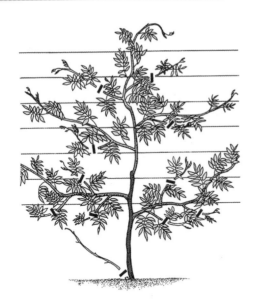

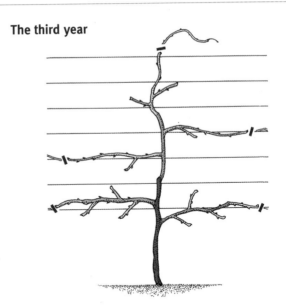

The third year

4 Early to late summer. Vigorous shoots develop. Train in the top one vertically as the new leader. Tie in other laterals at an angle of 45°. Remove any further basal growth. In late summer cut back any surplus laterals and sub-laterals to 15–13cm (6–9in).

5 Early to mid winter. Cut back the vertical leader to 75–90cm (30–36in) of the top lateral. Bring down the laterals to a horizontal position, and cut back their leaders by one-third. Cut back the leaders of last season's growth on horizontal branches by one-third.

The mature plant

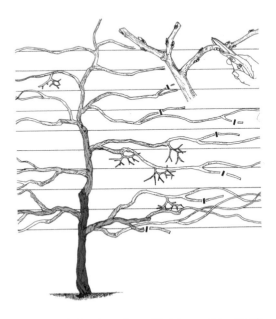

6 Every year in late summer prune all extension growths back to approximately 15cm (6in), leaving about 4–6 leaves on each spur shoot. Ensure that all laterals and sub-laterals are still tied in securely to their supports.

7 Every year, during the early to mid winter months, prune the same growths back to 8–10cm (3–4in), leaving only 2–3 buds on each spur shoot. Again, check that all laterals and sub-laterals are still securely tied in to their supports.

Climbing plants can be used to clothe house walls, fences, the sides of sheds, and garages. Apart from the obvious advantage of masking a less than beautiful construction, it is a method of merging house and garden. In addition, walls and fences provide shelter for slightly tender plants that are not totally hardy in the open garden. Aspect is very important in deciding what climbers to grow where. There is no point in planting a sun-loving wisteria against a dank north- or east-facing wall where it will not flower well, whereas a climbing hydrangea or ivy will cope well in such conditions. Never plant directly against a wall or fence, but about 45cm (18in) away (see page 79). The soil close to the wall is usually very dry and plant growth will suffer.

The pruning and training of climbing plants are affected by their vigour and their habit of growth. Take care to keep stems of vigorous climbers well clear of gutters and tiles, otherwise they can all too easily cause damage. The various growth habits can be divided into three basic groups.

Natural clingers

This group includes ivies and Virginia creeper, which support themselves by means of aerial roots or sucker pads. No support system is needed but make sure the building's structure and mortar is sound before planting one of these. Pruning is usually

IVY – AERIAL ROOTS

Ivies cling to surfaces by means of small roots growing from the stems. This habit means supports and training are unnecessary, although keep ivy clear of gutters and roof tiles.

a matter of keeping the plants within bounds, although they can be fan trained. Ivies can be sheared over every year in spring or summer, to produce a fresh flush of foliage.

Twiners

This is a large group. It includes plants that climb by means of twining stems – honeysuckle and wisteria (see pages 121–23), curling leaf tendrils (*Passiflora*), or leaf-stalks (*Clematis*, see pages 118–20). A support system to which they attach themselves is required (see page 248).

Scramblers and floppers

These clamber through other plants in the wild, using hooked thorns (roses: see pages 114–17), or by rapid elongation of the willowy shoots (*Solanum jasminoides*). A support system is necessary to which the growths can easily be tied (see page 248).

Supports for climbers

As most climbers require some sort of support, training wires or trellis must be in place before planting (see page 248). Make sure that the support and structure are strong enough to take the weight of the climber. Climbers can also be grown over pergolas, arbours, pillars, obelisks, and arches. The plants will need to be trained over the structure initially and new growth tied in at regular intervals. An alternative is to plant a climber to scramble through a tree or a hedge. In these cases make sure that the host plant is large and vigorous enough not to be swamped by the climber. Plant the climber beyond the edge of the tree canopy, and guide it into the branches by means of a cane or string, to reduce the competition for water and nutrients.

HONEYSUCKLES

Climbing honeysuckles can be divided into two groups for pruning purposes. The first group typified by *Lonicera japonica*, the rampant Japanese honeysuckle, produces flowers in pairs in the leaf axils on the current season's growth. The only pruning necessary is to restrict the exuberant growth by clipping away any unwanted growth in early to mid spring each year. This stimulates fresh young growth which quickly covers the sheared surface, and will flower later in the season.

The second group includes the Dutch honeysuckles (*L. periclymenum* and a number of related species, and hybrids such as *L. x americana*, *L. x brownii*, *L. sempervirens*, *L. x tellmanniana*, and *L. tragophylla*. These bear flowers on laterals produced from the previous season's growth.

If space allows they may be permitted to clamber through old trees, or on walls, and left unpruned. However they do tend to form "birds' nests" on bare stems – as do some *Clematis* – and if these are unsightly simply cut back some of the old weak growths and flowered shoots to a point where vigorous growth can be tied into a framework, or left to cascade down for an informal curtain of flowers.

Propagation: Softwood cuttings

Softwood is the most immature part of the stem, and, when propagating, it is the most difficult cutting to keep alive. However, softwood does have the highest capacity of all kinds of stems to produce roots: the younger and more immature the cutting, the greater will be its ability to develop roots. Soft stem growth is produced continuously at the tip of any stem during the growing season. Softwood cuttings are best taken in spring when the tips are fast growing.

Softwood cuttings

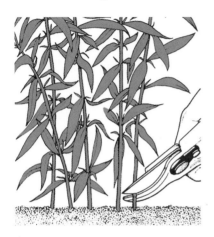

1 Prune woody plants hard in winter to promote the growth of new stems. These will have a high capacity to produce roots when taken as cuttings, as they appear in the spring.

2 Fill a container, a 9cm (3½in) pot will do, with a good quality, moist cutting compost. Without pressing too hard, gently firm the compost down to within 1.25cm (⅜in) of the rim of the container used.

3 Choose your cutting material. It should be a fast-growing, healthy, undamaged shoot with short internodes. Cut the tip of the stem one early morning in spring. Cut the shoot longer than the required cutting length.

4 To prevent the cuttings wilting, place them immediately into a closed polythene bag or in a bucket of cool water. Place these in a cool, shady position where the cuttings will not wilt.

5 Remove the cuttings one at a time as you deal with them. Cut the base of the stem 6mm (¼ in) below a leaf joint so that the cutting is no more than 10cm (4in) long.

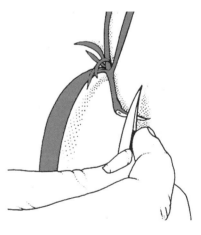

6 Alternatively, take the cutting with a heel by gently but firmly pulling it from the main stem, taking away a little of the stem as you do so. Trim this tail to a short heel.

Propagation: Softwood cuttings

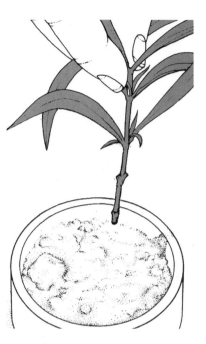

7 Remove the leaves cleanly from the bottom third of the cutting with a sharp knife. Dip the basal cut in a rooting powder or liquid to protect it against rotting and to promote efficient rooting.

8 Make a hole with a dibber in the compost near the edge of the pot. Insert the cutting up to its leaves in the compost, taking care not to damage the base of the cutting. Continue with more cuttings.

9 Label the cuttings clearly with the name of the plant. Firm the cutting compost around the cuttings. Water the cuttings from above with a fine-rosed watering can.

10 Keep the cuttings in a warm, well-lit position in a propagator. Alternatively, the complete pot can be enclosed in a sealed polythene bag. When they have rooted harden them off gradually.

11 When hardened off, plant the cuttings in individual pots of John Innes no. 1 compost or similar (see page 21), and clearly label. Keep in a protected position until they are well established.

HORMONE ROOTING

Rooting powders are based on talc to which low concentrations of rooting hormone is added and, in many cases, a fungicide. Most of the hormone is taken up through the cut base of the stem, so touch the base of the cutting on the hormone powder, ensuring none adheres to the outside of the stems.

If there is difficulty in getting sufficient hormone powder to stick to the cut surface of a softwood cutting, dip the cutting first in water.

Shrubs suitable for softwood cuttings include: *Abelia* (some), *Caryopteris*, *Ceanothus* (some), *Cestrum*, *Deutzia*, *Erica*, *Forsythia*, *Fuchsia* (some), *Hebe*, *Hydrangea*, *Kolkwitzia*, *Lavatera*, *Perovskia*, *Philadelphus*, *Spiraea*.

Propagation: Greenwood cuttings

The essential but subtle distinction between softwood and greenwood cuttings is the speed of growth. Externally they may appear to be similar, but greenwood cuttings are taken from the soft tip of the stem after the spring flush of growth has slowed down. The stem is then slightly harder and woodier. As the season progresses greenwood cuttings become harder.

Greenwood cuttings

1 Prune back woody plants hard in the winter to encourage strong, vigorous stems with a high rooting capacity.

2 Fill a container with cutting compost. Cut off as many vigorous shoots as you require early in the morning.

3 Place the cuttings at once in a bucket of water or a polythene bag, both kept in the shade to prevent the cuttings wilting.

4 Place the cuttings on a pane of glass or other hard, level surface. Reduce their length to 8–10cm (3–4in) using a sharp knife.

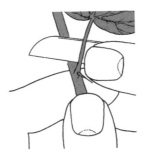

5 Trim the leaves from the bottom half of the cutting, shaving them flush with the stem to leave no snags.

6 Dip the base of the cutting into a rooting powder or liquid. These contain a fungicide which protects the cutting.

7 Make a hole in the compost with a dibber. Insert the cutting almost up to its leaves in the hole. Firm in and label.

8 Water the cuttings with a fine rose. Place in a closed environment that will control the loss of water and provide light shade.

9 Harden off the cuttings once they have rooted. Repot individually into a potting compost and grow on.

Shrubs suitable for greenwood cuttings include: Berry fruits, *Ceanothus*, *Chrysanthemum*, *Delphinium*, *Forsythia*, Gooseberry, *Pelargonium*, *Philadelphus*, *Vitis* (Vines, both fruiting and ornamental).

Right: An island bed demonstrates the structural quality of shrubs – those grown here include *Cotinus coggygria*, dogwood, heather, hibiscus, and rosemary.

Below: A pleasant woodland walkway lined with the bright and highly scented deciduous shrub *Rhododendron lutea*.

Left: Rose species such as the sweet briar, *Rosa eglanteria,* with their attractive hips, should only be pruned if they overrun a site.

Below: The informality of a cottage garden, in which climbing roses trained over an arbour play an important part.

Propagation: Semi-ripe cuttings

During the late summer, annual stem growth slows down and plant stems continue to harden. Cuttings taken at this time are called semi-ripe cuttings. As they are thicker and firmer than softwood and greenwood cuttings, they are more capable of survival. Semi-ripe cuttings have relatively high levels of stored foods and can survive and produce roots in poor light.

Semi-ripe cuttings

1 Prune the parent plant at the start of the dormant season to encourage strong stems to make good cutting material.

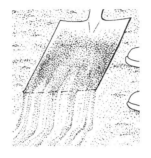

2 Prepare the soil in a cold frame by digging deeply. Add peat and grit. Cover with 3cm (1in) of fine sand.

3 Cut off a shoot with the current season's growth in late summer or early autumn. Remove the tip only if it is soft.

4 Shorten the cutting to 10–15cm (4–6in). Remove the leaves from the bottom 5cm (2in) of the stem by cutting cleanly.

5 Treat the basal cut with a rooting powder or liquid. Make a hole with a dibber and insert the cutting 4cm (1½in) deep.

6 Insert the remaining cuttings 8–10cm (3–4in) apart. Label and water with a fungicide. Seal and shade the frame.

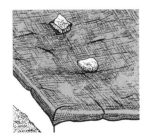

7 Rewet the soil if it dries out. Remove any fallen or rotting leaves. Insulate the cold frame with matting in cold weather.

8 Remove the insulation when the danger of frost is over and air the frame. Apply a routine liquid feed once growth starts.

9 Lift the new plants once their leaves have dropped in autumn, and transplant them to individual pots or a nursery bed.

Shrubs suitable for semi-ripe cuttings include: *Ribes (Currant, flowering), Deutzia, Diervilla, Cornus* (Dogwood, coloured bark), *Forsythia, Philadelphus, Prunus* (Plum, coloured leaf), *Weigela.*

Propagation: Hardwood cuttings

Propagating from hardwood cuttings is one of the easiest techniques of vegetative propagation. They are taken during the dormant season from the fully mature stem of a deciduous tree or shrub. Because the cutting has no leaves, the degree of environmental control required for propagation is minimal. The base of a stem has the greatest ability to develop roots.

Hardwood cuttings

1 Prune the parent plant hard during the dormant season to promote vigorous growth that is good for cuttings.

2 Run a hand down a leafy stem on the parent plant in autumn; if the leaves fall off then you can take cuttings.

3 Once the leaves have fallen off remove a hardwood stem at its base with a clean cut by a pair of secateurs.

4 Make a sloping cut just above the proposed top bud. The slope will be used to identify the top of the cutting.

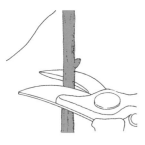

5 Make another cut 15cm (6in) below the first. This should be horizontal to identify the bottom of the cutting.

6 Dip only the basal cut in a rooting compound – this promotes rooting as well as providing a fungicide.

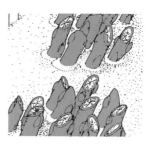

7 Heel in some bundles of cuttings with just their tips showing in a cold frame or box of sand, and clearly label.

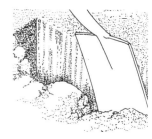

8 Dig the soil in a sheltered position just before bud break in spring. Dig a furrow 13cm (5in) deep with a spade.

9 Lift the cuttings and insert them individually in the trench, 10–15cm (4–6in) apart.

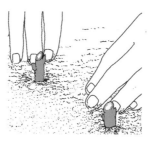

10 Fill in the trench and firm the soil, leaving about 3cm (1in) exposed.

11 If frosts lift the soil firm it back down again. Remove any weeds.

12 By the next autumn the cuttings can be lifted, and potted or put in a nursery bed.

Shrubs suitable for hardwood cuttings include: Black currant, *Cotoneaster*, large growing hybrids, *Ribes* (Currant, flowering) , *Cornus* (Dogwood, coloured-bark), *Prunus* (Plum, coloured-leaf), *Populus* (Poplar), Red currants, *Rosa* (Roses), *Spiraea*, *Viburnum*.

Propagation: Heel and mallet cuttings

Taking heel cuttings is a widely used method of preparing a stem cutting. It is quite possible to make heel cuttings of softwood, greenwood, semi-ripe, hardwood or evergreen stems. A young side shoot is gently pulled off with a thin sliver of bark and wood from the parent stem attached. Mallet cuttings have a hardwood plug at the base of each cutting that helps prevent fungal attack. Their use is restricted to semi-ripe and hardwood cuttings. *Berberis* is a good subject for this.

Heeled cuttings

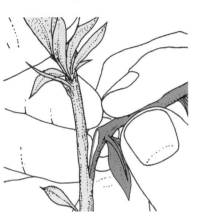

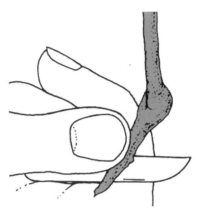

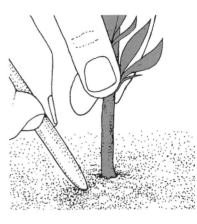

1   Hold the base of a side shoot between thumb and forefinger. Pull down, sharply removing the side shoot and part of the stem. These can be taken at any time of year.

2   With a sharp knife or scalpel neaten the tail on the heel by cutting across it. Remove the tip on semi-ripe and hardwood cuttings. Dip the cut base in a rooting powder or liquid.

3   Set the cuttings in a pot containing a good quality cutting compost. Make a hole, insert the cutting, and firm it in, completely filling in the hole. Clearly label. Water the compost.

Mallet cuttings

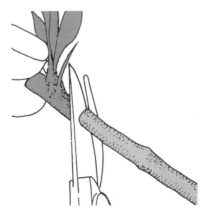

1   Cut horizontally through a stem just above a suitable side shoot, using a pair of scissor-type secateurs or a very sharp knife. It is important that the cut should be clean so as to avoid die-back.

2   Make a second cut about 2cm (¾in) below the first cut so that the side shoot is about midway between the two cuts. Split this "mallet" lengthways with a knife if it is thick. Remove any leaves at the base.

3   Dip the base in a rooting powder plus fungicide. Make a hole large enough to take the mallet. Then insert the cutting into a pot of cutting compost, firming it down gently. Label and then water.

Propagation: Conifer cuttings

Conifers are predominantly evergreen trees and shrubs, some of which can be propagated from softwood, greenwood, semi-ripe or ripewood cuttings. In general, spruces, firs and pines do not grow well from cuttings, and should be propagated from seed or grafted. Select cuttings from young, actively growing plants that have been clipped regularly which will help them produce strong, vigorous shoots. It is preferable to take cuttings from the top rather than bottom of the plant.

Conifer cuttings

1 Fill a container, such as a pot or a deep tray with fresh moist, good quality cutting compost. Level the surface by tapping the pot or container on the bench, and then, without too much pressure, gently firm it down to within 1.25cm (⅜in) of the rim of the pot or tray.

2 Cut off a vigorous leader or lateral shoot 5–15cm (2–6in) long of semi-ripe wood, including, from the upper part of the plant, about 5mm (¼ in) of brown barked wood at the bottom of the cutting.

3 Trim the leaves off the bottom 3–4cm (1–1½in) of the cutting, but retain the growing tip. Trim with a sharp knife or scalpel so that there are no snags. Also ensure that the bark is not damaged. Dip the area around the basal cut into a rooting compound with fungicide.

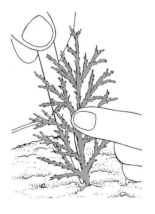

4 Make a 3cm (1in) hole with a dibber in the firmed down cutting compost. Insert the cutting right to the bottom of the hole. Gently firm it in so that there are no air pockets around the cutting. Insert any other cuttings at 4–5cm (1½–2in) intervals around the edge of the pot.

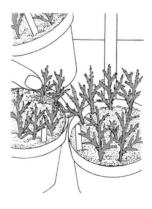

5 Label the pot clearly with the name of the plants and the date, then water them with a fine-rosed watering can. Place the container in a close atmosphere such as a propagating case or closed cold frame. A polythene bag can also be used as long as the cuttings do not touch the sides.

6 Once the cuttings start to produce new growth and have obviously rooted, harden them off. Pot them up individually in a suitable sized pot in a good quality potting compost, such as a John Innes no. 1, and grow on in a cold frame until they have become established.

Propagation: Air layering

Air layering can be used for propagating many different plants that have woody stems, and is a useful way of producing plants without specialised equipment or disturbing the parent plant. It is carried out either in spring on the mature wood of the previous season, in which case the air layer is placed close to the growing point, or, in late summer, on the hardening shoots of that season's growth. The layered stem will usually take at least a year, or possibly two, to produce adequate roots.

1 Trim any leaves and side shoots for about 15–30cm (6–12in) behind the tip of the stem to be layered.

2 Make an angled cut half-way through the stem to encourage root formation. Treat with rooting hormone and wedge open.

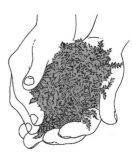

3 Squeeze two handfuls of wet sphagnum moss, or compost, together. Knead into a ball about 6cm (2 ½in) in diameter.

4 Then tease the moss, or compost, ball into two sections again, using the thumbs as if dividing an orange.

5 Place the two halves round the treated area of stem, and knead them together once more.

6 Hold the moss, or compost, in place with a square of black polythene. Secure with sticky insulating tape.

7 Prune back any new growth on the rooted layer towards the end of the dormant season.

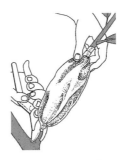

8 After a year check for roots before cutting with secateurs the stem just below the point of layering. Remove the polythene.

9 Loosen the moss ball and roots slightly. Then pot in John Innes no. 1 compost. Firm in gently, label and water.

Plants suitable for air layering include: *Ficus, Hamamelis, Citrus* (Lemon tree), *Magnolia, Rhododendron, Syringa* (Lilac).

Propagation: Stem or simple layering

Stem layering is one of the oldest techniques used to propagate woody plants. A stem is encouraged to develop roots before it is removed from the parent plant. This method does not need any complicated environmental control to ensure rooting takes place.

The condition of the stem will have a significant affect on the success of the process; vigorous, rapidly growing stems have the greatest capacity to root. When pruning, remember that the branches will have to be brought down to ground level.

Stem layering

1 During the winter dormant period, about twelve months before the intended layering, rigorously remove some of the low branches from the tree or shrub to induce young, vigorous shoots during the next growing season, which will provide the ideal layering material.

2 Cultivate the soil around the plant in the area where the layering will take place, thoroughly clearing away any weeds. Dig in plenty of well-rotted organic material into the soil and, if the drainage is poor, dig in some sharp sand or grit as well to improve matters.

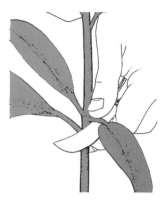

3 During the late winter or early spring, choose one or more of the vigorous young stems for layering. Trim off the leaves and side shoots cleanly with a knife so that there are no snags. Leave the foliage at the stem tip. The shoot should be bare from about 10–60cm (4–24in) below its tip.

4 Gently, without breaking it, bring the stems down one at a time to ground level and mark their position on the prepared soil. The position should be about 23cm (9in) behind the tip of each shoot, roughly at the point where the roots will be produced on the layer.

5 Dig a trench at each of the previously marked positions. Each trench should be dug in such a way that it slopes up towards the plant. It should be vertical at its further end where the tip of the stem will turn upwards. At its deepest it should be about 10–15cm (4–6in) deep.

6 Gently but firmly bend a stem into its trench so that the tip emerges from the soil at right angles about 23cm (9in) from the tip. Peg it down with a piece of bent wire to maintain the angle. The roots will then form where the stem bends.

Propagation: Stem layering

7 Carefully return the soil to each of the trenches in turn, so that the part of the stem without leaves is covered. Gently but firmly press it down well so that the stem is completely in contact with the soil, and to ensure that there are are no air pockets around the stem.

8 Water the area with a watering can fitted with a coarse rose. If the soil sinks, top it up with some more so that the surface is level. The soil should be kept moist throughout the spring and summer, and should be watered during prolonged dry periods. A mulch will help.

9 By autumn each of the layers should be showing signs of growth, the tip will be extending and new growth will have appeared. Cut through the stems that connect them to the parents at about soil level. If growth is not apparent leave for another year.

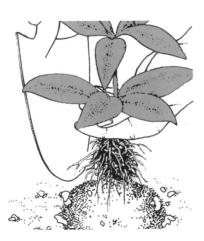

10 About three to four weeks after severing from the parent plant, cut off the growing tip of each new plant. This will encourage the roots to establish and the plant to bush out.

11 If the roots are well developed, the plant can be lifted and planted in its permanent position. If not, it can be left for another year or, if more convenient, planted in a pot of good potting compost.

12 Once a strong root system has developed each plant can be planted in the open ground either in a nursery bed or in its permanent position. Alternatively, each can be potted up for future use.

Plants suitable for stem layering include: *Actinidia, Amelanchier, Chaenomeles, Clematis, Erica, Hydrangea* (climbing*), Ilex* (Holly)*, Jasminum* (Jasmine)*, Lonicera* (Honeysuckle)*, Rhododendron, Viburnum* (some)*, Wisteria.*

GROWING IN CONTAINERS

City gardeners and flat dwellers are particularly reliant on containers to bring colour and plant interest to windowsills, steps, balconies, and patios, but even large gardens benefit from the addition of containers. Containers on terraces and beside paths add variety of scale to the garden design, and allow special plants to be singled out for attention and enjoyed in detail. However, container-grown plants need more care than those grown in open ground.

As a general rule, flower pots less than 20cm (8in) in diameter should not be used for plants that are to be grown on a hot, sunny patio. Such pots hold relatively little compost, and the plants will thus require frequent feeding and watering. The compost will also dry out exceptionally quickly, not only checking plant growth but also making more work for the gardener. In small pots plant roots are subject to excesses of cold and heat. The soil in containers may freeze, killing the roots of normally hardy plants. All containers must have adequate drainage facilities, and they should be stable when placed on a flat surface. Most plastic pots are held a fraction above the ground by a protruding rim, but clay pots have to be raised on bricks or special "pot feet" to prevent the drainage hole being blocked.

CONTAINER DISPLAYS

What you plant in containers is a matter of personal choice and the size of the container; how you plant them is limited to two choices. You can either mass different plants with similar requirements in one large pot or have a single species planting. The latter is easier to manage, allowing individual plant requirements to be indulged, and pots can be grouped together to create a mixed display.

Situation must also influence plant choice. In a sunny position you are spoilt for choice with a huge range of flowering plants, including pelargoniums, petunias and argyranthemums. Fewer flowering plants perform well in shade, but among them are begonias, busy lizzies, fuchsias, lobelias, mimulus, and tobacco plants. The use of plastic troughs or pots as liners makes changing planting schemes a simple matter of exchanging a liner full of faded plants with one full of fresh bedding. Thus a scheme need never look faded or undeveloped, especially if new plants are established some weeks before the changeover. This device is particularly suited to window boxes, using cheap plastic troughs to switch displays at the beginning of every season.

Another way to lift a display is to exchange one or two plants that are past their best for fresh ones in flower. With this in mind keep a few potted plants in reserve in a shady part of the garden. Regular deadheading (see page 52) and trimming straggly growth also prolongs summer displays. Don't be afraid either to do some judicious pruning if vigorous spreaders, such as *Helichrysum petiolare,* threaten to swamp their neighbours.

HANGING BASKETS AND WALL POTS

These are a versatile way of displaying plants, utilising space normally left empty. Hang them on walls, pergolas, single posts, and even trees, so long as their support is strong enough to hold the considerable weight of both the plants and wet compost. Baskets are cheap to buy and some are self watering. Use them to grow alpine strawberries, herbs, frilly loose-leaved lettuces, and tumbling tomatoes, as well as the usual flowering plants.

Types of containers

Containers are available in a variety of shapes, sizes, and materials. The shapes are very much dependent on their use and position, and the choice is largely a matter of aesthetic judgement. Even so, some attention must be paid to the choice as, for example, you cannot grow deep-rooted plants like roses in shallow containers.

Plastic pots tend to heat up more than clay pots, which are porous. However, this also means that moisture from the compost passes more quickly through the porous clay. Tubs, boxes, and planters are suitable for large plants. Those selected should be stable and capable of holding plenty of compost. Drainage holes may need to be drilled. Check that the hoops of round barrels are firm and the wooden sections held securely in place. Wooden containers should be painted, inside at least, with a "plant friendly" mastic or timber preservative. Wooden containers should also be raised on bricks.

TYPES OF CONTAINER

There is an ever-increasing variety of containers available for the gardener to use, varying from the ancient and traditional in style to the very modern. One of the most attractive materials used for containers is terracotta as it blends sympathetically with many plants. However it is expensive, heavy, and prone to frost damage, although less so if it is glazed. Although far less attractive, plastic is light and cheap. Plastic containers can be painted to improve their appearance or used as liners for large pots and window boxes. Artificial stone products are available in a wide range of shapes, are tough and, once they have aged, can look attractive. It is possible to age pots artificially by applying a lime wash. There are various recipes for encouraging lichens and mosses to encrust pots. These include painting the surface with yoghurt, sour milk or a paste of manure and water.

1. Terracotta strawberry barrel
2. Rusticated plastic barrel-tub
3. Plastic half-barrel
4. Wooden half-barrel
5. Plastic window box
6. Reproduction stone urn
7. Terracotta flower pots
8. Glazed ceramic jar
9. Terracotta window box

Prepare for planting by crocking the bottom of the container with pieces of broken terracotta or irregular stones. This will help with drainage, while at the same time preventing compost being washed through the drainage hole. Fill the container with a suitable compost. If the container is large then it is best filled in layers. Firm with fingers or knuckles to prevent over compaction. The surface should be about 3cm (1in) below the rim of the pot. For outside use, particularly when planting trees and shrubs, a loam-based compost is usually preferred. This has the advantage of holding moisture but at the same time it is difficult to over-water. Soilless composts are much lighter (making pots easier to move). But watering can be tricky and they should not be allowed to dry out. Water-retaining granules can be included before planting to help reduce the amount of watering needed. Slow-release fertilizers can also be added to the compost to avoid having to feed too often.

Planting containers

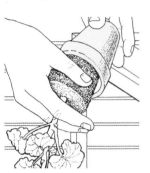

1 To remove plants from their growing pots hold the plant stem between the fingers and invert the pot. Tap gently on a table so that the rootball slides out into the palm of the hand.

2 With a trowel or the fingers, dig a hole large enough to accept the rootball. Insert the root system into the hole and fill in around it with extra compost.

3 Firm down the rootball and compost with hands or with the trowel handle, but do not over compact it. This will close any air pockets around the roots.

4 Continue adding other plants to the container. Level off the surface of the compost, adding or removing some as necessary. Water with a fine-rosed watering can.

Planting trees in containers

1 Fill the container with a good quality loam-based compost. Dig out a hole large enough to take the rootball of the plant. Allow space to spread out any extensive roots.

2 If the tree or shrub is going to need support, knock in a short stake to the bottom of the pot. If planting in a raised bed, hammer the stake down into the firm soil below.

3 Remove the plant from its pot. If the roots have become wound round the inside and rootbound, tease them out. Place the rootball in the hole and fill around it with compost.

4 Firm down the compost around the root area with the heel of your boot without over compacting it. Secure the trunk of the plant to the stake, allowing room for expansion.

Grouping plants

When considering the grouping of plants in containers it is worth remembering that one well-chosen plant can often look better than a mixed planting. Aim for as bold an effect as possible. It is usually preferable to plant a group of colourful seasonal plants in one large container rather than spreading them more sparsely between various smaller ones. The planting needs to be in scale with the container. For example, low-growing plants will look lost if planted alone in a wide-topped vase or urn, whereas if they are counter balanced by a tall central plant, the design comes into proportion. Combine upright plants of medium size with strong-growing trailers to keep the display in scale. Trailing plants will soften harsh outlines and hide unsightly containers, but do not obscure an especially attractive container. Simplicity in both design and colour is often the secret to well-planted containers. However, there are times when a riot of colour and tumbling plants are called for.

COMPOSITION

1. The tall central plant erupts like a fountain over the surrounding low-growing plants. It not only adds drama, but also brings the whole design into proportion with the container.

2. A single spiky plant in balance with its container makes a strong focal point. Such plants look effective in urns standing on a plinth of a wall. Take care in positioning them.

3. Keep planting in scale with the container. Often one well-chosen plant looks better than a fussy mixture. Flat, low-growing plants are acceptable only if the container is well below eye-level. Use shallow containers for this group of plants.

4. A tall, thin container always looks better if generously planted with trailing plants, especially if they spread outwards from the sides of the pot rather than hanging vertically.

5. Trailing plants soften an outline and are excellent for disguising dull containers. However, if the pot is ornamental in its own right the planting should not be allowed to obscure the decoration or form. Here, the mixed planting is in proportion with the container. In such mixed displays it is important that all the different plants used enjoy the same cultural conditions.

As well as purpose-built containers many other items can be adapted for container use. Obvious examples are containers that have been used for other purposes. Old galvanised buckets and baths are typical examples. Less obvious are objects such as tin cans. Good alternative containers include anything tubular from a pipe to a chimney pot. There are plenty of containers that can be made from junk and other discarded material. Old car tyres, for example, can be used in a variety of ways. Containers can be painted or left in a natural condition, but always make sure that there are drainage holes at the base.

IMPROVISED CONTAINERS

1. Chimney pots
These are available in a variety of sizes, shapes, and colours. A group of three or more, differing in height, can award a fine display but even one can make an impression if it is thoughtfully positioned. It is now also possible to buy fake chimney pots as planters.

2. Wheelbarrows
Old wheelbarrows and carts make ideal containers as they blend well with a rural garden. Most old wheelbarrows already have holes in them, but, if not, drill some for drainage.

3. Litterbins
Old litterbins can be transformed by lining them with plastic sheeting or a black bin liner before filling them with compost. Cut holes in the plastic so that the sides of the basket can be planted.

4. Car tyres
A stack of three tyres will make a good planter as long as it contains enough trailing plants to disguise it. They can be transformed by painting them in a strong single colour or with mosaic-like patterns.

5. Tree stumps
Old tree stumps are best removed but if you have one that is too large to remove, it can be hollowed out and used for planting. Woodland plants, like ferns, or trailers, such as honeysuckle, are the most appropriate plants.

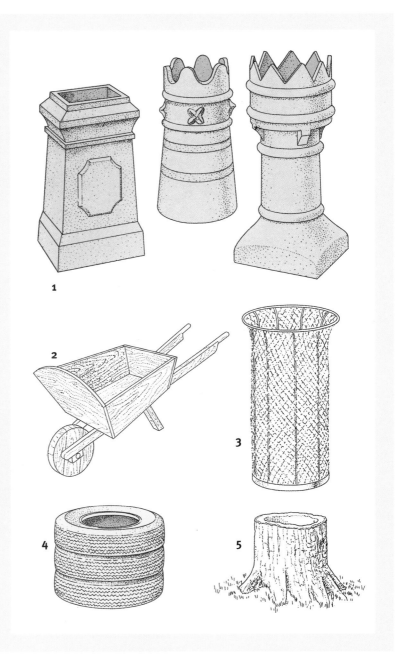

Planting window boxes

Window boxes can be used on windowsills if the windows open inwards or up and down (sash windows), or on brackets if the window opens outwards. They can also be used as decoration on any wall or fence. Wherever they are located they must be fixed on securely. Remember the higher up they are the more difficult they will be to water. It is sensible to stand them on drip trays if they are situated by a public right of way. Window boxes are treated as any other container, except that the linear shape means more drainage holes are required. They can be planted with just one kind of plant or a mixture of different types and colours. It is preferable to work to a design rather than dot the colour and shapes at random. As well as upright and bushy plants, trailing plants can also be used. These are particularly useful if the box is not very attractive and benefits from being hidden. Do not use long trailing plants in windy positions as they can be easily damaged by being blown about.

Planting a window box

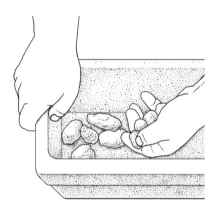

1 It is essential that the compost in the window box is free-draining. It should have several drainage holes and the base should be covered with small stones to help water drain out.

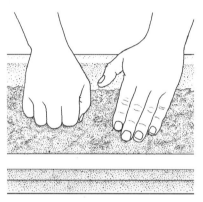

2 Fill the box with a good quality compost, firming it down gently with your hands. Since the box may be heavy when it is filled, place it in position before adding the compost.

3 Make holes in the compost with a trowel or your hands and put the plant in, continuing until the box is full. Add or remove compost so that the final level is just below the rim of the box. Level the surface.

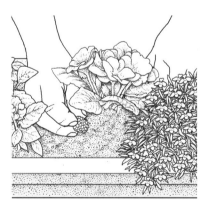

4 The compost will contain some fertilizer but this will soon be used up or leached out by the constant watering. The easiest way to supplement this is to push a plug of slow-release fertilizer down by the roots.

5 Once planting is complete, water the container. It will need watering at least once a day in summer, perhaps twice in really hot weather. Rainfall rarely provides enough water for window box plantings.

6 The plants will soon fill out and cover the compost. To keep the display looking fresh, remove flower heads as they begin to fade. As the season progresses cut back plants that have become straggly.

The solid bowl types of hanging basket are simply filled with compost, but a mesh basket needs to be lined in order to prevent the compost falling through. Traditionally a layer of sphagnum moss has been used but this is less widely available since conservation issues associated with its collection have become a cause for concern.

Polythene sheeting is a convenient alternative to moss as it is often already to hand. Polythene looks very ugly, but with the right plants, once they are fully grown, very little of the lining should be visible. Always use dark green or black polythene, as any other colour may look obtrusive. Polythene sheeting will help to retain moisture but it should be punctured with a few small slits to allow surplus water to drain away. Plants will not survive in waterlogged conditions. Trim the edges of the polythene sheeting before planting around the rim.

A good compromise between moss and polythene is first to line the basket with moss and then to place a secondary lining of polythene on top.

Other liners are made from recycled waste products such as foam, wood, coir fibre, and impregnated cardboard discs. When discs are used, slits are cut from the outer edge towards the centre so that the liner will take the shape of the basket when pressed down inside. The ready-made slits in foam, plastic or cardboard liners are conveniently placed for inserting plants into the side of the basket. Another form of liner that is widely available is a compressed fibre bowl, which fits neatly into a wire basket of the same size.

Planting baskets with moss

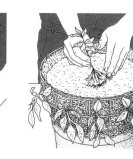

1 Cover the bottom half of the basket with a lining of moss or coir. Place an old saucer on this to help retain some moisture. Add some moist compost and gently firm.

2 Plant the sides of the basket first. Do this carefully by pushing the rootball of each plant through a hole so that it comes in contact with the moist compost.

3 Add more moss to the sides of the basket and continue to fill the basket with compost to about 3cm (1in) from the rim. Insert the remaining plants at the top of the basket.

4 Firm the compost, and add or remove compost so that the surface is just below the rim of the basket. Water with a fine rose, and add an extra thickness of moss around the rim.

Other basket liners

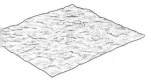

1 A sheet of green or black polythene can be inserted in the basket and then trimmed off around the rim. As it is impervious, make a few holes in the bottom to allow water out.

2 A cheap liner is one made from recycled pieces of plastic foam. It is very light and has slits to make it easy to fit the shape of the basket. The colours can be garish.

3 Better liners are made from compressed coconut fibres. These are brown in colour and slightly hairy, and look natural. Excess water passes through freely.

4 Premoulded, bowl-shaped liners are available made from recycled materials. They are similar to *papier mâché*, but will not dissolve when in constant contact with water.

Watering container plants

Plants in container dry out quickly and need frequent watering, usually daily, and more often in hot drying weather. Even when it rains water is unlikely to penetrate the compost as it is usually shed beyond the rim of the container by the density of the foliage (see below). One way of reducing the amount of watering is to incorporate water-retaining crystals or granules in the compost. These hold water without making the compost sodden, releasing it as the roots require it. This can reduce watering by up to a third, although you still need to water most days. Automatic watering systems (see page 147) are another option but they need careful monitoring. Some gardeners prefer to use rain water collected in a butt for specialised plants such as alpines. If this is not possible, run mains water into a barrel but use only once it has reached the ambient temperature and any gases, such as chlorine, have been given off. Use rain water for ericaceous plants where the mains water contains lime.

Watering containers

The quickest method of watering is to use a lance connected to the main water supply. This also produces a spray of varying intensity and is ideal to use with groups of pots.

A watering can does not require a hosepipe to be trailed around, but on the other hand has to be filled frequently and may be heavy to carry. Water the base of the plants.

Window boxes and hanging baskets are often high up and special pump-action watering devices can be used to push the water up through a long nozzle.

Watering hanging baskets

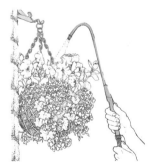

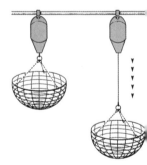

Hanging baskets can be difficult to water because of their height above the ground. A hosepipe stiffened by attaching a long cane to it is a simple way of overcoming the problem.

A similar but more expensive way is to buy a lance with a curved top that is attached to the hose. It is easier to direct the water to where it is needed with a curved nozzle.

A watering can may be used but it needs strength to lift it high enough. A long spouted one is easier. Using a pair of steps makes this method easier, although it is time-consuming.

One way to overcome the problem is to bring the basket down to a more comfortable level. This can be done by attaching the basket to a rise-and-fall system.

Once its pruning group is known, a clematis such as *C. macropetala* 'Rosie O'Grady' is easy to maintain.

Far left: The deciduous pear tree *Pyrus salicifolia* 'Pendula' only needs a light pruning in summer to keep it in shape.

Left: Wooden stepping stones set into the lawn reduce the amount of wear on the grass.

Below: Grass is always restful to the eye, not only when used as a lawn but, as here, as a wide path dividing two shrub borders.

Plants growing in containers depend on regular care, and the more they get the better they perform. Life in a pot is quite different from that in garden soil, where the plant's roots can search widely for water and nutrients and the soil largely insulates them from temperature changes. In pots plants are confined within a small body of compost, unnaturally crowded, and competing strongly for water and nutrients. Regular watering is essential. The compost must never be allowed to dry out, but overwatering must also be avoided. If the soil surface looks dry, feel what is like below the surface or use a moisture meter before you use the watering can.

Deadheading tidies up displays and encourages more flowers (see page 52). Do this at least once a week and at the same time take the opportunity to inspect the plants closely. Remove any discoloured or fallen leaves, and fallen flowers. Look under the leaves for any sign of pests or diseases. It is possible in hot, dry summers that red spider mite will attack; white powdery dust on leaves and shoot tips may indicate the presence of mildew. To help avoid these problems, which tend to be more prevalent in hot, still conditions, it is worth spraying the plants with water in the evening or early morning, and thinning out a dense display to improve the circulation of air.

Feeding

Daily watering washes nutrients out of the compost, depriving the plants of food. Although most composts include some fertilizer initially, this will soon be used up and supplementary feeding becomes essential. It is possible to buy compost specially formulated for the use in containers that includes a slow-release fertilizer – the "granules" resemble small golden eggs. In response to moisture and temperature levels suitable for growth, nutrients are released gradually over several months. Slow-release fertilizer can be added to any compost, either mixed in to it in loose granular form or as a plug, which is pushed down to root level. (A plug is simply a number of granules stuck together and should last for a whole season.)

To a certain extent, the use of slow-release fertilizers has reduced the dependence on traditional liquid feeding. Liquid feeds are added to one of the waterings at the prescribed rate of dilution, once every week or ten days, according to the instructions. A tomato fertilizer, designed to encourage fruiting and flowering, is very useful to keep displays of summer bedding flowering throughout the summer. A seaweed-based fertilizer also gives good results, and has a strengthening effect on plants, particularly when they are young.

Foliar feeding involves diluted feed being sprayed directly on to the leaves. Foliar feeds are quick acting and useful for displays that are recovering from a degree of neglect, disease or pest attack. Do not apply foliar feeds in sunny conditions.

Plants should only be fed during the growing season. Feeding should cease altogether in late summer, and no more should be given until growth recommences in spring.

Liquid and slow-release fertilizers

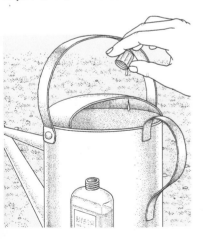

Liquid feeding should be carried out at regular intervals. The feed is diluted with water at the rate recommended by the manufacturer. Do not apply l quid feed to dry compost; water beforehand if necessary.

An increasingly popular method of feeding container plants, because it only needs to be done once, is to use slow-release fertilizer plugs. Push the plug or plugs well down to root level at the beginning of the season.

AUTOMATIC WATERING SYSTEMS

The permanent solution for watering containers is to install an automatic system operated by a timer. A range of kits is available and they can be linked to an outside tap. They consist of a hosepipe with branches of thinner tubing going off at intervals. Each of these tubes, or drip-lines, is run to a container and the dripper nozzle at the end is inserted into the compost. You can programme the timer to water your plants for a set period every day. In summer it is a good idea to water at night so the water can soak in thoroughly. Such a system ensures that your containers are watered regularly, even while you are away on holiday. These systems work best when the containers are grouped.

Supporting container plants

The size of plants used in containers should be in proportion to the size of the container, but there are cases for using tall or climbing plants that will need support. A container placed near a wall or fence can have trellis or wires fixed to the vertical face.

Free-standing pots should have unobtrusive stakes or other supports. The best are those where the plant completely envelops them. The supports should be in place before planting, or well before the plant reaches its ultimate width and height.

Supports in containers

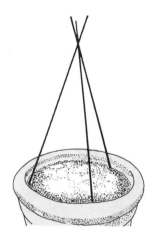 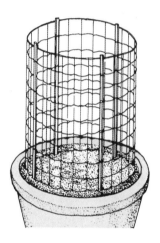 

Insert three canes into the compost and tie them securely at the top to form a tripod or pyramid to which the plants can be tied.

Roll netting into a neatly fitting cylinder. Thread canes though it and tie. Allow plants to grow so that they obscure the netting.

Insert twiggy sticks into the compost. Bend over the tops and tie with string to produce a cat's cradle through which the plant can grow.

Support in growing bags

 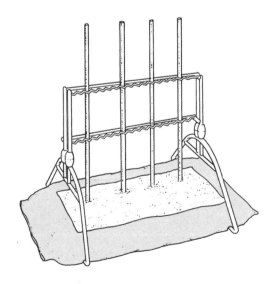

Wire frames are available for growing bags, held in place by the bag and its contents. Strings are stretched vertically, at intervals from the top bar to the bottom one, each providing support for one plant.

Alternatively, it is possible to buy a device specially designed to hold canes. The frame is held in place by the bag. The canes are gripped by cross members and the width between them can be adjusted.

Plants in large containers can be in isolated positions where they are prone to damage from frost or wind. Those against walls, which affords some protection, are less likely to suffer. One problem with prolonged cold spells is that the compost in the pot may freeze, severely damaging or destroying the plant's roots. It is as important to wrap up the container as it is the plant. If you can, sink the pot into the soil. Try and anticipate cold spells and protect the plants before they are injured.

Protecting plants

Tender plants can be protected from the frost by covering them loosely with a hessian or fleece. Cover the pot as well. Drape newspaper over the plant for short-term protection.

A more permanent winter protection can be achieved by plunging a pot in a sheltered spot outside, covering the plant with straw and bracken and then wrapping it in fine plastic netting.

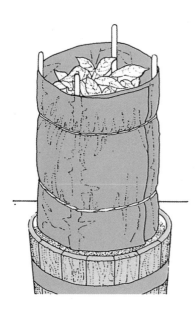

To protect a plant from the wind, place four or five canes around a free-standing plant, and then wrap plastic, hessian, a double layer of fleece, or plastic netting around the canes. Leave the top open.

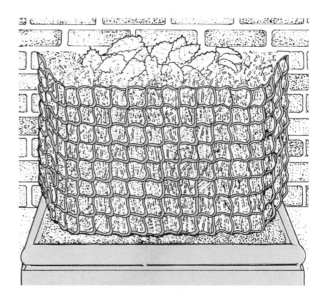

Alternative protection against cold winds is to cover the plant with straw or bracken, and then hold this in place with either rigid netting or plastic netting around a framework of canes.

LAWNS

A well-maintained lawn is a valuable feature of many gardens but to grow well grass needs sunlight. Grasses will not thrive in permanent shade, and in such situations another solution must be found, such as hard landscaping or shade-loving plants. It is also important not to make a lawn too small. An expanse of grass not only looks better, but is more useful than a patch barely big enough for a couple of deck chairs. In addition the amount of work entailed to keep a tiny lawn in good shape is not worth the effort.

The shape of a lawn is a matter of personal choice and style. In general, rectangular lawns are better suited to formal gardens than curving shapes. They are also easier to mow, but the edges must be kept straight and neat, and the corners right angled. Curved lines are more informal and versatile, and allow the lawn to flow seamlessly into a grassy path. For a natural look and easier maintenance, make the curves smooth and sweeping, rather than intricately undulating.

GRASS QUALITY

It is important to consider how your lawn will be used in order that it is made up of a suitable blend of grasses. One composed of fine soft grasses will look beautiful and mow well into stripes, but it will not stand up to boisterous ball games and heavy use. For these purposes you need a tougher mix. For general purposes, where the lawn is both a visual feature and regularly but not too heavily used, a utility lawn mix will be suitable. There are also grass mixes available that will thrive in light shade and that are drought tolerant.

Turf should always be purchased from a reputable company that can guarantee the quality. There are specialist growers who will supply hardwearing or utility grass, either by mail order or through garden centres. Top quality turf is also available, but it is very expensive. Nowadays, turf is often produced in rolls, which makes laying easier if you have a large or sloping area to cover. If you are using a local supplier, make sure that you will not be buying rough meadow grass, which will never make a good lawn.

SEED VERSUS TURF

Buying turf is expensive, but you get a result considerably quicker than you do from seed. Seed is much cheaper, but the lawn is slower to establish and you may have problems with birds, cats, and other animals scratching and roughing up the surface. You do, however, have much more control over the quality of the finished lawn. Whether you buy turf or sow seed, the soil must be thoroughly prepared beforehand.

PREPARATION

No amount of remedial work can undo a badly prepared lawn. It is essential to make certain that the area is thoroughly cleared of weeds and large stones. Prepare the soil, as explained on page 34, and, if possible, let it lie fallow for some weeks to give any remaining weed seeds a chance to germinate, and to be cleared before the lawn is laid. It is also important to level the soil. Tread it before raking to get rid of any humps and hollows. If the land slopes steeply terracing is worth considering, because the establishment and maintenance of grass on steep banks can be difficult.

Lawns on slopes

Grading major irregularities

1 Dig all the top-soil from the site and pile it to one side, leaving the sub-soil beneath.

2 Even out the level of the sub-soil, and then replace the top-soil.

Grading steep slopes

1 Remove the top-soil and transfer the sub-soil from the top to the bottom of the slope.

2 Level the sub-soil, firm it and then replace the top-soil and level that.

Levelling the site

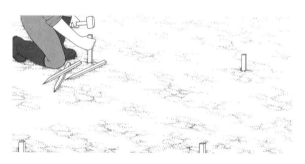

1 Hammer the master peg into the soil at a suitable point, leaving about 10cm (4in) of the peg above the surface. Then drive in the remaining pegs at 2m (6½ft) intervals to form a square grid.

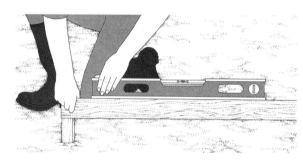

2 Adjust the height of the secondary pegs with a spirit level and a straight edged board, working away from the master peg. Continue until the tops of all the pegs are level with each other.

3 Add or remove soil until it is either level with the tops of the pegs or comes up to a predetermined mark on each peg. Ensure that all the soil has been evenly firmed before removing the pegs.

4 To create a uniform gradient establish the across-slope levels as above, then use further pegs to create the level of the slope. Add or remove soil so the level matches the marks on the pegs.

Laying turves

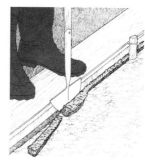

1 Apply a dressing of fertilizer a few days before laying the turf. Do not feed if the soil is already well manured.

2 Rake over the whole area, incorporating the fertilizer into the soil. Make sure that it is well worked in.

3 Mark out the exact shape of the lawn, using pegs and strings. When the turf is laid it will be laid slightly beyond this.

4 Leave the string in place, and, once the lawn has settled, the ragged edge can be cut back to this line.

5 Lay the turves in straight lines, ensuring that each turf is butted up as close as possible to the preceding one. Stagger successive rows.

6 If only part of a turf is needed to complete a row, lay a whole turf at the end and place the segment before it. Allow a 3cm (1in) overlap round the edge of the lawn.

7 Correct irregularities in the soil level and underside of some turves as laying progresses. Have some soil at hand for packing under any thin turves.

8 After all the turves have been laid, roll the lawn with a light garden roller, if one is available, or tread firm.

9 Apply a sandy top dressing mixture (see page 156) to the turves, distributing it across the lawn surface.

10 Work the dressing well into the crevices between the turves, using either a broom or the back of a rake.

Lawns from seed

How to grow lawns from seed

1 If you are sowing a small lawn by hand, first weigh out the quantity of seed to cover a square metre and put it in a carton. Mark the level on the side, and use this as a measure.

2 Divide the lawn into metre squares, using canes or strings tied between pegs. Then scatter half the seed from the carton in one direction, and the other half the opposite way to get even coverage.

3 To sow a large lawn by hand, divide the ground into bigger sections, and the seed for each section into halves. Broadcast one batch walking lengthways over the site and the other batch walking across.

USING A DISTRIBUTOR

4 For larger lawns it is more convenient to use a seed drill. Lay a sheet of plastic along the edge of the side and overrun each string. Sow half the seed lengthways, and the other half crossways.

5 After sowing, lightly rake over the entire seedbed, taking care not to bury the seeds too deeply, otherwise they will not germinate. Do not pull the soil into ridges or create an uneven surface.

Apply half the seed or fertilizer at a time, and make two applications, one up and down the site of the lawn, and the other across its width. Walk at a steady pace and in a straight line so that the content is spread evenly.

A good looking lawn depends on regular mowing and seasonal care. New lawns, especially, need to be looked after properly in their early stages.

New lawns from turf

It is essential to water newly laid turf in dry periods. If the weather is hot and sunny, water thoroughly in the evening so the moisture penetrates the soil. Although you can walk on newly laid turf, it is better to keep off for four to six weeks until it has bedded in. Make the first cut when the grass has grown to about 6cm (2in), setting the mower blades high.

New lawns from seed

Grass seeds should germinate within a couple of weeks of sowing. Once the lawn starts to grow it must be watered in dry weather throughout the first year and any weeds removed carefully by hand. Keep off the grass until it has grown about 8cm (3in), when it is time to make the first cut. A rotary mower is better than a cylinder mower, as it is less likely to tear the young grass. However, the cylinder performs as a light roller, gently firming in the young grass plants. Whatever type of mower you use adjust the blade to the highest setting. The grass should be ready for light use in about six months. Should there be any bare patches you can reseed them in autumn.

Established lawns

Once the lawn is established it will need a programme of regular maintenance to keep it in trim. At the height of the season it should be mown at least once a week, and even more frequently if you want a billiard table effect. The height of the cut will vary according to the season, and also according to the type of lawn (see chart). Set the mower blade high for the early cuts in spring, gradually lowering it to give a close finish in summer. Then, as growth slows in autumn, raise the blade again. Under drought conditions allow the grass to grow longer, even in summer. Fit the collecting box to the mower to catch the cuttings. If they are routinely left on the lawn they will encourage thatch and impede drainage. The exception is in summer when the weather is dry. In this case leave the clippings on the lawn where they will act as a light mulch.

To keep the grass healthy the lawn will need more attention than regular mowing. A spring feed, high in nitrogen, will encourage the grass to grow and green up. A second and third application can be made at about six week intervals. In autumn a low-nitrogen high phosphate feed will encourage a strong root system for the winter. (See also page 29.)

In addition to feeding, the lawn will need to be scarified to remove the dead grass and aerated, so that moisture and air can penetrate to the roots. Weeds and moss will need to be removed and the grass fed to keep it healthy. All these topics are covered in the following pages.

HEIGHT AND FREQUENCY OF CUT

This is the approximate height and frequency to which different quality lawns should be cut for the period late spring to early autumn. The figures should be varied according to the weather and the state of the turf. In other periods, the height of the cut should be increased by 1cm (½in).

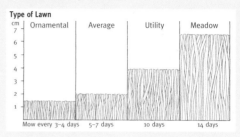

Type of Lawn

cm	Ornamental	Average	Utility	Meadow
Mow every	3–4 days	5–7 days	10 days	14 days

PRODUCING A BANDED FINISH

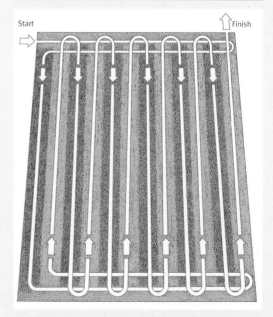

A neat, banded finish of contrasting light and dark strips can be obtained by using a mower with a rear mounted roller. On the whole cylinder mowers produce a better band than rotary machines. Start by cutting "headlands" at either end which will make a neat finish in the area where the mower turns. Then proceed to work up and down the lawn, mowing each succeeding parallel strip in the opposite direction to the previous one. To obtain a chequered effect, mow again at right angles.

Lawn maintenance

To keep lawns in first class condition carry out the following routine actions regularly every autumn. Scarify to remove the thatch, the layer of dead material that lies between the foliage and roots of the grass. Apply a top dressing to even out the irregularities in the surface and improve the soil. Aerate the lawn by spiking to allow air to enter the soil.

How to scarify

Pull the rake or scarifying tool vigorously along the surface of the lawn to remove as much thatch as possible. It is impossible to keep the tool pressed down on the surface when doing this.

Applying a top dressing

1 Broadcast a top dressing with a shovel, applying a fine loam/sharp sand mix or proprietary mix at a rate of 2kg per sq m (4lb per sq yd). On irregular turf apply up to 3.5kg per sq m (7lb per sq yd).

2 Work the top dressing into the lawn with the back of a wide wooden rake, spreading the top dressing evenly across the lawn, and filling in and levelling out hollows and other depressions.

3 As an alternative to a rake, a cheap and very effective home-made "lute" can be used. Construct one by fixing a pair of poles to a 1.5–1.8m (5–6ft) long plank of wood. It is easier to use by pulling rather than pushing.

Aerating with a garden fork

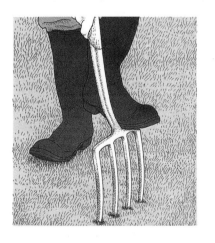

Small areas of lawn can be satisfactorily aerated with a garden fork. To do this, drive the fork backwards into the lawn to give vertical penetration, then ease it back and forward slightly before removing.

Aerating with a hollow-tine fork

Larger areas are best aerated with a hollow-tined fork. This tool is more efficient than a garden fork since it removes plugs of soil, which are deposited on the surface at the next penetration, ready to be picked up.

Aerating machines

Badly compacted large lawns can be treated with aerating machines. These machines have tines that are usually flattened and wedged-shaped, though they may also be cylindrical and solid or hollow.

The weeds most troublesome in established lawns are the creeping or rosetted perennials, which are unaffected by regular close mowing. Sowing or laying clean turves on a thoroughly cleaned site will ensure a weed-free start. Never rush the preparation of a new lawn. Allow plenty of time for the prepared ground to lie fallow so that if any perennial weeds have been left in the soil, they have a chance to reappear and can be removed before sowing or turfing takes place. If there are weeds in the lawn, always use a grass-box when mowing as this minimises the spread of their seed. Remove scattered weeds,

but remember to fill in any holes with top dressing (see page 156). For larger infestations, use a lawn weedkiller following the instructions on the packet exactly. Moss can be temporarily controlled by using mosskillers but, unless the underlying reason for the problem is addressed, often poor drainage (see page 40), the moss will return. If you need to use mosskiller, apply it in the cool conditions of autumn and spring when the moss is growing vigorously. Some lawn preparations combine a fertilizer, weedkiller, and mosskiller. Fertilizers for spring and autumn application are also available separately.

Spot-treating weeds

1 Spot treatment with a lawn weedkiller in an aerosol is a simple, economical method if there are only a few isolated weeds present. An aerosol leaves a foam on the weed after treatment, marking each plant.

2 Alternatively, use a stick of spot weedkiller. Apply both spot weedkillers at any time from spring to late summer, ideally during conditions when the soil is thoroughly moist and grass growth is vigorous.

Feeding and moss control: autumn

1 In early autumn apply a liquid mosskiller using a watering can with a dribble bar. A week or two later, rake out the dead moss, which will have turned black. Follow the instructions on the packet.

2 After treatment, apply an autumn turf fertilizer followed by a top dressing of 6 parts sharp sand, 3 parts sandy loam, and one part sieved leafmould. Apply at the rate of 2kg per sq m (4lb per sq yd).

Feeding and moss control: spring

1 In early spring apply a mosskiller in fine weather. One or two weeks later, rake out the dead moss, which will have turned black, taking care to disturb the young developing grass as little as possible.

2 After treatment apply a spring lawn fertilizer. Then apply a light top-dressing at the rate of 1kg per sq m (2lb per sq yd). Loosen the soil of bare patches, level to a fine tilth and reseed.

Lawn repairs

Repairing broken edges

1 Mark out a square piece of turf, enclosing the broken edge and, using a board, cleanly cut the turf free.

2 Use a spade to lift the turf slightly, and sever the underlying roots and soil so that the turf is of even thickness.

3 Slide the whole turf forwards, until all of the damaged part of it lies beyond the border of the lawn.

4 Cleanly trim off the broken edge of the turf so that the new edge is flush with the border of the lawn.

5 Fill the gap formed when the turf was moved forward with a new piece of turf, or add soil and sow seed.

Bumps

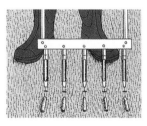 

1 Eliminate minor bumps by hollow-tining at intervals over the area. Gently tread or roll the area to make it level.

2 For larger bumps cut though the centre and peel back the turf. Remove some soil and replace the turf.

Hollows

1 Fill minor hollows by periodically applying light top dressings, adding at most a cm/in depth at a time.

2 For bigger hollows cut back the turf and add top-soil, then replace the turf, firm, and check that it is level.

Replacing bare patches

1 Mark out the smallest square of turf that encloses the bare patch and then cut it out and remove.

2 Break up the underlying soil surface with a hand fork or garden fork. Make certain that it is level.

3 Fill in the patch with new turves, and apply a sandy top dressing mixture to the crevices, brushing it in.

4 The exposed area may also be renovated by adding top-soil, and then sowing grass seed.

When faced with a neglected lawn the first step is to examine the turf carefully. If coarse grasses and troublesome weeds or mosses are predominant reclamation may not be possible. In this case it is best to clear the site (see page 260–61) and make a new lawn. If there is a predominance of fine grasses then renovation can be carried out. Spring is the best time for this.

Lawn renovation

1 The first step is to cut back the grass in the lawn in spring to a height approximately 5cm (2in) above the level of the soil.

2 After mowing, rake thoroughly to remove the cut grass and any accumulated dead material and debris.

3 After a week, mow with a cylinder mower with the blades as high as possible, lowering them over the next weeks.

4 After the first fine cut, apply a general purpose spring lawn fertilizer in order to stimulate fresh growth.

5 Apply a weedkiller 10–14 days after the fertilizer, taking care to avoid any recently reseeded areas.

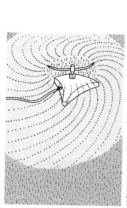    

6 In mid spring, apply seed to bare patches or sparsely grassed areas. Water thoroughly during dry periods.

7 In mid summer, apply sulphate of ammonia to keep grass growing strongly, unless fertilizer has been used recently.

8 In early autumn, fork out any patches of coarse grass, loosen the soil, and reseed the areas if necessary.

9 In early autumn, scarify and aerate any areas of the lawn that may require it.

10 Top dress with a sieved sharp sand/loam or compost mixture, and apply an autumn lawn fertilizer.

GROWING VEGETABLES AND HERBS

The ideal site for growing vegetables is sunny, well drained, and sheltered; although some vegetables, such as Jerusalem artichokes and summer salads, tolerate partial shade, they are in a minority. Avoid frost pockets and sites with overhanging trees. Ideally the soil should be deep, fertile, and slightly acid, with a pH of about 6.5 (see page 28). However cabbages, kale, and other brassicas enjoy slightly more alkaline conditions.

Initial soil preparation is important and this usually means digging. The technique is described on pages 34–39, and even if you are an afficionado of the no-dig method the initial preparation is vital. During initial digging, remove all perennial weeds and incorporate plenty of organic material such as rotted manure and garden compost. These contain nutrients, help to retain moisture, and improve the quality and structure of the soil. Vegetables take a lot out of the soil, so it is worth making your own compost (see page 30).

If the soil is basically in good condition you can smother weeds for a season or two with a light-excluding mulch of black polythene (see page 261). It is even possible to grow crops while this is taking place: potatoes can be grown by planting tubers as shown on page 172.

WHAT TO GROW

Grow the vegetables that you and your family enjoy; there is no point in growing crops no one will eat. If space is short, it is better to grow crops that need to be picked fresh, such as asparagus, runner beans, sweet corn, spinach, and salads, rather than those that occupy the ground for much of the year, like main crop potatoes and Brussels sprouts.

GROWING TECHNIQUES

Growing vegetables on the bed system has many advantages, especially in a small garden. They can look very attractive and it is easy to introduce crop rotation. Organic matter is concentrated where the plants are to grow, and the plants can be grown more closely and smother weeds as there is no need to leave space for treading; another plus factor is you can work and harvest in all weathers without compacting the soil.

Sowing little and often is described as successional sowing, and is a useful means of maximising your space. It should ensure you have young fresh pickings of salads, beans, carrots, turnips, and beetroots throughout the growing season, so avoiding those tiresome gaps and gluts. Intercropping is another useful way of saving space. A slow germinating crop, such as parsnips, is sown at stations with fast-germinating radishes or lettuces in between. Catch cropping is similar, except that the quicker-maturing crop is grown between rows of potatoes or brassicas; the catch crop will be harvested before the foliage of the main crop shades it out.

If space is limited, try growing vegetables among ornamental plants or in containers. Perennials, such as globe artichokes and rhubarb, have magnificent foliage. Some annual crops with colourful and decorative leaves, such as red or green loose-leaf lettuce, beetroot, chards, and spinach beet, can be fitted into gaps. Growing-bags are another useful method, especially for tomatoes, peppers, lettuces, and small salad crops. Broad beans, French beans, and new potatoes can be successfully grown in deep tubs.

Creating beds

In the bed system, the ground is divided up into a number of permanent beds separated by paths. The beds are narrow enough for all work to be done from the surrounding paths, so that there is no need to tread on the soil. While beds like this can be used for fruit, flowers and herbs, they are normally used to grow vegetables, and are particularly suitable for the no-dig method (see page 39).

This system has a number of advantages: it helps improve the soil structure because compaction caused by walking on the soil is avoided; you can plant, weed, and harvest in rainy weather when a conventional plot would be too wet to walk on; and garden compost and other organic materials are concentrated on the growing area, and are not wasted on soil used as paths.

Shapes and sizes

The beds are usually rectangular, although they can equally well be segments of a circle or any other shape, provided you can reach to the centre from surrounding paths. Most people find that 1.2m (4ft) is a comfortable width. Paths can be as narrow as 30cm (1ft), although you should make them at least 60cm (2ft) where you want to take a wheelbarrow.

A bed can be any length, although it is sensible to set a limit: 2.5–4m (8–13ft) is a good length for vegetable beds. If possible, orientate rectangular beds so their length runs roughly north-south, as this will minimize the shading effect of tall plants.

Edging

Unless they are artificially raised, beds do not have to be edged. However, a permanent edge helps to keep them defined, and prevents soil getting onto the paths, and loose path material, such as bark chippings, getting onto the soil. It will also protect newly sown or planted crops on the bed edges.

For most beds, an edging 10–15cm (4–6in) high should be sufficient. There is a wide choice of materials to use: wooden planks, scrap timber, bricks, or tiles.

Pressure-treated wooden edging is convenient for rectangular beds. Mark out beds and paths with pegs and strings, and cut wooden boards to fit their length and width. Wood 10–15cm (4–6in) high and 1.8–2.5cm (¾–1in) thick is ideal. Cut pegs 23–38cm (9–15in) long, from wood approximately 2.5 x 3.5cm (1 x 1⅜in) in cross-section to hold the boards in place. Cut one end of each peg to a point. Nail a peg to each end of all the boards, and, for a long board, at intervals along its length. Knock the boards into place.

For beds that are curved or irregular, frost-resistant bricks, tiles, or half logs set into the ground are much more suitable than boards.

Paths

The paths between beds can be left as bare earth and hoed, or they can be covered with a loose mulch such as gravel or bark, which will not only keep weeds down but keep your feet clean. Loose mulches need to be topped up regularly and can be underlaid with newpapers, cardboard, landscape fabric, or geotextile membrane.

In a formal garden, you could have brick- or block-paved paths. These are more expensive and require more skill to lay, but they are easy to maintain and very durable.

Creating the beds

1 Mark out the beds and paths with pegs and string. Beds measuring about 1.2m (4ft) wide by 2.5–4m (8–13ft) long are suitable for most purposes.

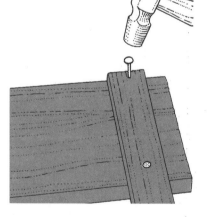

2 For the edging cut boards of pressure-treated timber to length before nailing on to 30cm (1ft) wooden pegs that have been sharpened to a point at one end.

3 Use a lump hammer to knock the boards into place. Both long boards and thin boards need extra pegs along the sides, as well as at each corner.

Vegetables such as lettuces that can be sown close together are intercropped here with sweet corn.

Right: Red cabbages can be grown for decoration – the leaves are blue-grey when young, changing to blue-red – and then eaten when mature.

Left: The gardener has to be constantly alert to the needs of the plants. Here, an overhead watering system ensures that the vegetables in this potager will thrive even in dry spells.

Spacing plants and using green manures

Since there is no need to have space to walk between them using the bed system, crops can be planted more closely, in blocks rather than in rows. This gives a higher yield, which should more than compensate for the space lost to paths. Close spacing means that weeds are quickly smothered and less weeding is necessary, especially for leafy crops such as beetroot and carrots.

Spacing out plants

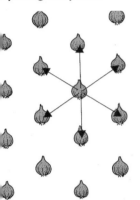 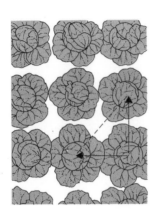 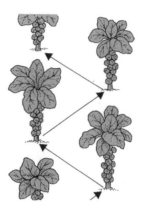 

1 Equidistant: Arrows show recommended spacing. This is the best layout for closely spaced crops like onions.

2 Square: An economical layout for cabbages as the in-row and between-row spacings are equal.

3 Staggered: The best layout for widely spaced crops, where there is only room for one plant in the width of the bed.

4 Wide spacing of crops such as cabbages gives large heads, reduced spacing produces smaller heads.

Using green manure plants

Green manures are plants, such as alfalfa, winter tares, mustard, or buckwheat, grown specifically to build up and improve soil structure, and fertility. As green manures grow, they take up plant foods that would otherwise be washed out of the soil and return them when they are dug in. The plants break the force of the rain, preventing capping and erosion. They also protect soil from extremes of temperature as well as smothering weeds. Try to include green manure into your crop rotation programme (see page 166).

1 Choose a green manure to suit the season and broadcast the seed over vacant ground. Plants will soon cover the area.

2 Shear off the foliage before flowers are produced and leave it to wilt before you dig it in.

3 Dig in the green manure. Allow a month or two for it to decompose before planting another crop.

Crop rotation

If the same vegetable is grown in one place year after year, the soil can become exhausted of vital nutrients, and pests and diseases will build up, reducing yields. If the crop occupies a different site over a three-year period, maximum use can be made of soil nutrients and disease problems are reduced. Group the crops and dress the soil as follows:

A: Legumes and salads Incorporate bulky organic matter in autumn; 3 weeks before sowing apply a general fertilizer.
B: Root crops Apply general fertilizer 2 weeks before sowing.
C: Brassicas If pH is less than 6.5 apply lime (see page 28). Apply general fertilizer 2 weeks before sowing or planting. Mulch long-standing brassicas with organic matter.

CROP ROTATION

First year

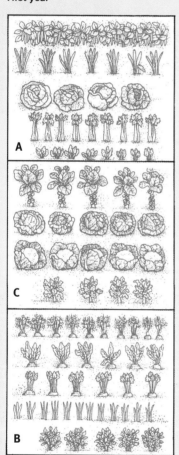

Second year

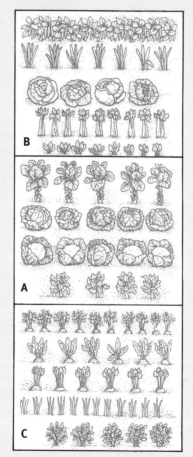

Third year

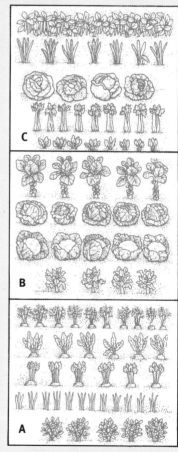

Section A: Legumes and salads.
Legumes: peas, beans.
Salads: lettuces; celery, celeriac, cucumber, tomatoes, endive, sweet corn, marrows, courgettes, onions, leeks, shallots, radishes, spinach.

Section B: Root crops.
Beetroot, carrots, leaf beet, potatoes, salsify, scorzonera, parsnips, swedes, turnips.

Section C: Brassicas.
Cabbages (including Savoys), cauliflowers, Brussels sprouts, broccoli, calabrese, kale, kohl rabi, chicory.

VEGETABLE SOWING AND PLANTING TIMES

Vegetable	Type	Sowing/planting	Distance apart	Distance between rows	Harvest
Asparagus	Hardy perennial	Sow or plant spring	30–38 (12–15in)	90cm (3ft) apart	late spring to early summer
Aubergine	Tender annual	Sow spring, plant early summer*	60cm (24in)	60cm (24in)	late summer onwards
Beetroot	Hardy annual	Sow spring	8–10cm (3–4in)	30cm (12in) apart	summer onwards
Broad beans	Hardy annual	Sow late autumn or spring	23cm (9in)	30–90cm (12–36in)	summer
Broccoli	Hardy annual	Sow spring, plant early summer	60cm (24in)	60cm (24in)	late winter onwards
Brussels sprouts	Hardy annual	Sow spring, plant early summer	50–75cm (20–30in)	75cm (30in)	autumn to late winter
Cabbage	Hardy annual	Sow spring to early summer, plant early summer to summer	50–75cm (20–30in)	75cm (30in)	throughout year
Carrots	Hardy annual	Sow spring onwards	8cm (3in)	20–25cm (8–10in)	early summer onwards
Calabrese	Hardy annual	Sow late spring	45cm (18in)	45cm (18in)	autumn onwards
Cauliflower	Hardy annual	Sow early spring or early summer, plant out early summer or summer	50–75cm (20–30in)	75cm (30in)	autumn onwards
Celeriac	Tender annual	Sow u/g in spring, plant early summer	30cm (12in)	40cm (16in)	autumn onwards
Celery	Tender annual	Sow u/g in spring, plant early summer	23–30cm (9–12in)	30cm (12in) apart	autumn onwards
Chicory	Hardy biennial	Sow in spring or early summer	15cm (6in)	30cm (12in)	winter
Chillies	Tender annual	Sow u/g spring, plant early summer*	45–60cm (18–24in)	45cm (18in)	late summer onwards
Courgette	Tender annual	Sow late spring, plant early summer	60cm (24in)	90cm (36in)	summer onwards
Cucumbers	Tender annual	Sow spring, plant early summer†	60cm (24in)	75cm (30in)	summer onwards
Endive	Hardy annual	Sow late spring or summer	25cm (10in)	35cm (14in)	summer onwards
Fennel	Hardy perennial	Sow early summer onwards	30cm (12in)	60cm (24in)	late summer onwards
French beans	Tender annual	Sow late spring onwards	10cm (4in)	45cm (18in)	summer onwards
Garlic	Hardy annual bulb	Plant late autumn or spring	15cm (6in)	25cm (10in) apart	mid-summer
Globe artichoke	Hardy perennial	Plant spring	75cm (30in)	120cm (4ft)	summer
Jerusalem artichoke	Hardy annual tuber	Plant spring	30cm (12in)	120cm (4ft)	autumn onwards
Kale	Hardy annual	Sow spring	45cm (18in)	60cm (24in)	late autumn onwards
Kohl rabi	Hardy annual	Sow spring onwards	20cm (8in)	30cm (12in)	summer onwards
Leeks	Hardy annual	Sow spring, plant early summer	15cm (6in)	30cm (12in)	autumn onwards
Lettuce	Tender/hardy annual	Sow spring onwards, plant spring onwards	23cm (9in)	30cm (12in)	early summer onwards
Marrow	Tender annual	Sow late spring, plant early summer	60cm (24in)	90cm (36in)	summer onwards
Onions	Hardy bulb	Sow u/g winter, plant spring	10cm (4in)	30cm (12in)	late summer
Parsnips	Hardy annual	Sow early spring	15–20cm (6–8in)	30cm (12in)	late autumn onwards
Peas	Tender annual	Sow spring onwards	5cm (2in)	60–80cm (2–2½ft)	early summer onwards
Peppers	Tender annual	Sow u/g spring, plant early summer*	45–60cm (18–24in)	45–60cm (18–24in)	summer onwards
Potatoes	Tender annual	Plant early to late spring	30–38cm (12–15in)	75cm (30in)	summer onwards
Pumpkin	Tender annual	Sow u/g spring, plant early summer	90–180cm (36–72in)	90–180cm (36–72in)	autumn
Radishes	Tender/hardy annual	Sow early spring onwards	2.5–5cm (1–2in)	15cm (6in)	late spring onwards
Rhubarb	Hardy perennial	Plant winter	75–90cm (30–36in)	75–90cm (30–36in)	spring onwards
Runner beans	Tender annual	Sow spring (u/g) or late spring, plant early summer	25–30cm (10–12in)	90–120cm (3–4ft)	summer onwards
Salsify	Hardy annual	Sow spring	15cm (6in)	25cm (10in)	late autumn onwards
Scorzonera	Hardy annual	Sow spring	15cm (6in)	25cm (10in)	late autumn onwards
Seakale	Hardy perennial	Plant spring	38cm (15cm)	45cm (18in)	early spring
Shallots	Hardy bulb	Plant spring	15cm (6in)	30cm (12in)	summer
Spinach	Tender/hardy perennial	Sow spring onwards	15cm (6in)	30cm (12in)	early summer onwards
Spring onions	Hardy annual	Sow early spring onwards	2.5cm (1in)	15–20cm (6–8in)	early summer onwards
Swedes	Hardy annual	Sow early summer	30cm (12in)	45cm (18in)	autumn onwards
Sweet corn	Tender annual	Sow u/g spring, plant early summer	30cm (12in)	30cm (12in)	autumn
Swiss chard	Hardy annual	Sow spring	30cm (12in)	45cm (18in) apart	late summer onwards
Tomatoes	Tender annual	Sow u/g early spring, Plant early summer†	60cm (24in)	60cm (24in)	summer onwards
Turnips	Hardy annual	Sow spring	15cm (6in)	30cm (12in)	summer onwards

u/g = under glass   *Should be planted under glass in cooler areas   †Some varieties are grown under glass and can be planted earlier

Sowing seeds

Dig the soil in autumn or early winter (see page 34), leaving the surface rough and exposed to the weather. In the early spring, or late winter, if it is workable and not sodden or frozen, the soil is broken down further into a fine tilth. A finer tilth is required for seed sowing than for transplanting. Also small seeds, such as those of lettuce, require a finer surface, than do large seeds of peas and beans. It is easy to produce a fine tilth on light soils, but more difficult on heavy clay soils. One solution is to draw out a wider and deeper drill than required, and line it with a potting compost or sieved garden compost. The seed is then sown into this. There is little point in sowing seed until the soil has warmed up to around 7°C (45°F). However, the soil temperature can be raised prior to sowing by covering it with cloches or fleece (see page 23).

The most common way of sowing seed is to sow it directly into the row, gently dropped from the hand or shaken from the packet. Most seeds need to be sown thinly. This prevents overcrowding at an early stage, as well as reducing the need to thin out the seedlings. Larger seed can be station or space sown, where individual seeds are placed at regular intervals. Pelleted seeds are small seeds, such as lettuce, pre-coated with a clay-like material, which allows seeds to be space sown.

Preparing and sowing a seedbed

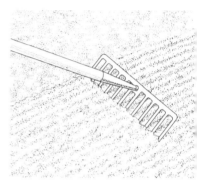

1 In late winter or early spring, hand cultivate the top 15–20cm (6–8in) of soil, using a backward and forward motion.

2 Roughly incorporate a base dressing of fertilizer into the top 10–15in (4–6in) of soil. If the soil has had plenty of organic material added this may not be necessary.

3 Consolidate the soil with the head of the rake and then rake to produce a fine tilth. Move backwards and forwards with as little soil movement as possible.

Sowing in drills

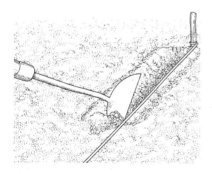

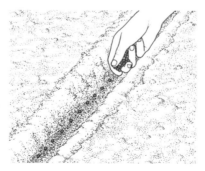

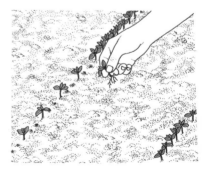

1 Stretch a garden line tightly between pegs at each end of the intended row. Keep the blade against the string and draw out a row with the corner of the hoe.

2 If the soil is dry, water the bottom of the drill. Allow the water to drain before sprinkling the seeds very thinly and regularly along it. Then cover with soil.

3 Remove unwanted seedlings as soon as possible, leaving the strongest plant at each station. Water the row of seedlings and, if necessary, firm afterwards.

Always plant vegetables with a line and use a measuring rod to mark the correct in-row spacings. Plant with a dibber, a hand fork or a trowel, depending on the type of transplant being handled. Plants raised in pots, soil, blocks, or seed trays have quite large root systems and the holes are probably best made with a trowel. Make the holes large enough for the roots and plant at the same depth as they were in the container.

Dibbers can be used for transplanting leek and brassica plants raised in outdoor seedbeds as these have smaller root systems. On heavy, wet soils, take care when using a dibber not to compress the soil at the sides of the hole because this can inhibit root spread and the establishment of transplanted plants. Water plants immediately after transplanting and again at regular intervals until they are well established.

Transplanting and aftercare

1 When transplanting or planting out always use a garden line as a guide to ensure that the row or block is straight. Because the plants should be evenly spaced a measuring rod or stick is a help.

2 A dibber is a useful tool for some vegetables, in particular onion sets, shallots, garlic, leeks, and brassicas. Make the hole right size for the plant and avoid air gaps around the roots.

3 For plants with a wider root system, a trowel is a better tool for planting. Dig a hole, spread the roots out, and then firm the soil back in, again making certain that there are no air pockets.

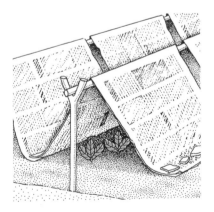

4 Once the plants are in the ground water them, preferably with a watering can. Be careful not to wash the soil away, thereby exposing the roots. Do not use a fierce jet of water from a hosepipe

5 It is best to transplant on dull, muggy days but should the weather turn fine and sunny then the newly planted seedlings will need some protection. Newspaper or fleece are both suitable.

6 Once the plants have become established, water them and then surround them with a layer of organic mulch. This will prevent water loss from the soil as well as keeping the roots cool.

Watering and special techniques

Vegetables depend on water in the soil to absorb the nutrients required for growth, and if insufficient water is available they cannot manufacture food. Water is also constantly lost through the leaves by transpiration and once this amount of water loss exceeds the amount taken in by the roots, wilting is possible, with a consequent reduction in growth and yield results. The timing of additional applications to certain vegetables is critical.

Water the crops in the evening or early morning when evaporation by the sun is low, and apply it in reasonable quantities so that it penetrates deeply into the soil (see also page 216). Digging in plenty of organic matter, such as rotted manure or compost, will help to preserve moisture where it is needed, by the roots. Mulching also helps as it reduces the amount of evaporation. Apply a mulch after rain or a thorough watering (see page 32).

Importance of watering

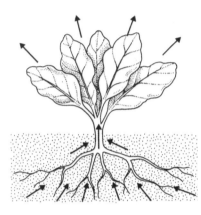

If water is applied in small amounts, the soil surface will harden and the plant will develop surface roots in an effort to reach the moisture in the top level. Always give the ground a thorough soaking.

Check the moisture content of the soil by digging a hole with a trowel. The state of the soil 23–30cm (9–12in) below the surface is the best guide to the watering needs of plants. It should be moist.

The plant's roots absorb water which passes up the stem and into the leaves. The water is then lost by the plant through its leaves by a process call transpiration. Without adequate moisture the plant wilts.

Catch cropping and intercropping

Some vegetables grow and mature more quickly than others so there are times of the year when gaps appear in the vegetable plot with nothing growing in them. These gaps can be used to grow – or catch – rapidly maturing vegetables. Thus the ground previously occupied by peas may not be needed for brassicas, for example, until the following spring and can be used in the meantime for growing crops such as radish or endive.

Rapidly maturing crops can also be intercropped or grown between slower maturing crops. For example, spinach can be grown between rows of slow-growing leeks (see left). Do not intercrop if one plant is likely to smother another crop growing nearby.

There is a number of gardening techniques that are unique to vegetable growing. None is particularly difficult but being able to do them enables the gardener to grow a wider and better selection of produce. Earthing up has several purposes. It can be used to protect young shoots from the frost or to support taller plants from wind-rock and it can also be used to blanch stems of certain vegetables, such as celery, to make them sweeter. The process is simple, it just requires pulling the soil around the plant as it develops. Blanching is an important technique for some plants as it makes them more palatable. There are ways of achieving this besides earthing up, all involving covering part of the plant in some way. Forcing is another technique used to bring on early crops, rhubarb for example, as well as blanching them to increase their tenderness and sweetness.

Earthing up

  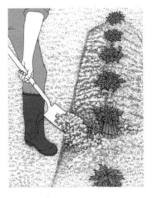 

To protect new shoots of asparagus from frost in spring, pull a little fine soil around them with a draw hoe or rake.

Support tall brassicas by forming mounds of soil round their stalks with a draw hoe, helping against wind damage.

Earth up celery every three weeks as the plants grow. Draw the soil gently up around the stems with a spade or hoe.

Rows of potatoes are earthed up, using a draw hoe, at ten day intervals during the early stages of their growth.

Blanching

Forcing

 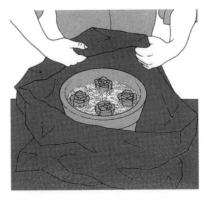 

Endive can be blanched by placing an inverted plastic pot over the plant, standing it on crocks to let air in. Place some tape or a flat stone over the hole to prevent light entering the pot.

To force rhubarb, chicory, or seakale during the winter, lift them from the garden and pot them up in a good compost. Cover the pots with a black polythene bag to exclude the light and store in a frost-free place.

Another way to force rhubarb is by covering the plants with a large bucket or dustbin in mid to late winter. Give the container a covering of straw as insulation. The tender shoots will be ready to pick in 5–6 weeks.

Special techniques

Further special techniques include how to grow potatoes by the no-dig method (see page 39). This system of growing plants is gaining an increasing number of adherents, but it does require different growing methods from the more traditional ones. Like most gardening techniques they are not difficult, especially once you understand the principles behind them. Growing vegetables in containers is another expanding field, especially as many people with small gardens now wish to enjoy the pleasures of fresh produce. Growing bags are one of the popular choices for this as they are prepared with specially formulated fertilizers and ready to use. Alternatively, large pots, buckets, or other containers can be used. Fill these with a good quality potting compost or use the compost from a new growing bag. Use compost from used growing bags and containers on the garden.

No-dig potatoes

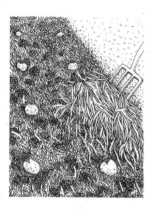 

1 The potatoes are placed on a thin layer of manure on the soil surface at the same spacing as with the conventional method. Cover them with a 8–10cm (3½–4in) layer of moist hay or straw.

2 When the plants have reached about 20–30cm (8–12in) high, add another thin layer of moist hay or straw around them. Make sure this covers the soil surface completely.

Growing bags

1 Place the growing bag on a flat surface. For tall plants this should be on the ground, but for shorter ones, such as peppers, it can be on the staging in a greenhouse. Cut out the slits as indicated on the top of the bag.

2 The bag is likely to contain a peat or peat-substitute based compost. It will need watering, but only with the amount given in the instructions on the bag. Never let it dry out nor over-water.

3 Water and feed the growing plants with care. It is easy to over-wet the peat or its substitute, and this may cause the plants to rot. Make drainage slits in the base of the bag to remove excess water. Feeding will be necessary as the plants grow. There will be some nutrients in the compost to start with, but this will be leached out by the constant watering, as well as being used up by the plants. Use a liquid feed following the instructions on the packaging.

There are two main reasons for storing vegetables, the first is to have these available in winter, when there are few fresh vegetables available. The second is to be able to store surplus vegetables in a time of glut, rather than throw them away. An additional reason is to make available vegetables when they are normally out-of-season; home freezers have increased our ability to do this.

The simplest way to store hardy vegetables, such as most of the root crops, is to leave them in the ground until they are required. In very cold areas these may need covering with straw. If periods of deep frost are forecast then it is advisable to lift some, and store in a frost-free place, as it may be difficult getting them out of the frozen ground. Most roots will keep well if placed in trays of slightly moist sand. Many of the winter brassicas, such as Brussels sprouts, can be left outside until required.

Other vegetables can be stored inside for varying lengths of time. All should be in good condition before storing. Remove any soil and make certain they are dry. Place in a cool, airy place so that they are not touching one another. Marrows, pumpkins, and gourds should be hardened off first in the sun, while onions, shallots, and garlic should be dried in the sun.

Most vegetables will stay reasonably fresh in a refrigerator for a few days, even those, such as peppers, that are usually impossible to store for long periods. Others can be stored by deep freezing. The flavour of most vegetables benefits from a brief blanching in boiling water before being frozen.

Storing and preserving

Carrots, parsnips, beetroot, and other root crops can be stored in a tray of slightly moist sand. The individual roots should not touch each other. Store in a cool, frost-free place.

Most root crops can be left in the ground. Some, such as celeriac, need to be protected with straw. Other root crops will also benefit from protection in very cold districts.

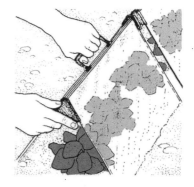

Certain leaf crops, such as winter spinach, will be available for picking given cloche protection. Make certain the cloches are wind proof.

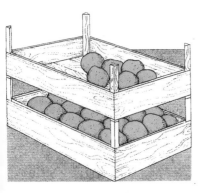

Potatoes, squashes, pumpkins, onions, and some other vegetables can be stored in trays. They should not touch one another. Potatoes need covering to exclude the light.

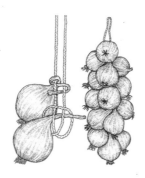

Onions can be stored in trays, net bags or, as here, in "ropes". Use the neck of the onion to attach it to the string. Garlic can be stored in the same way. Store in a cool place.

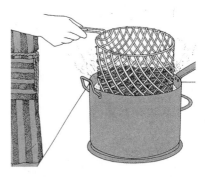

Most vegetables can be frozen, either as they are or in a cooked form. Many, such as peas and beans, need to be blanched briefly in boiling water to prolong storage life.

Herbs

Most herbs are easy to grow, and a selection of culinary types provides a variety of flavours to complement home-grown vegetables, and enhance the flavour of everyday food. It is not only the leaves that can be used. Flowers of chives and pot marigolds can be added to salads, borage flowers can decorate summer punches, young stems of angelica may be candied, and horseradish roots are grated to make a hot relish.

In the garden, herbs range in size from low-growing ground cover, such as thymes and marjoram, to angelica, which can reach 2m (7ft). Many of them are perennial plants with invasive habits, either by spreading roots or by self-seeding. The roots of mint and horseradish, especially, should be contained.

Most herbs like a sunny, sheltered position and well-drained soil. Many grow well in poor soils, such as sage, thyme, and rosemary. Bear in mind also that some thymes and rosemary are not reliably hardy. Plants in open ground benefit from a dry mulch over winter and those in pots should be moved to a protected position, cold frame, or cool greenhouse. As a precaution against losses it is well worth taking a few cuttings every year, as described below.

Herb gardens

Herbs can be grown alongside vegetables or flowers. Many herbs grow well in containers, provided they have adequate drainage holes (see pages 137–49). They can also be grown in their own separate patch, conveniently situated as near to the kitchen as possible. Some herbs, such as parsley, chives, and rosemary make excellent edging plants for beds. Space the plants about 30cm (12in) apart and pinch out the growing tips. Once established they will soon bush out to make a dwarf hedge.

Clip the hedge with shears once a year, immediately after flowering, to keep it in shape.

A separate herb garden makes an attractive garden feature. Popular designs for a herb garden include the wheel shown on page 176 and a chequerboard pattern of alternating paving slabs and blocks of herbs. Both these designs provide a means of collecting herbs without treading on the soil, and also separate the various plants, which can vary so greatly in their vigour.

Some herbs can sprawl and straggle, so once every three or four years it is a good idea to replant the herb garden using fresh stock, much of which you can raise yourself by dividing the plants (see page 58), taking cuttings (see pages 124–129) and by layering (see page 134). Parsley and basil can be raised annually from seed (see pages 43 and 168).

Routine care

Clean up the herb garden each spring to prevent the stronger plants from taking over, and weed it regularly by hand. Fennel, dill, lemon balm, and angelica seed freely and the self-sown seedlings will need to be thinned, transplanted, and removed.

After flowering is it is worth shearing over plants like thyme, chives, rosemary, and sage. This not only deadheads them, but also encourages a fresh flush of leaves and neater-looking plants.

Herbs for winter use

Some of the herbs listed on page 177, including basil, parsley and chives, can be lifted and potted up for winter use. Choose the herbs you use frequently and bring the pots under cover, into the greenhouse, or stand them on the kitchen windowsill. In this way you can have fresh herbs throughout the year.

Propagating rosemary

1 In mid or late spring strip a young side shoot from its parent stem so that a heel (a thin sliver of older wood) is left at its base. Treat as softwood cuttings (see pages 124 and 131).

2 Trim the heel and remove the lower leaves. Dip the heel in rooting hormone, insert immediately in cutting compost, and place in a covered propagator (see page 22).

Most herbs are no different to other plants in the way they are planted and maintained. Some are invasive, like mints, and need to be kept under control. Many herbs, especially the shrubby ones, are likely to be in the same position for many years and so it is important that the soil is thoroughly prepared before planting. It is particularly important that

all perennial weeds are totally removed. Do this by hand while preparing the ground in the autumn prior to planting, adding plenty of well-rotted organic matter such as garden compost (see pages 30 and 35). Rake it over in spring and remove any weeds that have reappeared before planting (see page 214).

How to plant invasive herbs

1 Plants with invasive roots need to be kept under control. This can be achieved by creating a barrier around the roots. One way is to sink a large pot or a bucket with holes in the bottom into the soil.

2 Put some soil in the bottom of the pot and stand the plant on the soil. Then fill the pot with soil, gently firming the soil around the plant. Water the plant thoroughly.

How to grow herbs for fresh winter use

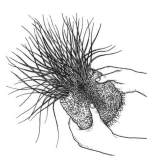

1 Some herbs, such as chives, die down over winter. However, if they are lifted in autumn, cut back, and taken into the kitchen or greenhouse, they will produce fresh leaves.

2 In the autumn the plant will be congested with the bulbs tightly packed. Split off a small clump, and then divide up the rest and replant it in the garden as required.

3 Plant the small clump of chives in an appropriate-sized pot, using a good quality potting compost. Firm the compost down and water. Cut back the leaves.

4 Stand it in a well lit position with a little warmth – a warm greenhouse is ideal. Keep watered without making the compost too wet. Use leaves as required.

Herbs in the garden

There are many ways of growing herbs. They can be integrated into flower beds or can be used to fill odd spaces in the vegetable garden. Another possibility, if there is space, is to create a special herb garden. This can be as large or as small as space allows. One very decorative way of doing this is to create a herb wheel out of bricks, as shown below. If space is really limited then a few of your favourite herbs can be grown in pots or window boxes (see pages 137–49).

Making a herb wheel

1 Work out the dimensions of a wheel that will fit into your garden design. Place a peg in the middle of the area. Attach one end of a piece of string to the peg and the other to a stick; the length of the string equals the radius of the circle. Score a circle in the soil, keeping the string taut.

2 Dig out the soil from within the circle to a depth of about half a brick length – 11cm (4½in). Cut round the edge of the circle very carefully as this will be the building line and irregularities will show. Keep the soil at the bottom of the circle as level as possible so the brick edge will be even.

3 Working a short section at a time, place a layer of cement on the soil around the edge of the circle. Place a brick vertically on the cement and tap into place. Put cement on the top face of a brick and set it next to the first, and so on round the circle, checking the level. Adjust the spaces slightly if necessary.

4 Place a ceramic pipe in the centre of the circle to form the hub and build out a low wall, two bricks high from this to the outer ring, cementing it as you go. No more than five "spokes" should be built. Although the bricks are cemented here for strength, the wheel can be constructed dry jointed.

5 Once the cement has set, loosen the soil in each segment, but be very careful not to undermine or loosen the brickwork, especially if it has been built without cement. Top up each segment with extra soil almost to the rim of the circle. The level will sink down slightly when the soil has settled.

There is a very wide range of herbs that can be grown in the garden. From a user's point of view, most of these are for culinary purposes. In the past, but to a lesser extent today, they were also grown for medicinal purposes. However, some gardeners grow herbs not so much for practical use but simply because they like to keep the tradition going and enjoy the sight and atmosphere of a herb garden. Listed below are the herbs that are mainly used for culinary purposes.

CULINARY HERBS FOR THE GARDEN

Herb	Uses	Type	Height/spread	Propagation
Anise (*Pimpinella anisum*)	Seed and leaves	Annual	45 x 20cm (18 x 8in)	Seed
Angelica (*Angelica archangelica*)	Stem, seeds and leaves	Biennial	2.5m x 90cm (8 x 3ft)	Seed
Basil (*Ocimum basilicum*)	Leaves	Annual	45 x 20cm (18 x 8in)	Seed
Bay (*Laurus nobilis*)	Leaves	Evergreen shrub or tree	Up to 4.5 x 3m (15 x 10ft)	Cuttings
Bergamot (*Monarda didyma*)	Leaves	Hardy perennial	90 x 60cm (3 x 2ft)	Division
Borage (*Borago officinalis*)	Leaves, flowers	Annual	75 x 45cm (30 x 18in)	Seed
Caraway (*Carum carvi*)	Seeds and leaves	Annual or biennial	60 x 20cm (24 x 8in)	Seed
Chamomile (*Chamaemelum nobile*)	Leaves	Hardy perennial	25 x 15cm (10 x 6 in)	Division
Chervil (*Anthriscus cerefolium*)	Leaves	Annual	38 x 20cm (15 x 8in)	Seed
Chives (*Allium schoenoprasum*)	Leaves	Bulb	30 x 20cm (12 x 8in)	Division
Coriander (*Coriandrum sativum*)	Leaves and seed	Biennial	60 x 20cm (24 x 8in)	Seed
Dill (*Anethum graveolens*)	Leaves and seed	Annual	Up to 1.5m x 25cm (5ft x 10in)	Seed
Fennel (*Foeniculum vulgare*)	Leaves and seed	Hardy perennial	2m x 60cm (7ft x 2ft)	Seed
Horseradish (*Armoracia rusticana*)	Root	Hardy perennial	60 x 45cm (2ft x 18in)	Root cuttings
Hyssop (*Hyssopus officinalis*)	Leaves	Hardy shrub	60 x 60cm (2 x 2ft)	Cuttings
Lemon balm (*Melissa officinalis*)	Leaves	Hardy perennial	90 x 60cm (3 x 2ft)	Seed
Lovage (*Levisticum officinale*)	Leaves and seed	Hardy perennial	2m x 75cm (6½ft x 30in)	Seed
Marjoram (*Origanum marjorana*)	Leaves	Annual or tender perennial	60 x 45cm (24 x 18in)	Seed
Mint (*Mentha* spp.)	Leaves	Hardy perennial	60 x 45cm (24 x 18in)	Division
Mustard (*Brassica* spp.)	Seed and young leaves	Annual	1.8m x 15cm (6ft x 6in)	Seed
Oregano (*Origanum vulgare*)	Leaves	Hardy perennial	60 x 45cm (24 x 18in) high	Division or seed
Parsley (*Petroselinum crispum*)	Leaves	Annual or biennial	15 x 23cm (12 x 9in)	Seed
Pot marigold (*Calendula officinalis*)	Flowers and leaves	Hardy annual	45 x 30cm (18 x 12in)	Seed
Rosemary (*Rosmarinus officinalis*)	Leaves	Evergreen shrub	Up to 1.8 x 1.5m (6 x 5ft)	Cuttings
Sage (*Salvia officinalis*)	Leaves	Evergreen shrub	75cm x 1m (30 x 36in)	Cuttings
Summer savory (*Satureja hortensis*)	Leaves	Annual	45 x 23cm (18 x 9in)	Seed
Sweet Cicely (*Myrrhis odorata*)	Seed and leaves	Hardy perennial	75 x 60cm (30 x 24in)	Seed
Tarragon (*Artemisia dracunculus*)	Leaves	Tender/hardy perennial	60 x 45cm (24 x 18in)	Cuttings
Thyme (*Thymus* spp.)	Leaves	Evergreen shrub	Up to 30 x 30cm (12 x 12in)	Cuttings
Winter savory (*Satureja montana*)	Leaves	Evergreen shrub	45 x 45cm (18 x 18in) high	Cuttings

GROWING FRUIT

Plant fruit in the sunniest site possible. Light and warmth are essential to ripen the fruits and the wood, and to promote the development of fruit buds for the next year's crop. Most fruit tolerates some shade, but crop yields may be affected, particularly with warm-temperature fruits such as apricots, peaches, nectarines, figs, and grapes, which must be in full sun, and preferably trained against a wall to benefit from the residual heat. Other tree fruits grow reasonably well in some shade as long as they receive sunlight for at least half a day throughout the growing season. Dessert fruits, in which colour and flavour are important, require more light than culinary fruits. Bush and cane fruits, such as raspberries, are the most tolerant of some shade, provided the soil is not too dry and the plants do not suffer from rain from overhanging branches.

SOIL PREPARATION

Most soils will grow fruit of some kind, provided the land is reasonably well-drained. The larger the plant the greater the depth of fertile soil required. Strawberries need a minimum of 30cm (12in), while fruit trees need twice that. A thin soil over chalk is unsuitable for all but the smallest fruit such as strawberries. Tree, bush, and cane fruits are a long-term investment. Once planted there should be no need to move them until their cropping life is over, which could be between 10 years for soft fruits to 50 years for tree fruits. It is essential therefore that the soil is well prepared, and for trees it is worthwhile double digging the site (see pages 34–36). Generous amounts of organic matter should be incorporated prior to planting to sustain the fruiting plants in their formative years (see page 32).

ROOTSTOCKS AND POLLINATION

The ultimate size of fruit trees is determined by the rootstock on which the chosen cultivar is grafted. Trees grafted on vigorous rootstocks will grow larger than trees grafted on dwarfing stocks, even those that may support the same cultivar. Nowadays, most trees are developed for small gardens, and are usually grafted on non-vigorous stocks, except for the half-standard or the standard forms. Before buying a fruit tree check with the garden centre or nursery that its vigour is suitable for your purposes, especially for container growing or where space is very limited. Most apples, pears, plums, and cherries need to be cross pollinated before they will bear fruit. So. unless there are fruit trees growing in neighbouring gardens, it is as well to buy more than one tree, first ascertaining that they will flower at the same time and will be compatible pollinators. For small gardens, a family tree is a good solution. This consists of three compatible but different cultivars grafted on the same rootstock. Although it is possible to graft a particular cultivar on a rootstock of your choice, it is easier and more reliable to buy exactly what you want from a reputable nursery.

TRAINED FORMS

Utilising walls and fences is another means of fitting fruit into a small garden. Fruit trees are available already trained as cordons, espaliers, and fans suitable for planting against a wall. Bush fruit can be similarly trained. Blackberries and their hybrids are vigorous, but can be kept under control if trained along a fence. Any supports must be strong and erected before planting takes place.

Siting and planting

Before any fruit is planted make sure the site is sheltered from wind and not in a frost pocket. Strong winds inhibit the movement of pollinating insects, damage growth, and cause fruits to drop prematurely. In exposed sites the gardener should provide a wind-break. On large scale plantings, such as orchards, a row of trees or tall hedge is appropriate. On a lesser scale, deciduous hedges, of beech or hornbeam, for example, form an attractive living wind-break, but they may cast shade and their roots will compete with those of the fruit trees for water and nutrients.

Where every bit of land is valuable, it is better to erect a fence against which fruit can be trained. A lapboard fence, for example, will reduce the wind just beyond the structure but may cause turbulence farther away. A more open fence is better if fruit is free-standing within the garden. When planting a wind-break or erecting a fence be careful not to create a frost pocket and, where such an obstruction already exists, it should be modified so that air drainage is improved, for example by creating a gap or removing some of the lower growth. Also avoid planting fruit in a hollow where frost can collect. If frost is likely to be a problem, plant late-flowering cultivars or seek advice on those that are the most frost-tolerant.

Although it is impractical to protect large fruit trees from frost, small plants or those trained against walls or fences can be draped with fleece when frost threatens (see also pages 219–20).

Frost pockets

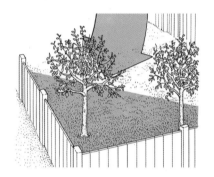

1 Avoid planting fruit trees and bushes in a frost pocket where cold air collects behind a fence, wall, or thick hedge.

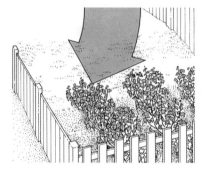

2 Improve air drainage by creating a gap to allow the cold air to flow away. Alternatively, plant later-flowering cultivars.

HEELING IN

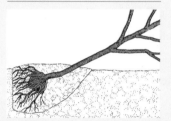

Bare-rooted trees are planted between late autumn and early spring. If they cannot be planted immediately, heel them in. Dig a shallow trench and lay the plant at an angle, covering the roots with moist, friable soil.

Planting bare-rooted trees

1 Prepare the ground (see pages 34–36). If the roots are dry, soak them in water for an hour or so before planting. Trim off any broken or long tap roots with secateurs.

2 Dig a hole deep and wide enough to take the roots when fully spread out. Drive in a stake. Heap a little of the soil in the middle to create a shallow mound.

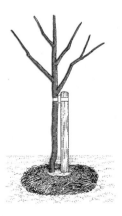

3 Set the tree on the mound and spread the roots. The graft union (page 188) should be about 10cm (4in) above the soil. Replace and firm the soil. Tie to the stake and mulch.

This gooseberry bush has been trained into a standard to make cultivation and picking the fruit an easier task.

Far left: The unusual but pretty American black raspberry is a vigorous plant that needs plenty of space.

Left: High bush blueberries are decorative shrubs that require copious watering in dry weather.

Below: Apples trained as single-layer espaliers to form a "stepover" require little pruning.

Where space is limited, apples and pears can be grown as bush trees, cordons, dwarf pyramids, or espaliers. Dwarf bush apples (between 2–4m/6½–12ft) are usually grown on M9 or M26 rootstocks, while a larger bush (between 4–6m/12–20ft) is produced on MM106 rootstock. Quince A is the most usual rootstock for pears, and makes a tree of 3–6m (10–20ft). The actual size will vary according to the growing conditions.

Commercial growers increasingly favour a central leader bush tree. Cordons have a single stem, but may be single- or multiple-stemmed. Because of their compact habit, cordons can be planted close together. The espalier is best described as a series of horizontal cordons on one plant. The dwarf pyramid is best described as a free-growing vertical cordon. It is easier to produce than the tightly pruned cordon.

Open-centre bush

Central-leader bush

Oblique single cordons

Dwarf pyramid

An open-centred bush, showing the 60cm (24in) main stem or trunk , and the radiating main branches, creating an open centre. This form of bush is sometimes compared to an inverted umbrella.

A central-leader bush differs from one with an open centre in having a main stem continuing vertically so that the branches arise over a greater length. This makes a denser bush and can be a lot more productive.

Oblique single cordons are trained at an angle of approximately 45° by securing them to canes fixed to wires placed at 60cm (24in) apart. The cordons should be planted 75cm (30in) apart.

A dwarf pyramid is a compact tree with a central leader and free-growing side branches. Its size makes it useful for planting in small gardens where a conventional tree-shape may be required.

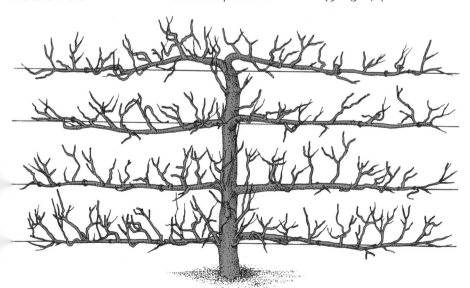

Espalier

An espalier is one of the more time-consuming shapes to create, but as well as being productive it is also a very attractive form. It is usually trained against a wall or fence on a system of strong supporting wires 40cm (16in) apart. The one shown has four tiers of horizontal fruiting arms, each one treated as a horizontal cordon. With patience trees can be created with many tiers, possibly arranged to cover the end wall of a house, for example.

Pruning apples and pears

When the framework of apple and pear trees has been formed, pruning is mainly aimed at furnishing the branches with spurs and flower-bearing laterals. Spurs will form naturally in many cases or they can be induced by pruning between late autumn and late winter or in the summer. The basis of spur pruning is to cut back lateral growth to the first flower bud. As the tree matures the spurs will become overcrowded and will need to be thinned. The other system is renewal pruning. This depends on the known tendency of both apple and pear varieties to produce flower buds on unpruned two-year-old laterals. The laterals are left until they have fruited and then they are removed.

Spur pruning: The first year

1 At some time from late autumn to late winter cut back a proportion of the laterals that developed in spring to four buds.

The second year

2 During late autumn to late winter of the second year cut back each lateral to a plump flower bud, removing the summer growth.

The third and fourth year

3 From mid summer to early autumn fruit will be carried on the laterals that have been pruned back. A spur system begins to develop.

Renewal pruning: The first year

1 Between late autumn and late winter select strong, well-placed laterals and leave them unpruned. Remove all others.

The second year

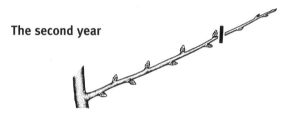

2 Flower buds have formed on the previous year's wood. Between late autumn and late winter cut back to where the new wood starts.

3 From late summer to mid autumn of the following season fruit will be carried on the pruned-back laterals.

The third year

4 In the late autumn to late winter, after fruiting, cut back the fruited laterals to leave a 3cm (1in) stub.

5 In mid autumn, at the end of the growing season new laterals will have developed. These are left unpruned to start the cycle over again.

The bush form of tree is widely used for apples and pears. There are slight variations between fruits, but the principles are the same. Training may take up to five years. Fruit buds are quite frequently set in the third or fourth years, but it is usually a further season before a reasonable crop is obtained. A one-year-old, or maiden, tree should be planted in the dormant season, from late autumn to late winter, in ground thoroughly prepared the previous autumn (see page 179–80). Take care not to bury the union. Pruning is also carried out between late autumn and early spring, but not when temperatures are below freezing.

Bush tree: The first year

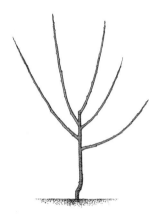

1 Between late autumn and late winter plant a maiden tree. Immediately after planting cut back the stem to about 70cm (27in) above the soil, making the cut just above a strong bud.

2 The tree as it appears in mid autumn, at the end of the season's growth. It has responded to pruning and has formed strong primary branches, which will determine the future shape of the bush.

3 Late autumn to late winter. Select four of the primary branches that have formed wide angles to the stem. Cut back vigorous ones by half, and the less vigorous ones by two-thirds. Remove unwanted branches.

The second year

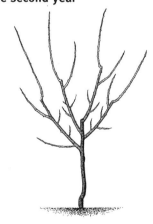

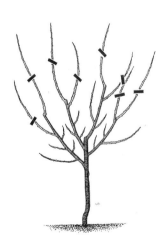

4 The bush in mid autumn, at the end of the season's growth. Strong secondary branches will have formed on the initial framework, and this will include new leaders on the main stems.

5 Late autumn to late winter. Select four well-placed new growths to form permanent branches. Cut back all leaders: shorten vigorous ones by half, less vigorous by two-thirds. Prune to outward-pointing buds.

6 At the same time prune back any laterals on the inner parts not required for secondary branches to four buds. Leave some laterals on the outside of the bush unpruned. Remove unwanted branches.

Pruning bush trees

The third year

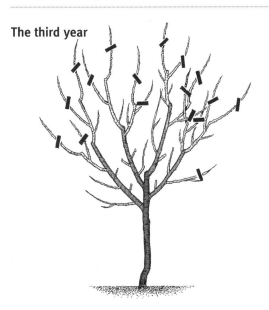

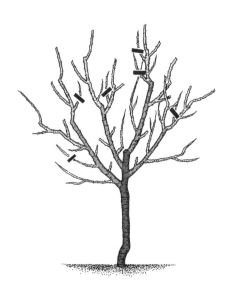

7 Late autumn to late winter. Cut back the vigorous leaders by about one-half and the less vigorous ones by about two-thirds. Always make the cut just above an outward-pointing bud.

8 At the same time as reducing the leaders, prune back all the budded laterals on the inside of the branches to four buds, cutting just above a prominent flower bud. Leave the laterals around the outside of the bush unpruned.

Fourth and subsequent years

9 Late autumn to late winter. The branch framework of the bush has now been formed and leader pruning can cease unless growth is weak. Leave laterals on the outer parts of the tree unpruned. Cut back the laterals on the inside to 10cm (4in).

10 At the same time, where prominent flower buds have already formed on well-placed unpruned laterals, cut back the stem to just above the topmost flower bud.

Renovating apples and pears

Pruning is a major contribution to the renovation of fruit trees. It is important to consider the state of excess vigour, apart from the possibility of scion rooting, because paradoxically a tree may be neglected by being subjected to over-severe pruning. Such a butchered tree is out of balance and over-vegetative. The remedy is to thin out crossing, broken, diseased, and over-crowded branches but to leave branches that are healthy and well-placed. The unpruned branches may well settle down to form flower buds and resume a fruitful career in two or three years. Remember that winter pruning stimulates growth, but summer pruning checks it. Yet another way to remedy the over-vigorous tree is to take advantage of the fact that shoots growing horizontally are fruitful, and shoots growing vertically are unfruitful. Horizontally inclined shoots should therefore be encouraged. The stunted tree is best remedied in the first place by measures involving staking and by removal of competition for water and nutrients. There is usually very little new wood to prune, but the thinning of spurs and the severe shortening of any one-year-old shoots, coupled with clearing weeds, feeding and mulching (see pages 29 and 32), will stimulate growth. It is often desirable to thin the fruit or to remove it altogether, as it sets, for a year or two to relieve the tree of the strain of reproduction. Fruit from a starved and neglected tree is not worth having anyway. Once a balance has been restored between growth and flower bud formation it should be maintained by sensible pruning and adequate control of pests and diseases.

Unfruitful growths

This is a case for the shredder or bonfire. Old age, neglect, and indifferent pruning have left only unfruitful vertical growths. There is very little that can be usefully done.

The over-vigorous tree

1 This tree has been left untended for a number of years, and it has now become very overcrowded and has ceased to produce much fruit, as well as looking unattractive.

2 Over the course of two winters the crossing branches and any dead material must be removed and fruitful horizontal growth encouraged.

Vigorous pear laterals

Horizontal or downward curving branches set better fruit. Here, vigorous pear laterals are seen in flower in the second year after they have been tied down and arched.

Stunted tree

1 This tree has very poor growth and bears little fruit. This has been caused by malnutrition, and competition for water and nutrients from the weeds.

2 The weeds have been cleared, avoiding deep digging. The tree is staked and a thick mulch has been applied. Fertilizers and water are used to stimulate growth.

Pruning cordons

The great beauty of the cordon form for apples and pears is that the trees can be planted closely, and can be kept compact and close enough to the ground to facilitate easy management. This offers the gardener the opportunity to grow a wide choice of cultivars in a small space. It is vital to control vigour and keep the trees within arm's reach so cordons are usually planted at 45°. To support the cordon it is necessary to secure canes to a post and wire fence, with wires spaced at 60cm (24in).

The first year

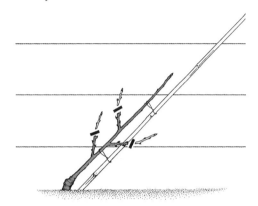

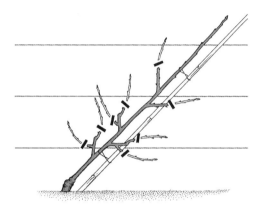

1 Between late autumn and late winter plant a one-year-old tree with the graft union (where a slight bulge or kink occurs) uppermost, against a cane secured to taut wire supports at about 45°. Do not prune the leader. Cut back any side shoots to four buds.

2 In late autumn, at the end of the first growing season, leave the leader unpruned. However, take the opportunity to cut back any laterals or main side shoots to four buds, and any sub-laterals to one or two buds, or to about 2.5cm (1in).

Second and subsequent years

3 In the spring of the second year remove any premature flowers as they appear, doing this carefully so that the basal rosette of leaves that surround the flowers are left intact. After the second year the flowers should not be removed.

4 From mid summer to early autumn, cut back laterals that are not needed for further extensions to three good leaves from the base, ignoring the basal cluster. Cut back the sub-laterals to one to two buds, or 2.5cm (1in).

Pruning espaliers

The first year

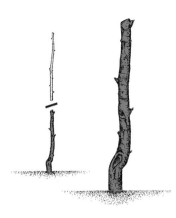

1 Late autumn to late winter. Plant a one-year-old unbranched tree. Cut back the stem to within 38cm (15in) of the ground. Leave room for a short leg and select three good upper buds.

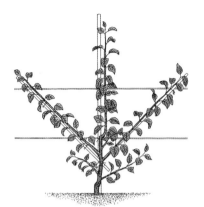

2 From early summer to early autumn, train the shoots from the top bud vertically, and those from the lower two buds at an angle of 45°. Tie them to canes fixed on wires spaced 40cm (16in) apart.

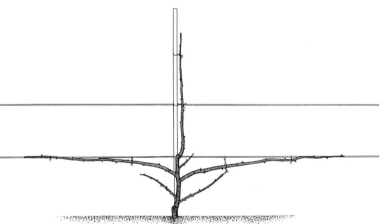

3 Late autumn. At the end of the growing season, lower the two side branches down to the horizontal. Tie them carefully to the first tier of wire supports. At the same time, cut back the central leader to within 45cm (18in) of the lower arm, leaving three good buds to form the new central leader, and two new horizontal arms that will form the next tier. Cut back the surplus laterals on the main stem to three buds. Prune back the horizontal leaders by one-third, cutting to downward-pointing buds.

Second and subsequent years

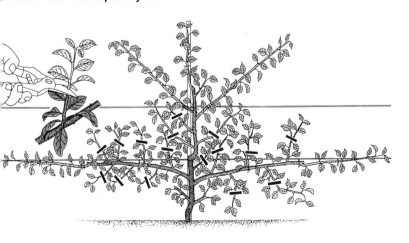

4 At some point in the late summer train the second tier of branches in the same way as in the previous year, by training the shoot from the top bud vertically and those from the two lower buds at an angle of 45° to the main stem. Once again, tie them to canes fixed to the wire supports. Cut back competing stems from the main stem to three leaves. Cut back laterals from the horizontal arms to just above the third leaf above the basal cluster.

Pruning espaliers

Espaliers (continued)

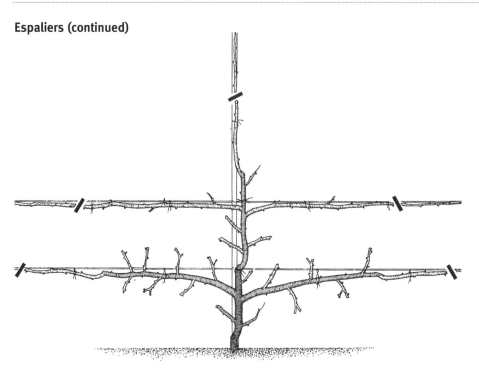

5 In late autumn, once growth has ceased for the year, cut back the central leader to within 45cm (18in) of the lower arm, leaving three good buds to form the new central leader and two new horizontal arms. Cut back the surplus laterals on the main stem to three buds. Prune back all the horizontal leaders by one-third, cutting back to downward-facing buds. Repeat this process in late autumn each year until the number of tiers that you require are all complete.

Mature tree

6 Once the tree has its required number of tiers and has filled its allotted space it is mature. From now on, during late spring, cut back the new terminal growths on the vertical and horizontal arms to their origins, so that the tree does not grow any larger, and prune the subsequent growths in summer as if they were laterals. Continue to prune the laterals back to three leaves as before.

Pruning dwarf pyramid plums

Plums, particularly gages, can be trained as fans against walls. But if wall space is scarce it is well worth growing plums as dwarf pyramids. The best rootstock for this is St Julien A. Choose a one-year-old tree of the required cultivar, with an even spread of undamaged side-shoots. Plant in the dormant season, in soil that has been thoroughly prepared (see page 179). Plums and other stone fruit belonging to the genus *Prunus* should not be pruned in winter because the risk of silver leaf disease entering through the wounds is much greater than in summer. Instead, carry out formative pruning in spring, just as the buds break, when healing will be fast. Then confine the pruning of mature trees as far as possible to the summer.

The first year

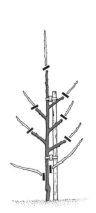

The second year

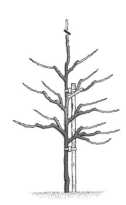

1 At some point between late autumn and late winter, plant a one-year-old tree with side shoots. Secure the tree to a stake using flexible tree ties.

2 Early spring. As the buds break, cut back the leader to 1.5m (5ft). Cut out any laterals up to 45cm (18in) above the ground. Cut back the remainder by half.

3 Mid summer. Cut back laterals growing directly from the stem to 20cm (8in). Cut back sub-laterals to 15cm (6in) above downward-pointing buds.

4 In early spring, just as the buds break, cut back the leader by two-thirds. Cut to a bud pointing in the opposite direction to the last pruning.

The third and subsequent years

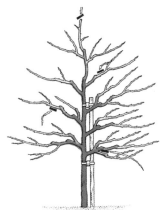

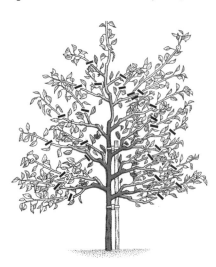

5 Mid summer. Cut back branch leaders to 20cm (8in) and laterals to 15cm (6in). Remove any extremely vigorous shoots. Tie down branches that are too vigorous.

6 In earely spring, just as the buds break, prune the leader as before until it reaches, for example, 2.7m (9ft), when it can be cut back to its base in late spring.

7 Mid summer. Cut back branch leaders to 20cm (8in) and laterals to 15cm (6in). Cut out any crossing laterals. Remove any vigorous shoots at the top of the tree.

Pruning bush plums

Plums, gages, and damsons are treated in the same way except that damsons are pruned less severely. Damsons are more tolerant than plums and thrive with gentle neglect, not suitable for the more refined plums and gages. Gages are merely dessert plums and should be treated as such. Bush trees make larger specimens than dwarf pyramids as they are grown on a half-standard trunk of about 1.2m (4ft). This form is suitable for plums with weeping branches to keep them clear of the ground.

The first year

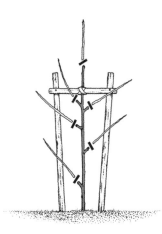

1 Late autumn to late winter. Plant, stake, and tie a one-year-old tree. In early spring, as buds break, cut back the leader to 1.5m (5ft) from the ground. Shorten all laterals or side shoots to about 8cm (3in).

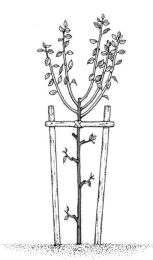

2 Mid to late summer. Four or five strong primary branches should develop towards the top of the main stem during the summer. No pruning is required at this point.

The second year

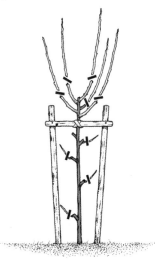

3 In early spring at bud break. Select four branches that have formed wide angles with the stem. Cut back by one-half to two-thirds, to outward-pointing buds. Cut back laterals to 8cm (3in).

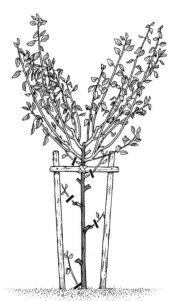

4 Mid to late summer. Cut back to 8cm (3in) laterals that appear below the first permanent branch. Remove any suckers that appear from below ground level.

Third and subsequent years (continued)

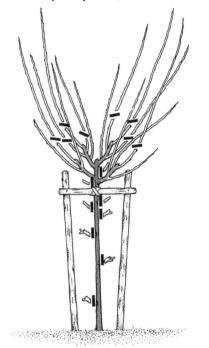

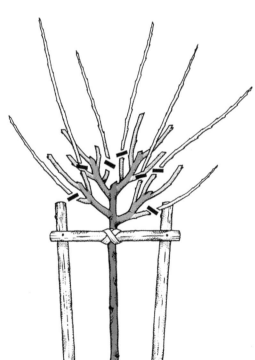

5 In early spring, at bud break, it will be necessary to repeat the procedures adopted the previous year (step 3, page 192), but this time allow more sub-laterals to develop to fill the increased space, allowing up to eight strong, well-spaced, and outward-growing, branches. Cut back these eight branch leaders by one-half to two-thirds to outward-pointing buds. At the same time remove all laterals that had been formerly reduced to 8–10cm (3–4in), as they have served their purpose and are no longer required.

6 At the same time as cutting back the selected laterals, cut back the remaining laterals on the inside of the bush to 8–10cm (3–4in). However, leave the laterals on the outside of the bush unpruned.

7 If the mature tree is growing well and the branches are strong and in their correct places, leader pruning can cease. However, in mid to late summer each year the laterals on the inside of the bush can be trimmed back to 8–10cm (3–4in). At the same time, cut out any vigorous or overlapping growths, and remove entirely any suckers that appear. No other pruning is required.

Pruning fan-trained trees

The first year

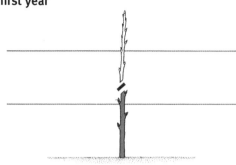

1 In the late winter or early spring, plant a one-year-old tree in soil prepared the previous autumn (see pages 179–80). When the buds begin to open cut back the stem to about 38 cm (15in) above the soil, just above a suitable bud.

2 At some point between late spring and early summer select two strong shoots close to the tip, and tie them to canes fixed to permanent wires at an angle of about 45°. Remove all the other shoots on the main stem.

The second year

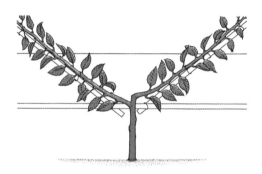

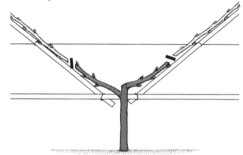

3 Mid summer to early autumn. Tie in the developing shoots. If necessary raise the shoots to increase their vigour, or depress them to decrease vigour and ensure even growth.

4 In early spring, when buds begin to open, shorten both of the leaders to about 30cm (12in), selecting suitable strong buds and cutting just above them.

5 At some time between early and late summer, train four to six strong shoots arising from each cut-back leader so that they are evenly spread on both sides of the fan. Tie each shoot to angled canes that are fixed to the permanent wires. Leave the centre of the fan unfilled. Prune back to 8–10cm (3–4in) any sub-laterals that develop.

The third year

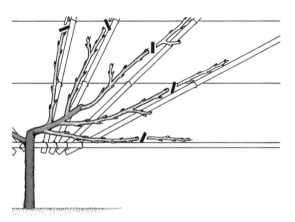

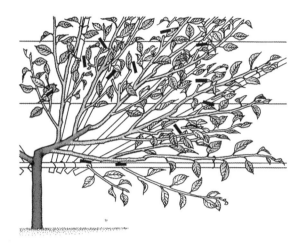

5 In the third year, at some point in late winter or early spring, when the buds begin to open, cut back all the new leaders to just above suitable strong buds, leaving about 45–53cm (18–21in) of the new growth. Tie this into the support canes.

6 In the summer or early autumn, select and evenly tie in three to six shoots from each pruned leader, gradually filling the space in the centre of the fan. Prune back any sub-laterals that develop to about 8–10cm (3–4in).

The fourth year

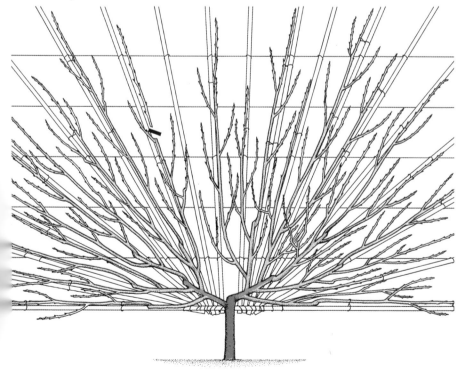

7 In late winter or early spring, when buds begin to open, check to see whether the leaders are spaced about 30–45cm (12–18in) apart at the tips. If any gaps remain, prune back selected leaders by one-half. Leave the remaining leaders unpruned. During the summer months each year, cut out all inward- and outward-growing shoots as they develop. Stop all other sub-laterals at 15cm (6in), or four to six leaves, to begin to form the spur system that will carry fruit in later years. In early autumn cut back all stopped laterals to 8–10cm (3–4in) to form spurs that will produce flower buds during the following year.

Renovating plum trees

Frequently old plum trees, particularly those on vigorous rootstocks, are neglected and become unkempt and unmanageable. They do not take kindly to severe pruning and are less tolerant of poor growing conditions than apples. They are also prone to the devasting silver leaf disease which can enter the plant through open wounds that are likely to result from severe pruning. Neglected plums may respond to generous feeding and mulching, once weeds are removed (see pages 29 and 32).

The first year

1 At some time during the summer cut out any large branches that upset the overall symmetry of the tree. Remove any crossing or awkwardly placed branches so that a framework of more-or-less evenly spaced branches remains.

2 At the same time, cut out any remaining dead, diseased or damaged wood. Remove any basal suckers and twiggy growths that have appeared at the base and on the main trunk.

Second and subsequent years

3 At the same time, thin out any lateral branches and twigs where crowded growth occurs to leave a well-furnished, evenly-spaced branch system. Finally remove any weeds, water the soil thoroughly, if necessary, and mulch around the base of the tree with organic matter.

4 During the summer months remove any over vigorous growths that threaten to spoil the overall symmetry of the tree. Thin out any remaining overcrowded branch systems. Cut out any further sucker growth and any weak water shoots arising from the trunk.

Protecting fruit on bushes

The simplest way to protect fruits and fruit buds from birds is to drape the bush with netting. Keep the netting off the branches by supporting it on canes. Cover the ends of the canes with flower pots or eye protectors.

Picking fruit

As a general principle, apples and other fruits are ripe and ready for picking when they come away easily in the hand. Hold larger fruit in the up-turned palm of the hand, grasp the fruit lightly with the fingers, and twist.

Storing hard fruit

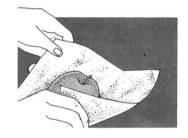

1 Place each sound fruit in the centre of a square of paper. Kitchen paper will do, but oiled or wax paper is likely to prolong the storage life of the fruit.

2 Fold the bottom point into the middle. Then fold in the two side points, followed by the top point to form a parcel.

3 Gently place the apple "parcel", folded side down into the box or tray. They are best stored in a single layer. Check from time to time and remove any rotten fruit.

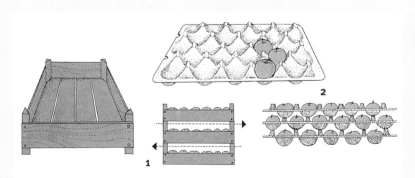

STORAGE BOXES AND TRAYS

Orchard boxes (1) have slatted sides and corner posts to allow air to circulate, and the slats have rounded edges to protect the fruit. Do not wrap fruit stored in polystyrene or trays (2). The moulded compartments prevent the fruit from touching and air can circulate freely between the rows.

Planting blackcurrants

Blackcurrants can be grown in a wide range of soils. Ideally, the soil should be slightly acid, about pH6.5 (see page 28), highly moisture-retentive and well-drained. Light soils need plenty of bulky organic material. The site should be frost-free and sheltered from strong winds. Most cultivars bloom early in the spring and the flowers are extremely vulnerable to frost.

Blackcurrants tolerate partial shade but prefer a sunny position. Buy two-year-old bushes certified virus-free. Select plants with at least three strong shoots. Plant between late autumn and early spring (see pages 179–80), spacing bushes 1.5m (5ft) apart in rows 1.8m (6ft) apart. Blackcurrants thrive on heavy manuring and high summer moisture. Clear weeds and mulch in spring.

Blackcurrants

1 In autumn, clear the ground of weeds. Dig in a 8cm (3in) layer of manure or compost. Rake in the surface a balanced fertilizer, such as a brand of Growmore, at 90g per sq m (3oz per sq yd).

2 Dig a hole wide and deep enough to take the roots when they are spread out well. Plant the bush about 5cm (2in) deeper than it was in the nursery. Fill in the hole and firm down the soil.

3 After planting, cut down all the shoots to within 5cm (2in) of the soil. Although this may seem drastic, new shoots will quickly be formed.

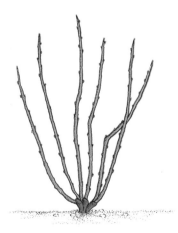

4 By late autumn, the severe pruning has resulted in strong new shoots appearing from the base. These will produce fruit the following year. No pruning is required at this stage is required.

5 Between late winter and early spring, apply a compound fertilizer, such as a brand of Growmore, at 90g per sq m (3oz per sq yd). A month later, apply 30g per sq m (1oz per sq yd) of sulphate of ammonia.

6 Mid summer. The bush fruits best on last year's growth. In late autumn, thin out weak and damaged shoots. In subsequent winters, remove one-third of the bush, cutting back fruited branches to a strong bud.

Apple trees trained as cordons.
A large number of such trees can
be included in a small space.

Far left: A dramatic archway is achieved by training and pruning a beech hedge.

Left: Box hedges play an important part in the design and atmosphere of this garden.

Below: Neatly-clipped box hedges are used to contain the vegetables in this potager.

The blackcurrant carries its best fruit on wood produced during the previous year, but it will also crop on older wood. It follows that the aim of the gardener should be to ensure a regular supply of young wood from the stool, the base of the plant, while the bush is young, and to encourage vigorous side branches from the older wood as the bush enters into middle age. As long as the bushes are healthy and certified virus-free, the first-year prunings can be used as hardwood cuttings (see page 130).

The first year

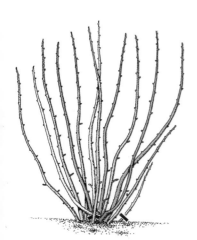

1 Late autumn to late winter. A one-year-old plant ready for planting. After planting cut down all shoots to within 5cm (2in) of the ground.

The second year

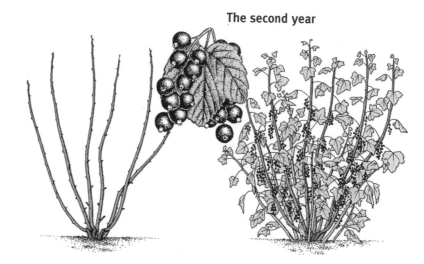

2 Late autumn. The severe pruning has resulted in strong new shoots appearing from the base. These will fruit in the following year. No pruning required.

3 In mid-summer the bush will produce a crop of blackcurrants on the previous year's shoots. New shoots are appearing from the base.

Third and subsequent years

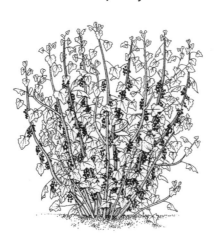

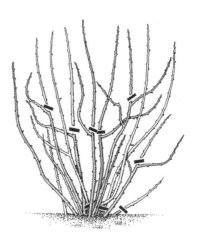

4 Between late autumn and late winter, cut out about one-third of the fruited branches to the base. Also cut out any damaged and weak growth.

5 In mid summer, the bush will produce blackcurrants, mainly on the previous year's growth. New basal growths and side branches are produced.

6 Late autumn to late winter. Remove three of the old branches entirely. Cut back other fruited branches to vigorous new side branches. Remove any damaged branches.

Planting red and white currants

Red and white currants are essentially the same, with the white being a colour variant of the red. They are both easy to grow and very fruitful. They require the same growing conditions and techniques. The fruit buds are produced in clusters at the base of the one-year-old wood shoots, and on short spurs on the older wood. Because of this fruiting habit there is a permanent framework of branches, unlike the blackcurrant for which a succession of young wood is needed.

Ideally the soil should be neutral to acid, about pH6.7 (see page 28). Red currants are less tolerant of poor drainage than black. Provided the soil is reasonably well-drained and not deficient in potash, the red currant is tolerant of a wide range of conditions. The flowers of the red currant are better able to cope with frost than those of the blackcurrant, so it is a useful bush for north-facing fences and walls. A sunny position is preferred if the berries are to acquire their full flavour but they will also grow well in moist shady areas not overhung by trees. Buy plants from a reliable source.

Red and white currants

1 In early autumn, prepare the soil by digging in a 4cm (1½in) layer of well-rotted manure (see pages 179–80). Then, rake in a compound fertilizer, such as a Growmore, at 60g per sq m (2oz per sq yd).

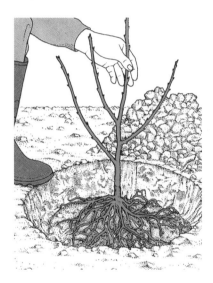

2 Plant from late autumn to early spring. Dig a hole large enough to take roots well spread out, and position the bush at the same depth as it was in the nursery. Delay planting if the ground is wet or frozen.

3 Every year in late winter, apply a balanced fertilizer, such as Growmore, at 60cm per sq m (2oz per sq yd) and sulphate of potash at 15g per sq m (½ oz per sq yd). On light soils apply a 5cm (2in) mulch of rotted manure or compost around each bush.

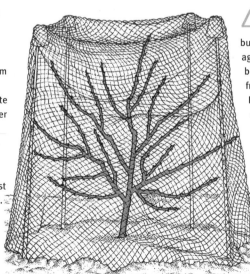

4 During the win protect the fru buds with netting against attacks by birds and against frost at blossom ti Remove the netti during the day when the plants flower so they can be pollinate

The main problem with red currants is that birds find both the buds and the fruit very tasty. This means that bushes must be protected by using nets, scaring devices, or, best of all, growing them inside a permanent cage. If bird damage does occur, defer pruning until the spring so that you can assess accurately the extent of the damage. White currants, typified by 'White Dutch', are treated in the same way as red currants. Red currants are usually grown as a miniature open-centred bush, with a short leg, and some eight radiating permanent branches. The leg is formed at the cutting stage by removing all but the top three buds from a hardwood cutting (see page 130). With their abundant clusters of bright red fruits, red currants are increasingly being used ornamentally. Plants are grown as upright cordons (see page 188) with two or four arms, as espaliers (see page 189), or even fans (see page 194). These can be trained against walls, fences, or wire supports to form a screen.

Red and white currants: The first year

1 Between late autumn and early spring, plant a one-year-old bush. Immediately after planting, cut back branches by one-half to outward-pointing buds.

2 In the following late autumn, prune leaders by a half to outward-pointing buds. Select well-placed shoots to form permanent branches and cut back by half. Cut back other side shoots to 5cm (2in).

Second and subsequent years

3 In mid summer the following year, cut back all unwanted laterals to 10cm (4in), to open up the bush and allow light to reach the fruit. No leader pruning is required at this stage.

4 Between late autumn and late winter, cut back all leaders by one-half to outward-pointing buds. Cut to 2.5cm (1in) laterals that were pruned previously to 10cm (4in).

Gooseberries

The gooseberry bears fruit on spurs on older wood, and at the base of the previous summer's lateral growth. For this reason they are grown with a permanent framework of branches similar to red currants, or as an upright or multi-branched cordon (see page 188). Gooseberries are easily propagated by hardwood cuttings taken in late autumn (see page 130). Remove the weak tip and all but four buds. The purpose of disbudding is to produce a smaller

open-centred bush on a short leg, a form which makes weeding, picking and pruning much easier given the thorny nature of the plant – left to its own devices it will sucker freely. As gooseberries are less vigorous than red currants it is advisable to grow on plants raised from cuttings for a year, or to buy two-year-old plants. As with all fruit the ground must be well-prepared prior to planting and moisture is important, particularly as the fruits begin to swell.

Planting gooseberries

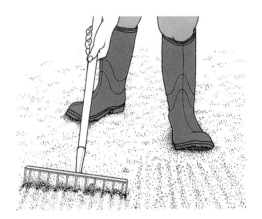

1 In early autumn, prepare the soil by digging and incorporating well-rotted organic matter. At the same time, clear the ground of perennial weeds. Before planting, rake the soil to level.

2 Between late autumn and early spring, dig a hole wide and deep enough to take the roots spread out well. Plant the bush. Remove any side shoots low down to leave a clear stem of 10–15cm (4–6in).

RENOVATING GOOSEBERRIES

Occasionally one has to deal with a long-neglected but healthy gooseberry bush. Such a bush is overcrowded with sucker shoots arising from the base, and frequently the tips of the weeping branches have not only touched the ground but have actually taken root.

In winter, cut out any very strong suckers, thin out the competing branches so that picking is made easier, and shorten appropriately any weeping branches.

Treated thus, the bush will fruit profusely on unpruned shoots formed the previous year. Once fruited these shoots should be removed completely to make way for their young and vigorous successors.

Thinning gooseberries

In late spring, when the gooseberries are large enough for cooking, thin the fruits by removing every other one. Cover the bush with netting to protect the fruits from the birds.

Pruning gooseberries

The gooseberry has the most exacting pruning requirements of all the bush fruits, and for this reason tends to be neglected and left to its own devices, which in view of the thorns is unwise. However, if it is properly pruned much larger fruits are obtained that are easier to pick. The more usual method of pruning is akin to that of red currants. They can, however, also be pruned in a manner similar to blackcurrants, but on a single stem. It is important to reduce the tendency of gooseberries to produce drooping branches by always pruning to an upward- and inward-facing bud. Cordons are spur pruned in the same way as each individual branch of bush, except that each cordon stem is trained vertically and staked (see pages 184 and 188).

Gooseberries: The first year

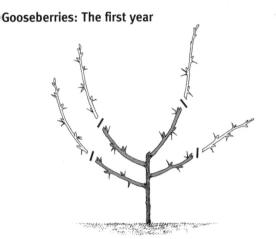

1 Plant a two-year old bush between late autumn and early spring when the weather allows. Cut back all the branches by one-half, cutting to an inward- and upward-pointing bud on each stem.

2 Prune the leaders by a half in late autumn. Select well-placed shoots to form further permanent branches, and cut back by a half. Cut back all other side shoots to 5cm (2in). Remove any suckers.

Second and subsequent years

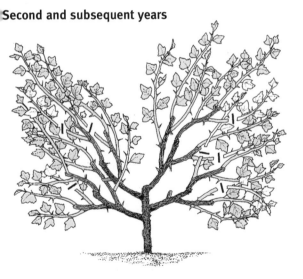

3 In mid summer, cut back all unwanted and badly placed laterals to 10cm (4in). The aim of this is to allow easy access for picking the fruit. Do not prune the leaders at this stage.

4 From late autumn to late winter, cut back all leaders by one-half. Also cut the laterals that were pruned last summer back to 5cm (2in). Cut out all dead, damaged or diseased wood.

Planting raspberries

Most raspberries flower in late spring, and the fruits ripen in early to mid-summer, depending upon the cultivar and weather: these are called summer-fruiting raspberries. Other cultivars have the characteristic of flowering on the first year's growth, on the topmost part, in late summer, and of fruiting in autumn. These are the autumn-fruiting raspberries. The two groups are cultivated in a similar manner but the pruning differs. Raspberries grow best on a slightly acid soil of pH 6–6.7 (see page 28) that is moisture-retentive but well-drained. They can be grown in light sandy and limy soil provided they are well watered in dry weather, and well-rotted manure is applied liberally before planting and in subsequent years. Although they prefer a sunny site they grow quite well in partial shade. Prepare the soil prior to planting (see pages 179–80). If possible plant in rows running north–south, so that one row does not shade another too much. Space canes 45–60cm (18–24in) apart with 1.5m (5ft) between single rows, and 1.2m (4ft) between double rows. To prevent the canes bowing over when heavy with fruit, it is necessary to support them. There are various support systems, and one should be in position before planting.

1 In early autumn take a trench in prepared ground. Cover the bottom with a 8–10cm (3–4in) layer of well-rotted manure or compost, and fork it in thoroughly.

2 Refill the trench and fork in a compound fertilizer at 90g per sq m (3oz per sq yd). Leave the soil slightly raised as it will sink down as it settles.

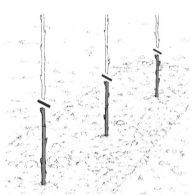

3 Between late autumn and early spring, plant the canes, spreading out the roots. Plant them about 8cm (3in) deep, then shorten the canes to about 25cm (10in).

SUPPORT SYSTEMS

Single post system
This is a method well suited to very small gardens. It consists of a single post to which each plant is tied. The posts (230 x 4 x 45cm/7½ft x 1½in x 18in) are driven 45cm (18in) into the ground at each planting station.

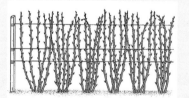

Single fence system
This is the most popular method, and consists of a post and wire fence with wires stretched horizontally at heights of 80, 100 and 165cm (2½, 3½, 5½ft). The fruiting canes are tied individually to the wires.

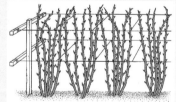

Double fence system
Drive 2m (6½ft) posts 45cm (18in) into the ground 4m (13ft) apart. Fix two 5 x 5 x 75cm (2 x 2 x 30in) cross bars to each post at 1 and 1.5m (3 and 5ft). Stretch parallel wires between cross bars, and cross-ties every 60cm (24in) along wires.

Raspberries are perennial plants with biennial stems. The aim of pruning is to encourage enough, but not too many, new canes to replace the old ones as they fruit and die. There are differences between summer- and autumn-fruiting cultivars that influence how they are pruned. Summer cultivars crop heavily on two-year-old canes, while autumn-fruiting cultivars crop less heavily on new wood. The annual canes required for autumn fruiting are encouraged by cutting down all canes in winter.

Summer-fruiting raspberries: The first year

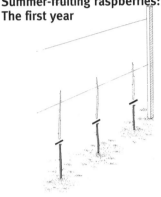

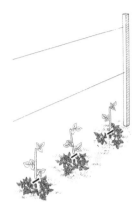

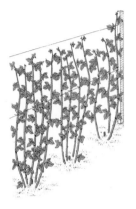

1 At some point between late autumn and early spring, plant the canes 45–60cm (18–24in) apart. Cut back each cane to within 25cm (10in) of the ground.

2 During the following spring new growth will appear at the base of the old wood as the new canes begin to develop. Cut down the old stumps to ground level.

3 Between early summer and early autumn, new canes develop. As they grow, space each cane 10cm (4in) apart and tie to a post and wire support. No fruit is produced this year.

Second and subsequent years

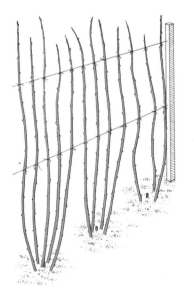

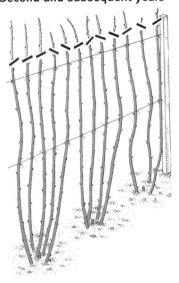

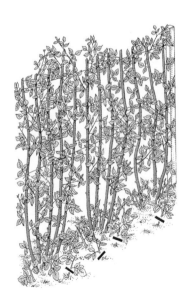

4 From mid autumn to late winter, complete tying in the canes 10cm (4in) apart. In windy areas do this in mid autumn. Loop over the tips to form a series of arches if necessary.

5 In late winter, cut back all dead and weak tips to about 1.5m (5ft) from the ground. This will encourage the development of fruiting laterals.

6 By mid-summer, new growths will have emerged from the base of the existing canes. Remove excess and misplaced ones, leaving new canes 10cm (4in) apart.

Pruning raspberries

7 From mid to late summer, raspberries are carried on the laterals that formed on the previous year's canes. The new canes continue to develop from the base, and should be tied to the wires in in windy areas.

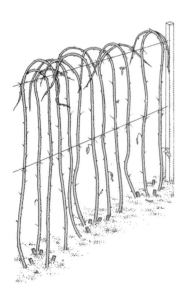

8 In mid autumn, cut back all fruited canes to ground level. Tie in the new canes at 10cm (4in) intervals. If growth is vigorous loop the new canes over at the top.

AUTUMN-FRUITING RASPBERRIES

Autumn-fruiting raspberries produce fruit on the laterals carried towards the ends of the canes grown in the current year. In the first year, the newly planted canes are treated as the summer fruiting varieties, tying in the canes at 10cm (4in) intervals. A few fruits can be gathered in the first autumn.

In the second and subsequent years, all the canes are cut down to ground level in the early spring. This encourages the new canes to grow rapidly and fruit from early autumn onwards. After fruiting cut the canes to the ground.

Growing blackberries and hybrid berries

Blackberries and hybrid berries such as loganberries and Tayberries, will grow in most soils. Prepare the ground in autumn (see pages 179–80) and plant as for raspberries (see page 206). The one-way system of training is particularly suitable for vigorous blackberries. Although the technique is simple it does require plenty of space, so in small gardens train plants along a fence. Plant canes about 4.5m (15ft) apart and, after planting, cut the stems back to within 25cm (10in) of the ground.

The first year

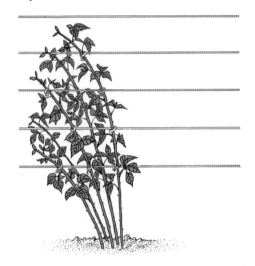

1 In summer, as the young rods appear, tie them with string to a strong post and wire support. Tie them into the wires to one side of the plant. Continue to tie in as they grow. Leave the other side clear. No fruit will be produced in this first year.

The second year

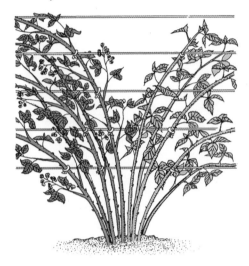

2 In the following summer, new rods will appear from the base of the plant. These should be trained along the wires in the opposite direction to the previous year's growth. Blackberries will be carried on the laterals formed on last year's rods.

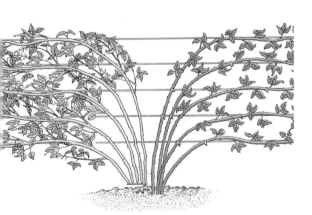

3 In autumn, usually about mid autumn, once fruiting has finished, untie the rods that have fruited and cut them out completely at ground level. If dealing with a thorny cultivar it is wise to wear thick gloves to protect your hands against scratches.

The third year

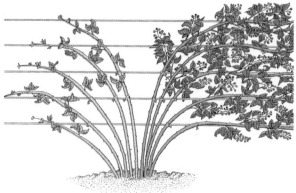

4 In the summer of the third year, train in the new rods as they appear along the now empty wires, and in the opposite direction to those of the previous year's growth. A crop of blackberries will be carried on the laterals of the old rods, which are cut out after fruiting.

Propagating blackberries and hybrid berries

Blackberries, loganberries, and other hybrid berries are easily propagated by tip layering. If a shoot tip is buried in the soil it will naturally develop roots, and quickly establish itself as a new plant. Tip layering is a useful technique for propagating a few

plants as it can be carried out *in situ* without disturbing the fruiting ability of the rest of the plant. The best time to do this is in late summer and early autumn when plants will be ready for transplanting during winter. Tip layer only from virus-free stock.

Tip layering

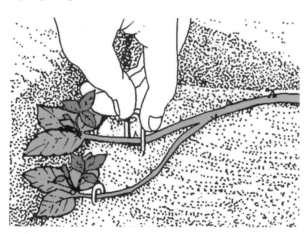

1 In late summer cultivate the soil. Add organic matter and grit, to improve drainage. Dig a trench at the layering point: 10cm (4in) deep and vertical at the furthest end, and sloping towards the plant. Use staples to pin down the tips in the deepest part of the trench.

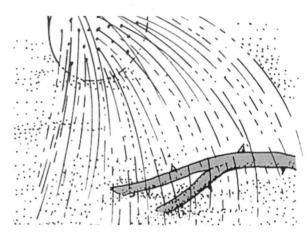

2 Replace the removed soil back into the trench so that the tips are completely covered. Gently but firmly press down the soil so that there are no air pockets around the tip. Water with a watering can fitted with a coarse rose. If the surface sinks top up with more soil.

3 After about three weeks or so shoots will start to appear above ground. In early autumn, cut through the original stem right back at the crown of the parent plant so that the new layer can be free to establish itself as an independent plant.

4 Later in autumn, after leaf fall, lift the rooted layer with a fork, taking as much surrounding soil as possible to avoid damaging the fine fibrous roots. Replant the layer carefully in its permanent position. Firm in and water thoroughly.

Strawberries are divided into three categories. The ordinary summer-fruiting cultivars and the perpetual strawberries, which crop in irregular flushes throughout the summer until stopped by autumn frosts, can both be raised from runners (see page 59); and alpine strawberries, which are raised from seed (see page 54). Summer-fruiting strawberries vary widely in flavour, yield, and the time they crop. It is important to buy and propagate from plants certified as virus-free. Perpetual strawberries are best replaced annually and summer-fruiting strawberries every three years. Replant all types of strawberry on a fresh site.

1 In mid summer, clear perennial weeds and prepare soil for planting (see pages 179–80), digging in well-rotted manure.

2 Just before planting, in mid or late summer, fork into the soil a balanced fertilizer at 90g per sq m (3oz per sq yd).

3 Space plants 45cm (18in) apart in rows 90cm (3ft) apart. Spread out the roots, keeping the crowns level with soil. Firm in.

4 For the first few weeks and during dry spells in the growing season, water regularly. Protect flowers from late frost.

5 When the fruits begin to swell, keep them clean and dry by covering the soil under and around the plants with straw.

6 Protect the fruit from birds with netting stretched over cloches, or supported on posts at least 45cm (18in) high.

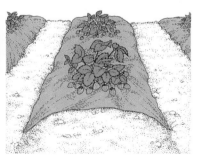

7 As an alternative to the use of straw, plant the strawberries through slits in black polythene raised on a slight mound.

8 Another alternative is to use special mats, made out of roofing felt, laid on the ground to form a collar round the plant.

9 In late summer, after cropping, cut off all the old leaves 8cm (3in) above the crown, and rake off the straw and other debris.

PLANT CARE

Planting a garden and then leaving it to get on by itself is a recipe for disaster. It is important to undertake a regular maintenance programme. It need not be an arduous schedule: "little and often" are the watchwords. The key to success is to keep on top of things.

A REGULAR ROUTINE

The easiest and most enjoyable way of keeping an eye on the garden is to take a leisurely stroll round it regularly looking at the plants. Ask yourself how the garden looks overall. Does the growth look healthy and lush, or is there a dullness to the foliage? Then look more closely – check anything untoward; feel the leaves and inspect underneath them; poke your fingers into the soil to see whether it is dry below the surface. In this way you will get to know your plants and garden, and quickly notice any changes – for better or for worse.

Within most gardens there are slight variations of climate, or microclimates – sunnier or shadier, wetter or drier places. During your regular observations you will become increasingly aware of these variations, which enables you to take advantage of them in your choice of plants.

This regular stroll is also a good time to pull out any weeds before they get to the flowering stage or out of control, and to snip off any dead heads. Regular deadheading helps to keep the garden tidy, and improves the appearance of plants by encouraging a bushier shape, better looking foliage, and more flowers (see also page 52).

Check tree ties and loosen them if they are too tight. If a bulge starts to appear above the tie, cut it away completely. If the constriction is allowed to continue, growth will suffer and ultimately the tree will die. Where trees, shrubs, or climbers are trained against supports, tie in new growth regularly before it becomes wayward. Use special plant ties, or raffia or soft green twine, tied quite loosely in a figure of eight knot. By this means the soft tissue will not be damaged, as it could be if wire or nylon string is used. Neither of these "give" or break down so there is danger of them strangling branches in time.

EXTREME WEATHER

In hot, dry summers drought is bound to be a problem and you will need to water. It is better to give vulnerable plants a good soaking once a week than a dribble every day, which will only encourage roots to grow at the surface rather than penetrate deeply in search of moisture. In view of the frequent hosepipe bans it is worth installing a water butt or two. You can also recycle household water. This "grey water", as it is known, should not be watered directly onto plants or used on plants in containers, but directed onto the soil – you could hoe out narrow channels and water into these. Not all waste water is suitable; don't recycle water which contains bath oils, bleach, or other harsh household chemicals.

It is just as important to visit the garden in the winter months as in summer. After a fall of snow, go out and knock it off the branches of conifers, evergreens, and hedges. If this is not done, the weight of the snow can break branches and spoil the shape of a hedge. Check the weather forecast, and when frost is threatened protect plants that are vulnerable; this is especially important late and early in the growing season.

Weeding

Weeding is one of those jobs that never seems to end. Every time you think you have cleared an area, you find more have appeared on your next visit. It is important to keep on top of them though, especially during the spring when growth is fast, otherwise they will thrive at the expense of other plants robbing them of nutrients, moisture, and light.

Weeds can be cleared in several ways: by hand; by hoeing; by smothering and by using an appropriate chemical according to the manufacturer's instructions (see page 260–61).

Annual weeds

Annuals are plants that complete their life cycle within a growing season, but many annual weeds are often able to undergo more than one life cycle in a season. They are also characterised by the production of very many seeds so that the weed seed population in the soil is constantly replenished. Annual weeds are relatively simple to deal with. If they are prevented from seeding, then, once the reservoir of seed in the soil has been used up, there is less of a problem. So the most effective time to weed is before the plants flower and set seed.

Perennial weeds

These are the real nuisance. Perennial plants live from year to year and usually have underground stems or roots which enable them to survive through the winter. Thus docks and dandelions have thick, fleshy tap roots, and couch grass, ground elder, and creeping buttercup have creeping stems, or rhizomes. Any piece of root or stem left in the soil is likely to produce new weeds, often spreading into surrounding plants and making it difficult to extract them.

Controlling perennial weeds

Certainly a thorough ground preparation in the first place helps considerably. Although you can compost the leaves of perennial weeds, the roots need to be disposed of, and not put in the compost bin. Because every piece of root is capable of regenerating, rotovating weedy ground is a bad idea. The machine may break up the soil, but it also chops up the weeds into many small pieces increasing their number and aggravating the problem.

Controlling annual weeds

As the soil is turned over annual weeds continually reappear. This is a particular nuisance when sowing seeds for not every one can recognise the difference between weeds and the desired plants in their early stages. There are two ways forward, apart from spraying. You can employ the no-dig method of gardening (see page 39) or make a stale seedbed. The latter involves preparing the ground ready for sowing flowers, grass or vegetables, then leaving it for 10 to 14 days, by which time any surface weed seeds will have germinated. These can be hoed off or sprayed before sowing your chosen plants (see page 261).

Smothering weeds

Weeds can also be smothered. Covering weedy ground for a season with old carpet or black plastic should clear it of most weeds as it starves them of light. The same effect can be achieved by mulching with organic matter, such as bark, rotted-manure or leafmould, or a non-biodegradable material such as gravel (see pages 32–33). The soil should be cleared before mulching round plants, but germination of new weeds will be suppressed due to the lack of light.

Weeding

Carefully hoe annual weeds, keeping the level blade just inside the surface layers of the soil. Choose a warm, drying day, so that weeds shrivel, and keep the blade of the hoe sharp.

Perennial weeds are best dealt with by removing them completely. Dig them out during the winter, removing every piece. Do not compost these as they will infest the compost.

A mulch helps to keep weeds down by smothering seedlings, but does not stop perennials if they have been left in the ground. Either an organic or polythene mulch can be used.

With neglected areas the only way to clean the ground may be to use a weedkiller. Choose one appropriate to the problem and always follow the instructions as given on the packet.

Much is expected of garden plants in terms of yield and flowering ability, and they are concentrated in gardens in a way not found in the wild. Plants massed together make great demands on soil nutrients. The soil will soon become impoverished, and the plants decline in vigour, unless the nutrients are regularly replenished. This is particularly true where vegetables and fruits are grown. In order to produce reasonable yields of good quality crops they need a ready supply of vital nutrients. Bush roses, which flower prolifically throughout the summer and into autumn, make similar high demands.

Nutrients can be provided at the time the bed is prepared. Well-rotted organic material added to the soil at that time breaks down to provide variable amounts of nutrients for the plants, and in addition it will help to retain moisture and improve soil quality (see page 32).

However, organic matter does not always supply sufficient nutrients, or, in the case of plants showing a deficiency, a particular nutrient. In these cases a more concentrated source of a nutrient or nutrients is found in fertilizers, although organic matter should continue to be applied regularly.

Base dressing crops

Dressings of base fertilizers are applied during the final stages of soil preparation before sowing or planting. They include materials like Growmore, sterilised bonemeal and fish, and blood and bone, all of which break down fairly slowly to help keep plants in good condition over a season (see page 29). Rates of application usually range from 30–120g per sq m (1–4oz per sq yd), and the material must be spread evenly. Divide the fertilizer into two lots, and rake one lot from up and down, and the other from side to side. This helps with even distribution. Very small quantities can be bulked up by mixing with soil or sharp sand.

Top dressing crops

Top dressings are most commonly applied in solid form around the base of plants. Most fertilizers are formulated as fairly coarse granules, but care is needed to ensure that they do not land in the middle of developing plants, because they can burn and scorch the young tissue. This is a particularly important consideration when applying nitrogen and potassium fertilizers. Phosphates, however, are best placed close to the seeds or the roots of young plants. Always apply top dressings as close to the ground as possible, and water them immediately to ensure that they have a rapid effect on plant growth.

Liquid fertilizers and foliage feeding

A number of proprietary foliar and liquid feed materials are available, some of which are of organic origin. Liquid feeding is a convenient way of top dressing plants but the effects are rarely as rapid and dramatic as using granular fertilizers where major elements of NPK (nitrogen, phosphate and potassium) are required. However, liquid feeding is very effective for correcting particular deficiency symptoms, particularly of magnesium and various minor elements; an example is sequestered iron, often used to "blue" hydrangeas. Liquid feeds based on seaweed are useful for young plants and seedlings as they seem to have a beneficial strengthening effect if used regularly. Foliar feeds are most useful for giving plants a quick boost. They are probably most effective on young plants growing in pots or massed summer displays in containers (see page 147).

Feeding

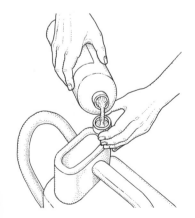

One method of feeding plants is to use a liquid fertilizer. This is added to water in a can at the recommended dosage.

This device fixes on to a hosepipe and dispenses fertilizer at a fixed rate into the flow of water. Useful for large scale feeding.

The traditional way of feeding is to use dry fertilizer. Spread this on to the surface, preferably just before rain is forecast.

Watering

Plants depend on water in the soil to absorb nutrients; if insufficient water is available they cannot manufacture food. Water is constantly lost through the leaves by transpiration and once the amount lost exceeds the amount taken in by the roots, wilting, with consequent reduction in growth and yield, results. Water also evaporates from the soil surface around plants in sunny and windy weather.

Soil moisture can be conserved in ways other than watering and choosing drought-resistant plants. Organic matter dug into the soil increases its moisture-holding capacity (see page 25). Mulching the soil is a great help as long as the mulch is sufficiently thick and overlays thoroughly moist soil (see pages 32–33). Keeping down weeds reduces the competition for water. Plants grown as ground cover, so that their foliage forms a canopy over the intervening soil, and close spacing of vegetables (see page 165) also reduce water loss.

Applying water

Water is often a scarce commodity and should only be used where and when it is necessary. Watering in the cool of the evening or early in the morning is better than in the heat of the day as evaporation will be less. Water heavily every so often rather than a daily light sprinkling; apply around 12l per sq m (2–5gal yd^2). Rather than use sprinklers, which are wasteful and inefficient, try to get the water directly to the roots where it is needed. To this end seep hoses can be laid along rows of plants, in borders, or even buried in the soil. Perforated hoses can be used in a similar way, but if buried lay them in a channel of gravel to prevent the holes from clogging up. They are also useful for watering lawns. You could link up a series of seep hoses to an automatic timer (see page 147), so that it is possible to water at a set time.

Watering priorities

Certain plants have high demands at various times of their lives when they should have priority. These include seedlings, new lawns, and newly established plants, particularly trees and shrubs, which are expensive and long term. Fruit and vegetables also benefit most from generous watering at flowering time, when fruit sets, and also when fruits and pods are swelling.

Watering

A watering can is the most versatile of watering devices. It can be used with or without a rose.

A hosepipe with a lance on the end is a good method of watering individual plants. Make certain that the soil is thoroughly soaked.

In order to prevent water flowing away from where it is required, build a low wall of soil around the plant to create a reservoir.

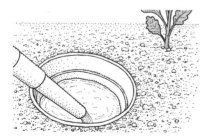

Sink a flower pot next to individual plants and fill this with water. This ensures that it goes where it is needed, down by the roots.

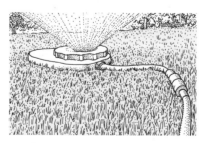

Using a sprinkler to water a lawn or large area is non-selective and wasteful. It takes hours to soak the ground thoroughly.

A perforated or seep hose allows water to trickle out slowly. It is more efficient than a sprinkler, as it only waters where it is laid.

Left: A dark-coloured formal hedge is the perfect foil for setting off light-coloured flowers in a border.

Right: Railway sleepers that have been cut to length are used as the risers for this sweeping set of steps.

Right: The tranquillity of an informal and naturalistic setting for a water feature.

Far right: A stream descending a cascade of waterfalls in a woodland garden.

Below: A natural-looking rock garden merging with an artificially made scree bed.

Many plants are marginally tender, that is they will stand a certain degree of frost but not too much. Others are hardy as long as the ground around them does not freeze. Both these categories are frequently left in the ground, but given some form of protection during the winter months. In milder areas they are only covered when cold weather threatens, in others where the cold is more constant, they are kept covered.

A third problem is one that most gardeners dread, late frosts. Here perfectly hardy plants will suffer because a severe, late, and often unexpected frost cuts back all the new growth. This is particularly a problem after a mild winter when growth is early and well advanced. The only answer here is to be aware of the type of weather that will produce such frosts, and listen to weather forecasts during vulnerable times. Should a late frost threaten, then place a temporary cover over as many of the vulnerable plants as possible. As long as the frost is not very severe even a light covering of material such as fleece or newspaper will protect the plants. Since frost at this time of year is not usually accompanied by wind several sheets of paper can simply be draped over the plants without being anchored.

Some gardens suffer from frost constantly, sometimes even in the summer if they form a frost pocket. Cold air drains down slopes and gets trapped within the garden keeping it cold. If the garden is at the bottom of the hill, little can be done, but if it is on the slope, a hole can be made in the hedge or fence to allow the cold air to continue down the slope away from the garden. Another ploy is to put a hedge at an angle above the garden to deflect the cold air around it.

If a garden is on a slope, plant the more tender plants towards the top. South-facing slopes are warmer than north-facing ones. Walls will also give protection against frost, especially house walls.

Frost protection

As temporary frost protection, lightweight fleece can be draped over the plants.

Vulnerable crowns and plants below ground can be protected with a covering of straw.

To prevent the dry straw from being blown away it can be placed in an upturned box.

Cloches help to protect many vegetables from the more extremes of weather.

FROST PROTECTION OF ORNAMENTALS

Most rock garden plants are hardy and need protecting from rain rather than the cold. However, frost-tender border plants and sub-shrubs may need protection. The plants need to have air circulating around them and should not be smothered. Hessian or matting over a cloche works well as does newspaper as temporary covering.

Vulnerable shrubs can be covered in straw and then wrapped in plastic or fleece.

Fruit can be grown against a wall with a sheet of plastic or fleece to protect early blossom.

Wind protection

The best protection against wind is a living windbreak of trees and shrubs, or a hedge (see pages 80 and 82–83). But such plants are not always feasible. Fences are a good alternative. Chosen with care they will filter wind effectively but they are not so tough nor as long lasting as plants. Wood is still the preferred material for most garden fences, although wire or wire-netting is a cheaper alternative and will disappear behind a planting of shrubs or climbers. A solid, boarded fence can create turbulence, so a more open design is preferable, as they allow the wind to filter through. Wattle hurdles are attractive but short lived.

A solid windbreak

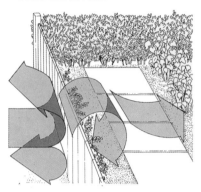

A solid, close-boarded fence halts the wind, which then tumbles over it creating turbulence on the far side. This is often far more destructive than a steady wind as it thrashes plants around in all directions.

An open windbreak

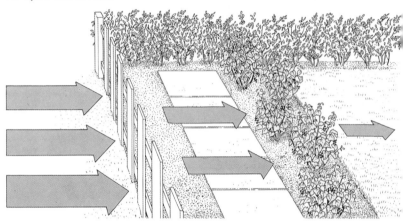

A picket fence, or one built in such a way that it has gaps in it allows the wind to filter through. This slows the wind down, but does not create the turbulence of the solid fence. Because the wind can filter through, the pressure on the fence is less.

Wire fencing windbreak

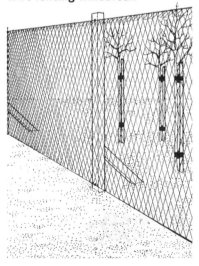

Wire netting, or special plastic netting, can be used for creating a windbreak, the latter being useful for a temporary screen.

Attaching netting to posts

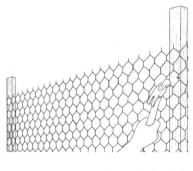

Wire- or plastic-netting can be stretched between posts to create a boundary fence while windbreak-planting is becoming established. The fence is stronger if wire is first stretched between the posts at the top, middle, and bottom of the netting. The netting is then attached to this at regular intervals with wire ties.

The wire-netting can be attached to the upright wooden posts with galvanised staples that will not corrode. Strain the wire netting as tight as possible before hammering in the staples.

The climate of an area is determined by the prevailing conditions over a period of time, as opposed to weather that changes day by day. Your local climate depends firstly upon major factors such as latitude, distance from the sea and prevailing winds, and secondly on the local topography. Within the garden the climate can vary quite widely from the local norm, and small-scale variations can exist side by side, known as microclimates. The secret of coping successfully with a particular microclimate is either to modify it, by planting or erecting windbreaks, or to grow plants capable of surviving in the particular conditions it provides. The aspect and soil (see page 26–27) both influence what plants can be grown, but a plant's tolerance of frost and wind and its ability to adapt to the seasonal cycle that prevails – its hardiness – is all important.

Frost

Cold air, like water, seeks the lowest level, and areas at the foot of sloping ground will be far more susceptible to frost than land higher up the slope. Do not position tender plants, especially fruit trees with early blossom, in frost pockets, and avoid creating pockets by erecting solid fences or hedges across a slope. Cold air flowing down the slope will gather behind such obstacles, and also collect in hollows, leading to frost damage to plants. Permeable barriers such as open fences allow cold air to seep through, and are therefore to be preferred (see page 180).

Wind

Frost may be the main problem in low-lying gardens, but strong winds are a constant hazard in exposed or hilltop places where they will physically damage trees and shrubs, and cause water to be lost from the soil and foliage more rapidly. The answer is not to erect a solid barrier, for wind cannot simply be halted – its energy has to be dissipated. A solid wall or fence presented to the wind will cause the air currents to rise up and then fall directly behind the wall, creating damaging down-draughts and turbulence (see page 220). The way to cut down damage from strong winds is to erect a relatively permeable barrier, such as a deciduous hedge or open screen. This will reduce the force of the wind to a level which plants can tolerate. A permeable barrier will effectively reduce the wind speed for a distance equal to ten times its height, thus a 1.2m (6ft) screen will protect up to 12m (6oft) of ground on its leeward side. For example, the prevailing wind in Britain usually comes from the west or south-west, so windbreaks are best erected to run from north-west to south-east. Rows of trees, fences or buildings running in the same direction as the wind can create a funnelling effect, and should, if possible, be planted across its path to diffuse the force – a wire-netting fence planted on the leeside would work well. Wind tunnels created by buildings and walls, such as occur in many side entrances to houses, should have their entrances sheltered by shrubs, trees, or open screens.

Rainfall

The wind plays an important part in the distribution of rainfall. Frequently ground at the base of walls or trees to the leeward side will remain dry; and that below south- and west-facing walls will dry out due to shortage of water and its sunny aspect. It is essential to take this into account before planting and to improve the moisture-retaining capacity of soils in these situations with plenty of organic matter (see pages 27 and 30).

Altitude

The higher the ground the colder it will be. For every rise of 75m (250ft) above sea level, the temperature drops by about one degree and the growing season is shorter.

Urban heat

Large urban areas give off heat day and night which can artificially lift temperatures, particularly in winter, and allow a wider range of plants to be grown. Within the garden sunny walls act as storage heaters allowing less than hardy plants to survive over winter.

Types of windbreak

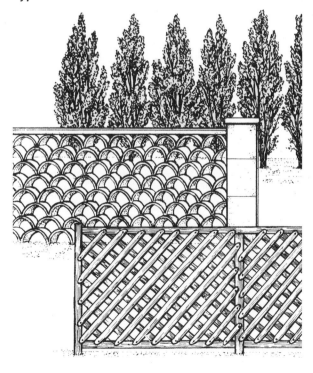

The best windbreaks allow some wind to filter through. They can be planted screens of wind-tolerant, usually deciduous, trees and shrubs; wooden fences, or walls constructed of perforated concrete blocks.

CONSTRUCTION WORK

Gardening is about making and maintaining structures as well as planting. The "do-it-yourself" approach to ponds and paving is invariably less expensive than employing professionals, and there is a great deal of satisfaction to be gained from constructing something oneself. However, not all gardeners will feel competent to tackle these jobs. The best advice is that you should take on only the tasks you feel confident you can finish. But even if your prefer to call in the experts, a clear understanding of what is involved will help you to get the job done to your satisfaction. It is also important to site these permanent features correctly. An ill-placed pool or patio will prove a permanent and costly mistake. So plan them carefully beforehand. Mark their outline on the ground with spray paint to help you visualise their extent and position.

PONDS AND WATER FEATURES

Avoid siting a pool under trees. Not only will the shady conditions result in poor plant growth, but the pool will become clogged with fallen leaves, which can be harmful to fish and laborious to remove. An open site, sheltered from strong winds, is best, where the reflections on the water's surface can be enjoyed. If lights or a pump are to be installed, make sure that the pool is within reach of an electricity supply. Larger areas of water look better and are easier to manage than smaller ones, and the depth should be no less than 45cm (18in). Flexible liners have made pools of any shape and size much easier to construct and maintain than out-moded concrete pools. These liners have also facilitated the construction of rills and waterfalls. If you don't feel you have space for a pond, a wall

fountain or sunken reservoir feature can be fitted into the smallest of gardens, and in sun or shade.

RAISED BEDS AND ROCK GARDENS

Both these features should be carefully planned within the garden design. Raised beds not only allow you to grow plants that require special conditions, but they can be used to divide the garden into sections. Rock gardens, like pools, need an open, sunny, sheltered spot. They must be constructed with thought if they are to work well, both visually, and for the rock or alpine plants they are designed to support.

PATHS AND PAVING

Useful paved areas should conform to some basic rules. Paths should cover the shortest distance between the two points to be linked, and be wide enough to take whatever traffic is likely to pass over it. Patios should be large enough to take a table and chairs with room for people to move freely round them. All paved features look best if they use materials that blend in with the style of house and garden. They need adequate foundations to ensure stability, and should also allow surface water to drain away, and away from house walls.

FENCES AND GATES

Choose fences and gates with care, especially if you live in a windy area (see page 220) and once erected look after them. Those made of wood will last longer if they are painted with preservative every two or three years. Using posts and gravel boards of tanalised timber or concrete will also prolong the life of a fence. Gates need to be sited with care, and erected at the same time as a fence.

Making a pool with a flexible liner

The three main types of flexible liner are butyl rubber, PVC, and polythene. Butyl is very tough, long-lasting, flexible, and the most expensive; PVC is less durable and may crease, but is cheaper.

Polythene is the least expensive, but easily damaged, and very short-lived if exposed to ultraviolet light. However, if it is buried under a layer of clay it lasts longer.

Making a pool with a liner

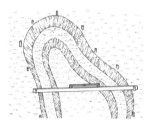

1 Use a series of pegs around the proposed pond to ensure that the levels are correct during the excavation.

2 After marking out, dig down in even layers, incorporating a marginal shelf if one is desired.

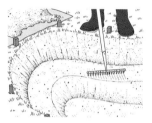

3 Remove any sharp stones from the excavation that may otherwise puncture the liner. Rake the surface smooth.

4 Line the pool with fleece, geotextile, or polyester matting. Spread it over the site, moulding it into the contours.

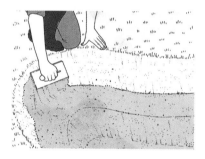

5 Alternatively, plaster the excavation with a 3cm (1in) layer of damp sand, making sure it adheres well to the sides.

6 Lay the liner over the excavation, making sure that it is centred. Anchor it with large stones around the edge.

7 Fill the pool with water. The liner will stretch into the shape of the hole; gradually lift the stones to release the liner.

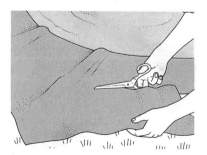

8 Using a pair of sharp scissors, neatly trim the liner, leaving a margin of approximately 15cm (6in).

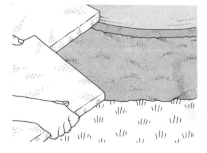

9 Bury the edge of the liner in up to 15cm (6in) of soil. Set paving slabs on cement so that they slightly overhang the pool.

TURF EDGING

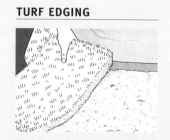

In areas that have a heavy soil, turf can be laid right up to the edges of the pool. Trim grass with care.

Preformed pools are only available in a limited range of shapes and sizes, but interlinking modules are available for making streams and multiple pools. Fibreglass shells are rigid and much easier to manage than thin plastic or PVC shells, both of which are likely to distort during the installation process. It is important to get the pool perfectly horizontal and disguise the edges.

Preformed pool installation

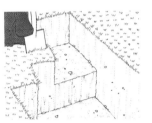

1 Mark out and excavate a rectangle or a contoured hole that will easily embrace the preformed unit.

2 Remove any sharp stones or roots, and tamp the soil down with your feet by treading the earth with regular footsteps.

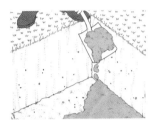

3 Place a layer of damp sand across the floor of the excavation. This will act as a cushion for the unit.

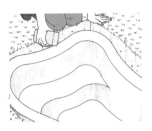

4 Position the unit in the excavation, building up any areas not touching the ground with bricks and stones.

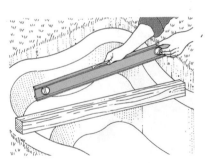

5 Once installed, check the unit is completely level by spanning it with a plank of wood with a spirit level laid on it.

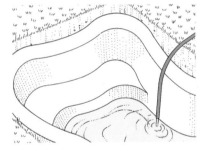

6 Using a hosepipe, fill the pool with approximately 10cm (4in) of water before backfilling around the unit.

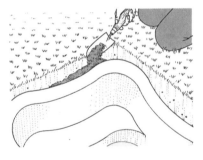

7 Fill the gap around the pool by feeding and firming a small quantity of sand at a time as you work round the pool.

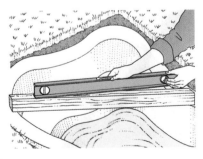

8 After each full circuit, check that the unit is still level. Backfill the top layer with soil if the edge is to be planted.

9 Once the unit is firmly installed, lay a bed of mortar approximately 3cm (1in) thick around the edge of the pool.

10 Position each piece of paving so that it overhangs the edge of the pool, and point the cracks between each.

Planting aquatics

Preparing and planting a basket

1 Line the basket with hessian or special lining material. Fill the basket with top-soil to within 2.5cm (1in) of the rim and firm down. Trim off the excess lining material.

2 Before planting, use a watering can with a fine rose to soak the soil. Use ordinary garden soil that has not been enriched with rotted manure or fertilizer.

3 With a trowel or your hands, dig a hole in the compost large enough to take the roots of the plant when spread out, and place the plant into the hole.

4 Cover the roots with the planting medium, ensuring that there are no air pockets. Firm down the surface of the compost, especially around the roots of the plant.

5 Cover the soil surface with a 1–2cm (½in) layer of washed pea gravel. This will prevent fish from disturbing the soil and soil particles floating off after the basket is submerged.

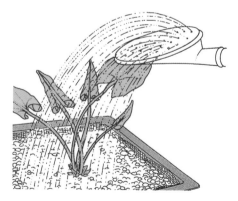 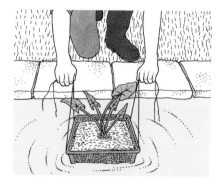

6 Always soak the soil in planting baskets thoroughly to remove all the air before putting them in the pool. If this is not done properly, streams of air bubbles will bring up debris and cloud the water.

7 Position the basket in the water. For deep water planting use cords to lower a basket on to bricks, so it sits 15cm (6in) below the surface, then, as the plant grows gradually lower it to the bottom.

Planting aquatics

Making planting sacks

1 Mix some aquatic compost or some heavy garden soil with enough water to make it into a mud-like consistency.

2 Take a generous handful of the mixture, and pack it around the roots of the plant in a 10cm (4in) layer.

3 Place the plant on a square of hessian and, using string, loosely tie the hessian around the neck of the plant.

4 Carefully lower the sack containing the plant into the pool, making sure it is in the desired location.

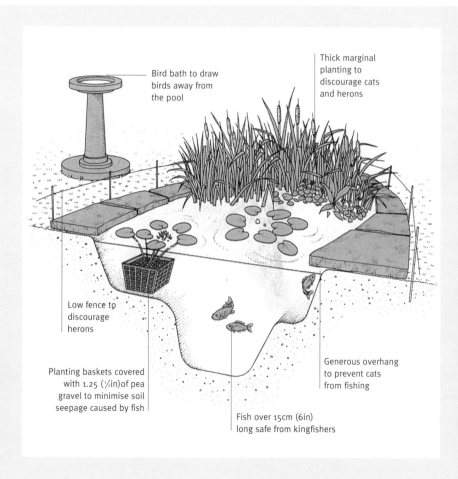

Bird bath to draw birds away from the pool

Thick marginal planting to discourage cats and herons

Low fence to discourage herons

Planting baskets covered with 1.25 (½in) of pea gravel to minimise soil seepage caused by fish

Fish over 15cm (6in) long safe from kingfishers

Generous overhang to prevent cats from fishing

PROTECTING THE POOL

Although a large pond, well-stocked with oxygenating plants, is generally a self-sustaining and stable environment, a smaller one may need help to prevent one or more elements becoming dominant or, conversely, from dying out. Fish, for example, can become easy prey for birds such as herons and kingfishers. An overhanging edge, floating leaves, and marginal planting will give some protection. The plants will also help the larvae, of dragonflies for example, and tadpoles by giving them hiding places from fish. Pools can become overrun by vigorous plants and algae, and these should be thinned or cleared regularly (see page 231).

Installing electricity outdoors

If you have, or are planning to have, a pond the chances are you will need a pump. A pump is essential to circulate the water to operate a fountain, a waterfall, and some filtration units. Underwater lighting can create magical effects at night, and special pool heaters will keep an area of water ice-free in winter so that fish have adequate oxygen. To operate any of these features you will need a source of electricity. Electricity is potentially lethal, and stringent safety measures are essential if electrical equipment, especially that associated with water, is to work correctly without endangering life. Therefore, however self-sufficient you are in DIY, the one area you should always leave to a qualified professional is the installation of outdoor electrical wiring.

Cables and power points

A power source run from a house to a garden pool will almost always be laid under ground. A fully-armoured cable should be used that will stand a certain amount of damage should it be struck inadvertently when the garden is being dug. To minimise the likelihood of such an accident, all armoured cable should be buried in a trench, excavated to a depth of 50cm (20in) under paths and hard surfaces. If this is not possible and they need to run under beds, borders, or lawn, bury them to a depth of 60cm (24in). Before the cable trench is filled in, tiles and warning tape should be laid on top of the cable. The circuit must have its own fuse or miniature circuit breaker (MCB), and a residual current device (RCD). All switches, sockets, and plugs used outdoors must be waterproof; those used indoors are not suitable.

Pumps and lights can operate through a transformer on a 12- or 24-volt system; these low voltage systems are very safe and can be housed indoors. Any joins in the cables must be through a purpose-made outdoor waterproof connector housed in a chamber that can be easily accessed for maintenance.

You can save a lot of money and avoid possible damage to garden plants by excavating the trench yourself, but before you start, check the specifications with the electrician who is to carry out the wiring. A permanent plan should be kept of the position of the underground cables, and this should be passed on to the new occupant when a property changes hands.

SAFETY

WATER AND ELECTRICITY DO NOT MIX: ALWAYS USE WATERPROOF ARMOURED CABLE AND A WATERPROOF CONNECTOR

Always follow the manufacturer's instructions exactly when installing pumps, lighting, or any other electrically operated equipment. All electrical equipment must be operated in conjunction with a circuit breaker to protect against electric shocks; this device cuts off the electrical supply within 30 milliseconds should problems occur. Most pumps work directly from the mains 240 volt electricity supply. Armoured cable must be laid in a 50–60cm (20–24in) trench to protect it from being cut or damaged. Only install specially designed underwater lighting.

Digging trenches for underground cables

1 To avoid damage by digging, cables should be buried in a trench at least 60cm (24in) deep, or 50cm (20in) under paths and other hard surfaces.

2 The cable should be further protected by laying a row of old roofing tiles over it, or running it through special protective plastic conduits.

3 As a further precaution lay a warning tape, coloured with yellow and black stripes, along its length. This indicates the presence of a live cable.

Always use a special plug-in residual current device (RCD). Cables should be joined only with a purpose-made weatherproof connector.

A pool fountain is powered by a submersible low-voltage pump, to which the power cable should already be attached. Place a few concrete slabs in the deepest part of the pond. Lower the pump on to this plinth, so that the fountainhead protrudes just above the waterline. Run the cable out of the pond by the least noticeable route, taking it under the slab edging. Where the cable enters the house through a drilled hole, it is best fed through a length of conduit fixed to the surface every metre (3ft).

Fountains

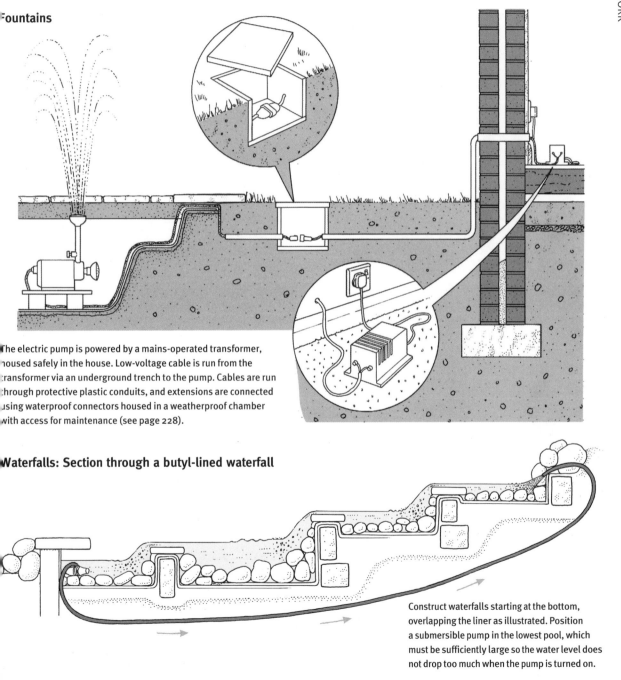

The electric pump is powered by a mains-operated transformer, housed safely in the house. Low-voltage cable is run from the transformer via an underground trench to the pump. Cables are run through protective plastic conduits, and extensions are connected using waterproof connectors housed in a weatherproof chamber with access for maintenance (see page 228).

Waterfalls: Section through a butyl-lined waterfall

Construct waterfalls starting at the bottom, overlapping the liner as illustrated. Position a submersible pump in the lowest pool, which must be sufficiently large so the water level does not drop too much when the pump is turned on.

Installing a sunken reservoir fountain

A sunken reservoir fountain can be fitted into gardens that are too small for a pond. They also make attractive and safe water features for children to enjoy. This example uses a millstone, but the same principle can be adapted to other styles of bubble fountain. For a lined excavation illustrated below, mark, and then dig out, a circular hole slightly larger than the diameter

of the millstone. Alternatively, use a plastic dustbin, excavating a hole deep enough so the lip is flush with the ground. Dig a margin around the excavation about 10cm (4in) deep and 15cm (6in) wide. Check the excavation is level before lining the hole or lowering the dustbin. To keep the pump stable, stand it on bricks placed on a double layer of geotextile, to protect the liner.

Millstone fountain

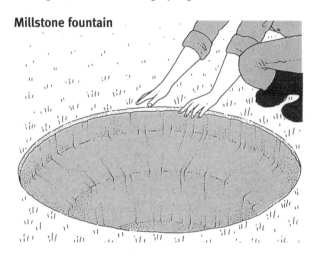

1 Dig a circular hole about 1m (3ft) deep and 2–3cm (1in) larger than the diameter of the millstone with a wide margin around it. Line the excavation with a butyl rubber liner, pleating it smoothly.

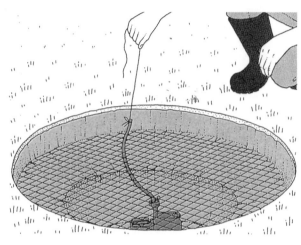

2 Having installed the pump, place a circle of reinforced wire mesh over the excavation to support the millstone. Feed the delivery hose, attached to a piece of string, through the mesh.

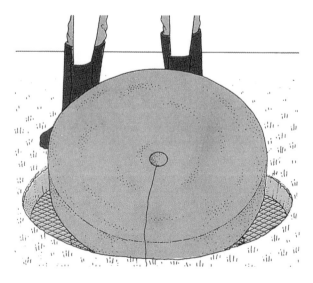

3 Position the millstone on the wire mesh so that it sits centrally over the excavation, feeding the piece of string and the delivery hose through the central hole. Part fill with water and test the flow.

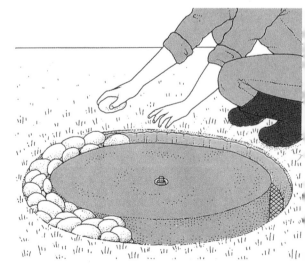

4 Once the millstone is installed and the jet unit correctly positioned, top up the reservoir with water. Cover the margins with cobblestones so they cover the pump cable, liner, and the mesh.

Protection from falling leaves

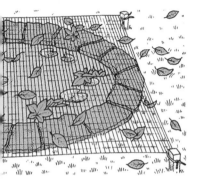

In autumn before the leaves fall, secure a net over the pool, pegging it to the ground. Regularly remove the fallen leaves and make compost or leaf-mould (see pages 30–33).

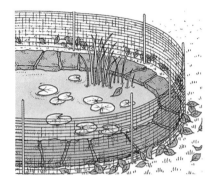

The leaves can also be stopped by a low fence. Push strong canes in the ground, and bend wire-netting round them, securing it with string or wire. This also deters herons.

Cleaning the pool

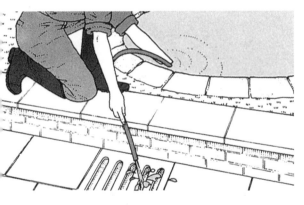

1 Empty the pool of water by pumping, siphoning, or bailing it out with a bucket. When siphoning, make certain that the pipe is not blocked by weed covering the end of it.

WINTER CARE

Keep an area of the pond ice-free, otherwise noxious gases will build up that could kill the fish. Keep a patch open by using hot water or a special electric pool heater (see page 228).

2 Next, using a bucket, remove all the dirty remaining water, remove the plants, and scoop out any fish with a net.

3 Place fish, water snails, and waterlilies in separate containers of pond water, but leave marginal plants in their baskets.

4 Once you have dug out all the mud and debris, clean the pool with a stiff brush and clean water. Do not pierce the liner.

Routine pool care

Repairing a butyl rubber lining

1 Empty the pool of water. Thoroughly clean the damaged area. Make sure it is free from dirt and algae, otherwise the patch will not stick properly. Clean around the area of the damage as well as the puncture itself.

2 Thoroughly dry the area around the damage. Roughen the surface with sandpaper to help adhesion. Using a paintbrush, spread the adhesive on and around the puncture.

3 Cut a patch larger than the puncture from spare liner. Spread one side with adhesive. Once it and the adhesive on the liner are tacky, put the patch over the hole and firm down, avoiding air bubbles.

CARE OF PUMPS AND FILTERS

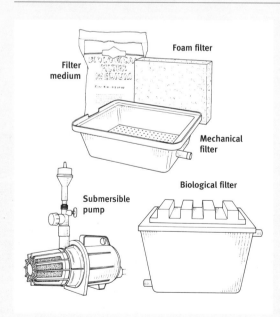

Foam filter

Filter medium

Mechanical filter

Biological filter

Submersible pump

Submersible pumps

These are the most popular type of pump and they will operate most garden water features. They are silent and easy to install, but must sit level. In late autumn, take them out of the pond and store over winter. Take this opportunity to give them a clean and service in line with the manufacturer's instructions. In spring reinstate the pump in the pond.

Filters

Mechanical filters simply sieve out debris and can be run as necessary. They consist of a foam filter covered with gravel or charcoal. The inlet pipe and inner tray should be cleaned weekly in summer. A separate algal tray can be incorporated, and this must also be cleaned regularly.

Biological filters are used to clean and enrich the water and usually operate from outside the pool. Water passes through the filter medium, which contains beneficial bacteria; these change the organic waste into useful nutrients. Run the lfilter constantly except in hard winters. Clean out the filter thoroughly before starting it up again. Some filters combine mechanical and biological systems.

Making a bog garden

A bog garden may form an integral part of a water feature, which abuts the pool and is sited at a slightly lower level. It may also form a separate unit in a shady, low-lying part of the garden. For either type it needs a minimum depth of 30–45cm (12–18in), otherwise it will dry out too quickly. Separate bog gardens require regular watering to keep the soil saturated or the plants will quickly die. An integrated bog area draws water from the pool, which must be topped up regularly.

Making an integral bog garden

1 Mark out the proposed pond and bog garden using a hosepipe as a guide to achieve an irregular shape.

2 Dig out the pond and bog garden, leaving a ridge of soil between them, about 8cm (3in) lower than the pool edge.

3 Remove any stones, and line first the pond, and then the bog garden, with fleece, geotextile, or polyester matting.

4 Place the liner over the pool and bog area, centred over the middle of the two excavations.

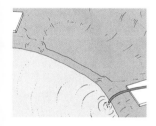

5 Fill the pool to just below the level of the wall between the two.

6 Put a layer of gravel for drainage in the bog garden, and partially fill with soil.

7 Build a barrier of rocks and stones along the interconnecting wall.

8 Place a layer of fine mesh along the back of the barrier on the bog side.

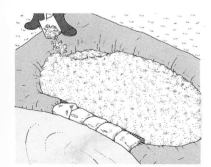

9 Shovel more soil into the bog garden, until its surface is level with the surrounding soil.

10 Continue to top up the pool with water. Water will seep through the rocks into the bog garden.

11 If either the pond or bog garden has a sloping edge, rounded pebbles can be placed on soft sand to form a beach.

Raised beds

In the overall design of a garden, raised beds are useful as they introduce planting on different levels, and make the garden more interesting. Raised beds are ideal for growing rock plants, alpines, or other plants that require special conditions, as they allow the gardener to have control over the composition of the soil and to ensure that it is very free draining. For elderly and disabled gardeners, raised beds are particularly useful and labour-saving as they eliminate a certain amount of bending, and make it possible to work from a wheelchair. Construct beds from brick, stone, or wooden railway sleepers. The sides of each should be 45–60cm (18–24in) high, and no wider than 1m (3ft) if the bed has access on only one side; 1.8m (6ft), if it is accessible from both sides. Where wheelchairs are to be used, ensure the paths are smooth and wide enough.

Types of raised bed

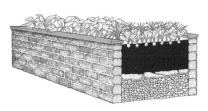 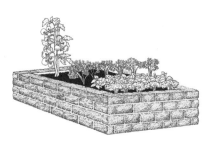 

Brick-built raised beds are relatively straight forward to build as long as you are competent at bricklaying. Such beds will need a proper concrete foundation. The walls should be capped with a layer of coping stones. If possible, the bricks should match those of the house.

Proprietary walling blocks are easier to lay than bricks. They are available in a variety of colours and finishes; some are made from reconstituted stone. Again, foundations will be needed to prevent the wall subsiding and cracking. In areas where stone is a local material, this can be used to great effect.

Wooden raised beds are the cheapest to make. They have the advantage of not needing foundations, but the disadvantage that in time they will decay. They should be made from pressure-treated wood. Thin planks can be used but thicker wood, as here, looks better and will last longer.

Constructing raised beds from railway sleepers

 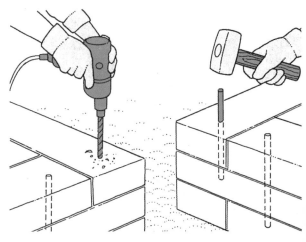

1 Railway sleepers are ideal for building raised beds, and can be purchased from garden centres. They are tough and durable, and do not require foundations. Laid in a single or double layer they require no fixings. For higher beds, stack them so the vertical joints are staggered in alternate rows, and butt-join them at the corners.

2 Once stacked up most sleepers are usually heavy enough to remain in position. However, it is safer to tie them together in some way. The most unobtrusive way is to drill through the stack with a long auger bit, and then to knock metal rods into the holes. Railway sleepers are impregnated with preservative to give them a long life.

Right: This forged metal gate
makes a good contrast to the
planting in this informal setting.

Below: Fences need not be ugly
as the simplicity and elegance
of this post and rail fence amply
demonstrate.

Right: Mixing materials such as bricks and large stones in a path can have a dramatic effect.

Far right: An ornamental path covered by a simple wooden pergola festooned with roses.

Below: Crazy paving, made from irregular slabs, makes an informal but solid path.

One of the advantages of a raised bed is that the gardener can have control over the soil conditions. This means that if you wish to grow, say, rhododendrons in a garden with chalky soil, then an acid soil can be used in the raised bed making this possible. Soil control is particularly important for alpine gardeners. With a raised bed they can create very free-draining conditions, perhaps with small pockets of more moisture-retaining soil for those plants that need it. Provision must be made for excess moisture

to drain away. Loosen the soil at the bottom of the bed, and add a layer of rubble covered by one of coarse gravel before you add the soil or compost. In brick and stone beds a few vertical joints at the base of the wall should be left uncemented so water can drain out if the base of the bed becomes compacted (see page 40). A good gritty soil also helps with drainage. Mix your own by combining two parts loam or good quality top-soil with one part gravel, and one part leafmould or peat substitute (see page 31).

Filling the bed with compost

Mix the soil on a flat area, and then barrow it into the raised bed, using a stout plank as a ramp. Alternatively, mix it in a clean concrete mixer, standing beside the bed, and tip it straight in.

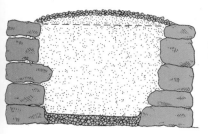

Even with firming down, the soil level will sink over time. To overcome this, mound extra soil or compost in the centre of the bed.

As an alternative to humping up the centre, add an extra row of uncemented bricks and remove them once the soil has sunk.

FOR ROCK PLANTS

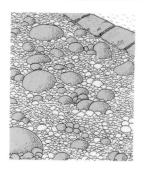

Set rocks into the surface of the bed. They will create a miniature landscape but also provide shade and cool root-runs for the plants. Tilt and part bury them to resemble exposed outcrops.

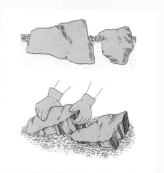

A softer-looking finish can be given to the bed by covering it with rounder stones, such as pebbles, varying the size to produce a more interesting surface in which to plant small plants.

Making rock gardens

Site your rock garden with care. The outcrop should be on a free-draining open site facing south, if possible, as most rock plants need sunlight and do not tolerate shade. Avoid building near trees, which cast shade and shed drips and leaves, which can encourage disease problems. If necessary, improve the

drainage (see page 40). Use a local stone for preference to blend in better with the surroundings, and select the rocks carefully with the finished outcrop in mind. Rocks are heavy and there is a knack of manoeuvring them into position (see page 239). When the construction is complete infill with gritty soil mix (see page 237).

Building a rock outcrop

1 Start to build the outcrop by bedding in the largest and most attractively weathered as the keystone. Dig out a seating deep enough for the rock to be stable while tilting at a gentle angle. Pack in or scrape away soil to adjust the position.

2 When the keystone is set firm, build up the body of the outcrop. Use the larger, better shaped rocks alongside the keystone to form the front face. They must align with the keystone and tilt at the same angle, between 5° and 10°, but avoid a too neat and regular effect.

CORRECT

To imitate the cracks and fissure of a natural outcrop, keep vertical joints in line and horizontal joints parallel, although they can occur at differing levels. The outcrop should tilt at a slight but uniform angle.

INCORRECT

When rocks are staggered, the result is more like a poorly constructed brick wall than a natural outcrop. Rocks laid haphazardly on a mound of soil results in a plum-pudding effect that is visually disturbing even when planted.

3 After the front face or "key" rocks are in place, start to build the sides. The outcrop should form a wedge shape that appears to be rising out of the soil, with a uniform slope. Align the blocks vertically and horizontally. Stand back to view the structure from time to time.

4 The top face should be reasonably flat. Trim the rocks where necessary. Pack soil and small stones between the larger blocks to adjust their position and keep them stable. Position a few smaller rocks alongside but in alignment. Allow the rocks to settle.

There is much physical effort involved in moving rocks, and safety matters must be taken seriously. Any lump of stone exceeding 25kg (55lb) in weight should be regarded as too heavy for physical lifting without some aid. For many people the limit is considerably lower. Stout leather gloves should always be worn when handling rock, and footwear must be strong enough to protect the toes. Rubber boots are inadequate; far safer are heavy hiking or working boots, preferably with steel toecaps. The rock-moving methods illustrated may be time consuming, but they should help to prevent accidents.

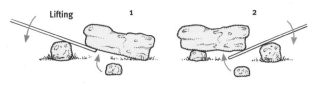

Increased leverage can be achieved by using a small rock as a fulcrum. Raise one end of the block so a small rock can be slid underneath, then lever up the other end to position a second rock. In this way a very large rock can be manoeuvred on to a plank and roller track (see below).

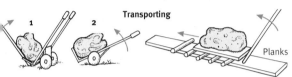

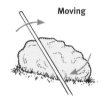

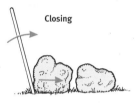

First create a gap for the truck plate, using a lever. Push the truck plate into the gap and tilt the truck backwards to take up the load, placing another chock behind the wheels.

Use a system of rollers on a plank track to move a large boulder with a face flat enough to run on the rollers, or lever irregular rocks onto a slab. Lever, or push, the load forward.

Manoeuvre heavy rocks by driving in a crowbar hard against the face. Push forwards to slew the rock on its base.

Butt heavy rocks together by driving in a crowbar hard against the face. Push forwards until the gap is closed.

CONSTRUCTING A ROCK GARDEN POOL

Rock gardens are often associated with pools as they are a means of utilising the excavated soil. They work well together as both need a sunny open site free from overhanging trees. To look convincing, however, the wedge of rocks should be carefully positioned so it faces south and appears to rise out of the water, and the pool and rock garden should be in scale with each other. First construct the pool, using a flexible butyl liner for strength, as described on page 224. Drape the liner over the pool, anchoring it around the edge, before slowy filling with water. Then build the rock garden, as described on page 238. The keystones should sit on the line and overhang the pool edge. A turf edging gives a natural finish (see page 224), perhaps with one or two rocks tilted at the same angle as the outcrop.

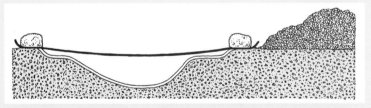

Stack the topsoil on a plastic sheet to one side of where the outcrop is to be built. Anchor the liner in position and fill the pool; the weight of the water will ensure the liner fits snugly.

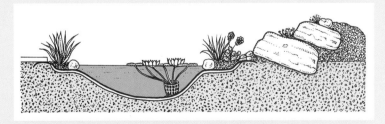

Allow the rocks to overhang the pool edge, or make a boggy planting pocket in front (see page 233), filled with some of the top-soil to disguise the the transition between rock and water.

Planting rock gardens

After the rocks have settled, and at least a week has passed since soil was added, add more gritty soil mix (see page 237) to restore the level. Once this has been done planting can begin. The best time to plant is late spring when the soil has dried out from winter and the weather is increasingly warm. The enemy of rock plants is not drought but wet, which can encourage diseases that cause rotting, particularly to the "neck". A gravel mulch spread over the soil, 2–4cm (1–1½in) deep, helps to overcome this.

Planting alpine plants

1 Using a trowel or handfork, dig a hole in the relevant position. Make sure it is large enough to take the plant's rootball comfortably.

2 Place the plant in the hole, adding soil if necessary, so that the top of the rootball is level with the surface of the bed. Fill in the gaps around the roots, gently firming down with the hands.

3 After planting a mat-forming or cushion plant, in particular, gently work gravel under the foliage and round the stem. This will improve drainage and prevent the foliage sitting on damp soil after rain.

Planting behind a rock

Some plants, such as some of the saxifrages, need protection from the hot midday sun. Rocks can be positioned to provide shade.

Planting in a crevice

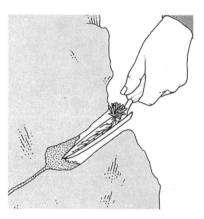

Use a narrow-bladed trowel, or folded length of card, to insert roots, plus a little compost into crevices in rocks or dry stone walls.

PLANTING IN WALLS

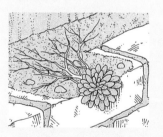

Some rock plants will thrive in walls. Spread the roots fanwise over a layer of moist compost. Cover roots with more compost and place pebbles to keep the joint open when the next course of bricks is laid.

The garden may be full of fascinating features and beautiful plants, but if wet ground has to be crossed to reach them the earth will quickly turn into a muddy mire. Sheds, greenhouses, vegetables, herbs, and fruit have to be visited regularly in all weathers and at all seasons, so a path providing clean and easy access is essential. Apart from linking the most visited parts of the garden by the most direct route, a path should allow surface water to drain through or else be given a slope or camber so the water runs off. It should also be sufficiently wide and stable.

Patios are frequently the hub of the garden and get the kind of use lawns will not tolerate. A hard level surface is essential to provide stability for a table, chairs, and barbecue. A patio should be built where it will receive the most sunshine, although it is also desirable to site it close to some shade. As a rough guide, you should allow sufficient space to accommodate garden furniture for four people in addition to permitting passage through to the garden. The minimum practical size is about 4m² (40ft²).

It is likely your patio will cover existing drain runs and manhole inspection chambers. You will either have to build up the walls of an inspection chamber to set the manhole cover at the new surface level, or else cover the existing manhole with a loose-laid slab.

The runoff of rain water must be considered. The entire patio must slope slightly, about 3cm in 2m (1in in 6½ft), towards the garden, but not towards the house walls or you could create a damp problem. If the ground slopes naturally towards the house you will have to incorporate a drainage channel (see page 40–41).

Materials and edging

There is a wide choice of paving materials, varying in cost and appearance, but all should provide a firm surface which is easy to walk on and to maintain. Materials that blend in with the style of the house and garden look best. You should also consider local materials or seek out second-hand paving slabs, which are often reasonably priced.

It is not essential on a narrow path to incorporate edge restraints to prevent the surface materials from creeping. However, a decorative edging of frost-proof bricks, tiles, or pressure-treated timber does look attractive. The edge is set in a slim trench and does not have to be set in mortar. Where concrete is used the edging is best put in position inside the framework before the mixture is laid.

Preparing the ground

Set up stringlines and pegs to mark out the shape of the patio, or shape and route of the path, then skim off turf and top-soil, and any large stones. Where the paved area joins a lawn, plan to set the paving about 2.5cm (¾in) lower so you can mow to the edge without damaging the mower blades.

Ram down the exposed sub-soil with a stout timber post, or compact thoroughly with a timber post, sledge hammer, or garden roller. If the area is large, hire a plate compactor. Check the base is level, using a spirit level on a long straight timber plank laid on edge. Allow a drainage crossfall to one side, and away from house walls. An easy way to do this is spanning across the area with a spirit level set on a long plank. Place a small offcut of wood 1–2cm (½in) thick underneath the end of the plank at the lower side. Adjust the ground so the spirit level registers horizontal. Tip barrowloads of sand onto the sub-base, and spread it 5–8cm (2–3in) thick, using a straight-edged length of plank the width of the path.

Hardcore foundations

In a patio, driveway, or heavily used path, or where the soil is soft, you should lay compacted hardcore on the sub-base. Tip hardcore over the rammed soil to a depth of 8–10cm (3–4in). Compact and level the hardcore with a sledgehammer or garden roller, or hire a plate compactor if you are dealing with a large area. Top with a 3–5cm (1–2in) thick blinding layer of sand, and rake level. The base is now ready for laying the paving material.

Laying the foundation

1 Dig out the soil within the lines, which are set 5cm (2in) wider than the final width.

2 Compact the soil in the base of the area with a stout timber or garden roller.

3 Add 8cm (3in) hardcore to the base. Ram this down with a sledgehammer or roller.

4 Blind the surface with a 5cm (2in) layer of sand, filling any gaps in the hardcore.

Laying paving slabs and cobblestones

Loose-laying paving slabs

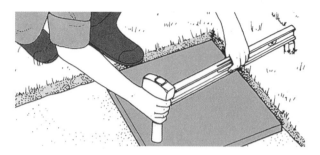

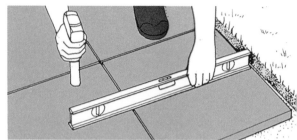

1 Lay the first slab on the sand bed, and set level with the top of a datum peg which will be used to determine the height of the path. Check the slab with a spirit level to ensure that it is level.

2 Continue to lay the slabs one at a time, levelling each by tapping them into the sand with the handle of a club hammer. Add more sand if the slabs are set too low. Check they are level.

3 The gaps can be filled in with sand, but weeds may grow in them. Instead, fill with a dry mix of cement, brushing this into the gaps and tamping it down with a narrow stick before adding more cement.

4 To cut slabs, first score them along the line of the cut with a bolster chisel. Place on a piece of timber over a flat surface, and break along the scored line by firmly tapping with a club hammer.

Laying cobblestones

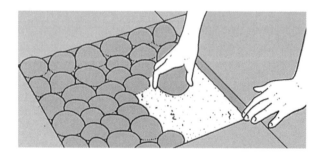

1 Cobblestones can be set in mortar in feature areas within slab or brick paving. Spread out the mortar, then push in the individual cobbles about halfway, varying the colour mix.

2 Bed the cobblestones evenly by placing a straight-edged length of timber across the top of them (resting it on the surrounding paving stones), to press down any high stones.

Concrete paving blocks, known as "flexible" pavers because they are laid dry, without mortar, on a sand bed over hardcore (see page 241), can be used to create an attractive patterned and textured hard surface for a patio. They are also a good choice for paths and drives, where they can support considerable loading from vehicles. The paving must be set within kerbstones or other edging, and, to allow for compaction, blocks should be laid 10mm (⅜in) above the top of the edge restraints. Begin laying the blocks at one corner, and work across and along the area, following your chosen pattern.

Flexible paving

1 Check the position of downpipes and other obstructions in relation to the finished level of the paving blocks. Special manhole lids are available to allow access to inspection chambers.

2 Starting from one corner, place the blocks on the sand in your chosen pattern. As the surface progresses, work on a board placed over the blocks in order to spread your weight.

3 Stretch stringlines between pegs across the paving as a guide to laying the blocks symmetrically, especially when creating a diagonal effect. Lay blocks up to the line, then move it 1.5m (5ft) on.

4 Lay whole blocks first, leaving the cut ones round the edge until last. Mark the blocks for cutting by holding them over the space, and scribing with a bolster chisel against a straight edge.

Laying flexible paving

Flexible paving (continued)

5 To consolidate the surface, you should hire a motorised plate compactor fitted with a rubber bottom or "sole" plate. This will vibrate the blocks into the sand bed without damaging them.

6 Finally, brush sand into the joints between the blocks, and vibrate the surface again, using the plate compactor to form a firm, flat patio. If necessary, you will still be able to lift individual blocks.

LAYING PATTERNS

Herringbone pattern
This popular pattern is created by a series of zig-zagging rows of blocks laid end to side; it can be laid straight or diagonally.

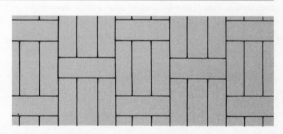

Cane-weave pattern
This comprises staggered rows of three blocks laid on end, alternated with one block laid across their ends.

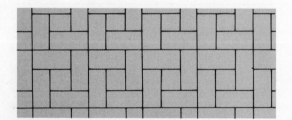

Squared design
In this design whole blocks are laid in a square box pattern with the gap in the centre filled by a half block cut to fit.

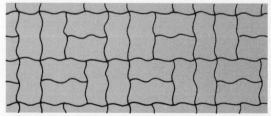

Fishtail blocks
Wavy-edged blocks laid in a parquet design to give a characteristic rippling effect of being underwater.

Erecting fence posts

Whatever the type, all fences have supporting posts in common. These may be of pressure-treated timber, concrete, or metal. Posts are traditionally erected in a hole and encased in concrete, although metal fixing spikes are increasingly used to support timber posts because they are so easy to install. As the timber is not set in the earth, it lasts longer as rotting is far less likely.

Timber posts that have rotted at the base may be bolted onto a precast concrete spur, which is set in concrete at the base. Posts are available in set lengths. Buy them tall enough so they can extend above the fence by a few cm/in and sunk in the ground deep enough to give stability: posts up to 1.2m (4ft) are sunk 45cm (18in) deep; taller posts 60cm (24in).

Driving in a post

Posts driven straight into the ground with a heavy hammer are only suitable for low, lightweight fences. A thick pad of wood will protect the post from splitting.

Installing a fence spike

1 Drive the fence spike into the ground using a sledgehammer, protecting the top with an offcut of post or a proprietary fixing accessory.

2 It is important to check that the spike is vertical by holding a spirit level against each side in turn, at frequent intervals, as you knock it in.

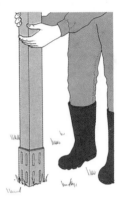

3 Once the fence spike is firmly in the ground, push the post fully into the collar. In some models integral bolts have to be tightened to secure.

Concreting in a post

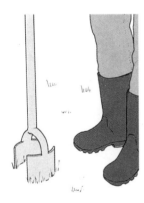

1 Dig the hole 15cm (6in) deeper than you require, using a spade or hired post-hole borer. Ensure the hole is in the correct position.

2 Prop the post in the hole on a brick. Nail temporary braces on to the post. Adjust the position until it is vertical by checking each side in turn with a spirit level. The braces should be strong enough to hold the post without it moving.

3 With a spare piece of post, ram hardcore into the hole around the post. Check that the post does not move out of the vertical. The post should be held rigid by the hardcore, which should stop short of ground level by 15cm (6in).

4 Trowel in fresh concrete over the hardcore, and compact it to dispel air bubbles. Shape the mound so that the top is above ground level and rain water will quickly run off. Leave the braces in position until the concrete has set hard.

Chain-link fences

Chain-link fencing can be used as an unobtrusive boundary marker or a means of keeping animals in or out. It is stretched between vertical posts of timber, concrete or steel, erected as described on page 245. It is available in rolls in a choice of chain-link mesh (which may be welded for extra strength), a lightweight galvanised chicken wire, or a more decorative mesh with a hooped top. Most suppliers will sell a kit containing all

the hardware required for the type of mesh fence needed. Wire fencing is less expensive than timber. Although it is not particularly attractive, wire mesh is very low maintenance and makes a good support for climbing plants and shrubs. For a more solid appearance you can create a "fedge", which is ivy growing completely over the wire fence, and clipped in such a manner as to make it look like a conventional hedge.

Erecting a post-and-wire fence

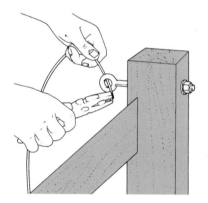

1 Fit an eyebolt to one of the end posts, but do not tighten the nut, leave it near the start of its thread. Attach a wire through the eye. Three wires are needed, one each at the top, middle, and base of the mesh.

2 Thread a stretcher bar through the loops of wire in the end of the mesh roll. Then attach the bar to the brackets fitted to the eyebolts. Run out the mesh, tying it loosely at intervals to the straining wires.

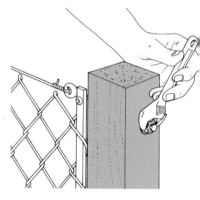

3 Once all the line wires are in position tension them by tightening the nuts at either end of each of the lines. Check them every so often and, if they become slack, tighten up the nuts.

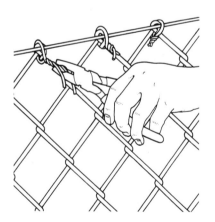

4 Use twists of galvanised wire or special clips to hold the mesh tight to the line wires along the length of the fence, to prevent it sagging. Attach the mesh to the middle and bottom wires in the same way.

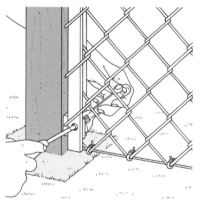

5 At the far end of the fence, thread another stretcher bar through the mesh, and pull the fence tight so that the bar just reaches the end post – this is easier with two people. Attach the stretch bar to the eyebolt brackets.

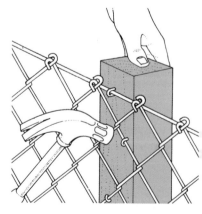

6 When the wire mesh is taut, and has been secured at the ends and clipped to the straining wires, it can be stapled to the wooden posts. On metal or concrete posts secure the mesh with wire stirrups.

Before you erect a fence, mark out the run on the ground, using pegs and stringlines; for a boundary fence, all the posts and fencing must be on the property side of the line. Although you can insert all the posts first, spaced at the correct distance apart, it is often easier to fix them one at a time, using the next panel in line as an accurate spacing guide. This avoids the problem of misaligned posts. It is easier to adjust a post before it is firmly fixed than discover that a post is in a wrong position and the panel will not fit. It is better to set posts in spikes than in concrete for this type of progressive construction (see page 245).

Erecting a panel fence

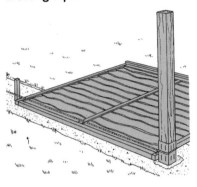

1 Mark out accurately the line of the fence run, using pegs and string. Put the first post in position, either in a fence spike or set in concrete. Use the next panel as an accurate guide for fixing the distance of the next post, and the stringline as a guide to keep it straight.

2 Use two-piece metal brackets to fix the panel to the posts. Make a T-shaped gauge to set the first bracket at the correct distance from the edge of the post.

3 Fix the second half of the bracket to the post about 3cm (1in) above the first, using galvanised nails. Ensure that they are fixed squarely or the panel will not fit.

4 Feed the fence panel into the gap between the two brackets from below, then pivot it downwards, and slot it into the channel formed by a lower pair of brackets.

5 Stand the panel on a brick so that it does not come into contact with the damp soil. Secure the panel by nailing through all the bracket flanges. Remove the brick.

6 Fix the subsequent posts on the fence run by laying a panel on the ground, one end, butted up against the previously-fixed post. Then drive a metal post spike into the ground at the other end of the panel. Pause frequently to check with a spirit level that the spike is entering the ground perfectly straight, or the panel might not fit.

Fence maintenance and plant supports

Check over your fence every winter to make sure it is sound. Take the opportunity to make repairs before serious damage occurs: replace any broken panels or rotten gravel boards; make good loose fixings; and tighten and replace plant supports if

necessary. Timber posts that show signs of rot should be braced with a concrete spur (see page 245). To prolong the life of wooden fences and trellis, treat them with preservative every two or three years in winter when the plants have died down.

Weatherproofing the fence

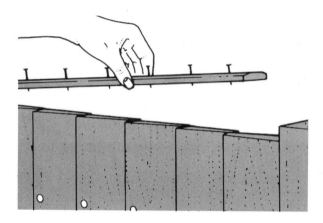

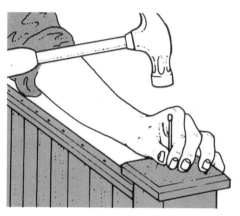

1 Fit bevelled coping strips to throw rain water off the fence. Cut lengths of coping to fit between the posts, and place them on top of feather-edged boards or fence panels. Carefully drive galvanised nails through the copings, and into the fence top at regular intervals.

2 If post tops are left square, protect them with a bevelled cap nailed on the top, so rain water is thrown clear. The tops can also be rounded, angled, or pointed in order that rain water runs off fast, before it can soak into the vulnerable end grain.

PLANT SUPPORTS ON WALLS AND FENCES

Most fences and walls require some kind of plant support if climbers and wall shrubs are to be grown against them. Wooden trellis panels treated with preservative can be fastened to fence posts or to a wall that has been drilled and plugged to accept screws. Use cotton reels or door stops to keep the trellis a few cm/in away from the surface. This space allows climbers to twine freely, and makes tying in shoots easier. Plastic-coated wire netting is an alternative to trellis.

Horizontal training wires are another means of support. Space them about 45cm (18in) apart. The wires are stretched taut between masonry nails driven into the mortar or, more permanently, between metal vine eyes inserted into drilled plugged holes. The wires are held about 5cm (2in) clear of the wall.

Fix trellis panels with long screws. Use door stops or cotton reels as spacers to hold panels clear of the wall or fence.

Attach training wires to masonry nails or vine eyes fitted to drilled and plugged holes, or screwed into fence posts.

Gates should be erected at the same time as fences. Position gates carefully, taking into account the dimensions of regular traffic. If possible they should be in a material which matches or complements the fence. When hanging a gate, make sure the necessary hinges, hinge brackets, bolts, and catches are to hand. Allow for any slope in the ground. When the gate is fully open, it must clear the path, even if the path slopes. Make the latch side of the gate slightly higher than the hinge side. Fit a spring-closer where the safety of children and pets is a consideration. Wooden gates need the support of strong posts (see page 245) and benefit from regular care. Oil hinges and check latches regularly, and every year or two treat the wood with preservative. Metal gates are easier to hang than wooden and can open wider, but their structure is more open.

Hanging a gate

1 Check the gate fits by propping it vertically, on wedges, between the posts. Adjust the height to the right position, about 5cm (2in) above the ground. Knock in further wedges down the sides so that there is a gap of 5mm (¼ in) at either side. Check the gate is vertical.

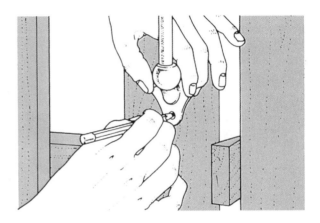

2 Remove the gate to attach the strap hinges. Prop the gate back in its correct position. Place the lower hinge cup in position with the hinge pin. Mark the position of the screw holes. Remove the gate and drill pilot holes. Replace gate and screw the lower cups into position.

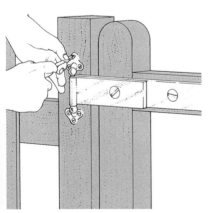

3 Fit the top hinge cups to retain the hinge pins. Remove the wedges and the gate should swing freely without binding on the posts. Note: If the gate has a diagonal brace it should be on the hinge side.

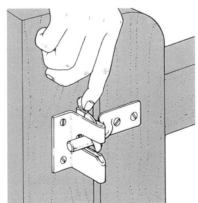

4 A self-closing latch is screwed to the gate post before the corresponding locking bar is attached to the gate, so that the two align. A thumb-operated lever releases the bar to open the gate.

FITTING A SPRING-CLOSING DEVICE

A spring-closing device screwed across the gate and post on the hinge side will close the gate automatically, and a self-closing latch will hold it shut.

AVOIDING PROBLEMS

In order to prevent problems happening in the first place, adopt a "whole-garden strategy". This entails selecting vigorous plants, growing them in the right place, and making sure your soil is healthy. Build up a healthy, well-structured soil (see pages 25–29) in order to provide plants with a balanced diet and a regular water supply. Such plants will be less susceptible to attack, and more able to resist problems that do arise. The key to a healthy soil is the regular addition of organic matter such as well-rotted manures and garden compost (see page 26).

Watch what's going on in your garden by walking round and nipping problems in the bud. Deal with pest and disease problems and weeds at first sight, before they get out of hand. Good hygiene is all important, so remove all diseased plant material, fallen fruits, spotted leaves, and similar detritus. Put them straight into a plastic bag so that disease spores are not wafted around. Pests such as aphids, slugs, and caterpillars are easy to spot and can be handpicked or squashed.

PLANTS AND PLANTING MATERIAL

Buy the healthiest plants available. Young vigorous plants will establish more quickly than those that are old and pot bound. Bare-root plants should have a good fibrous root system. While bedding plants in flower may look more attractive, those not yet in flower are a better buy because the plants will be able to establish themselves before they flower. Choose bulbs that are firm and show no sign of mould. Always buy certified virus-free seed potatoes and fruit plants, where available.

Inspect all new plants for pests and disease before you buy, especially those destined for the greenhouse, as this is the way that many greenhouse problems are brought in.

Seeds should be as fresh as possible. Most seeds sold commercially are sealed in foil packets to keep them fresh, but check the date on the packet before buying in case it is old stock, and don't buy packets of seeds from racks that have been standing in direct sun. Old seed and seed stored in poor conditions may produce plants lacking in vigour; the faster a seedling grows, the less it is at risk.

A GOOD START

Give plants a good start in life and they will grow healthily and be more likely to withstand most problems. Sow and plant correctly, and in conditions that suit. Poor planting can result in reduced growth and poor performance in the future.

Choose the right plant for the right place: (see pages 26–28). Test your soil and ascertain the prevailing conditions in your garden and then choose plants to suit them (see pages 26–28 and 221). This is a much more successful strategy than buying the plants first and then trying to keep them growing in conditions that are less than appropriate. For example, a rose or honeysuckle planted in poor dry soil up against a house wall may suffer from mildew; hostas may suffer from slug damage if planted in a dark wet corner, whereas a fern will thrive. Different fruit types and cultivars suit many different locations, and there are even some vegetables that will grow in the shade. Always think about the situation in which a plant is to grow (soil type, shade or sun, exposure to wind) before you buy or plant.

Avoiding problems: 1

Prevention is better than cure. By following the good garden practices recommended in this book, and planting a range of plants to suit your particular garden conditions, many problems can be avoided. If a problem does arise, first identify what it is. Do not jump to conclusions: remember that poor growing conditions can cause as much damage as pests and diseases, and that not every creepy crawly is a pest – it may be a friend.

Watering (see page 216)

Too much or not enough water can damage plant growth. Poorly drained soil can encourage root problems. Growing on raised beds will help (see pages 162 and 234), but if the problem is severe consider improving the drainage (see page 40). Wilting is an obvious sign of water shortage, but other side effects can occur before this. Powdery mildews are worse when the soil is dry; an answer is to improve the water-holding capacity of the soil by adding organic matter (see page 34).

Most established plants should thrive without regular watering, except in long periods of drought.

Soil pH (see page 28)

Altering the pH of a soil can help in the control of certain diseases. For instance, raising the pH of an acid soil by adding lime can help to reduce the incidence of club root infection on brassicas and wallflowers. Plants that have a particular requirement for an acid or alkaline soil may grow poorly and with yellowing leaves. This may be a sign of mineral deficiencies caused by an inappropriate soil pH. Rhododendrons growing on chalky soils are a case in point. The answer is to grow these plants in raised beds or containers filled with a lime-free compost, and choose plants that suit the soil for the open garden.

Good airflow around plants

Diseases thrive in the moist air around overcrowded plants. Encourage a good airflow by thinning seedlings before they become overcrowded. Fruit trees and bushes, and roses will suffer less from mildew if the centre is kept open by pruning correctly (see pages 105 and 183). Good ventilation is particularly important in a greenhouse, even during cold weather.

Natural predators

Encourage natural predators into your garden by providing them with suitable food, shelter, and breeding sites and, of course, not killing them with sprays. Winter digging (see page 34), for example, will expose pests such as root flies, millipedes and slugs to birds. The work of these predators – ladybirds, ground beetles, and bluetits, and many more – often goes unrecognised. They may not always achieve the level of control that we would like so other measures may also be required, but they should be given a chance to do their bit.

ENCOURAGE BENEFICIAL INSECTS

Include some of the following plants in your garden. The nectar and pollen they provide will encourage not only natural predators, such as hoverflies, lacewings, and ladybirds, but also bees and other pollinating insects.

ANNUALS

Calendula officinalis (Pot marigold)

Convolvulus tricolor (Annual convolvulus)

Eschscholzia species (Californian poppy)

Helianthus annuus and cultivars (Sunflower)

Limnanthes douglasii (Poached egg plant)

Nemophila menziesii (Baby blue eyes)

Phacelia tanacetifolia (Phacelia)

PERENNIALS

Achillea species and cultivars (Yarrow)

Anaphalis species (Pearl everlasting)

Aster species and cultivars (Michaelmas daisies)

Echium vulgare (Viper's bugloss)

Erigeron species and cultivars (Fleabane)

Fragaria vesca (Alpine strawberry)

Leucanthemum x *superbum* (Shasta daisy)

Solidago cultivars (Golden rod)

HERBS

Angelica	Lovage
Chervil	Sweet cicely
Fennel	Thyme

BENEFICIAL ANIMALS

Encourage these creatures as they will eat all manner of pests including slugs, snails, and caterpillars. Although birds may damage buds and fruit they also eat many pests.

Bats	Newts
Birds	Shrews
Frogs	Slow-worms
Hedgehogs	Toads

Above: A dry stone wall used for terracing the garden is complemented by steps made from sympathetic materials.

Right: A formal set of curved steps that have become informal by being planted with grass and heather.

Self-sown plants, such as the upright, clump-forming perennial *Verbena bonariensis*, add to the informality of a garden.

Resistant cultivars

Plants vary in their susceptibility to pests and diseases and those that show some resistance provide a valuable means of preventing specific recurring problems, such as black spot on roses, or one that has no cure, such as cucumber mosaic virus. Use resistant cultivars as part of an overall pest and disease management strategy; they are less susceptible but not altogether immune to attack. Although examples of disease-resistant cultivars are given below, the range changes all the time, so consult catalogues for an up-to-date selection.

Diversity

A monoculture – a large area of plants of one type grown together – is a paradise for a pest or disease, because once it has discovered one suitable host plant, it will be surrounded on all sides by more of the same. It is a good idea to mix plants. Do away with some of the divisions between fruits, flowers, and vegetables in a small garden. Vegetables can look good in an ornamental border; lettuce, beetroot, chard, carrots, rhubarb, and courgettes, for example, have very attractive foliage.

Interspersed among unrelated ornamentals they are less likely to be discovered by pests or diseases. Fruit trees and bushes are also attractive, and a few flowers in the vegetable garden can liven up a plot while also attracting beneficial insects that can help with pest control (see page 252).

Rotation

In general never grow the same crop on the same site in successive seasons. Fruit trees, roses, and some bedding plants, such as pansies, are prone to replant disorders, and the replacement may grow poorly or even die.

Barriers and traps

Netting plants against birds and other pests, and using other forms of barriers to protect against pests can be most effective. Traps can be used to reduce pests in a small area and to monitor new arrivals so that the timing of an appropriate spray or introduction of a biological control can be made accurately. The use of barriers and scaring devices to keep pests at bay can help to reduce damage to plants.

RESISTANT CULTIVARS

FRUITS

Apple *Powdery mildew*: 'Sunset', 'Blenheim Orange'; *canker*: 'Newton's Wonder'; *scab*: 'Discovery', 'Sunset', 'Ashmead's Kernel'.
Black currant *Powdery mildew*: 'Ben Sarek', 'Ben Nevis'; *frost*: 'Ben Nevis', 'Ben Tirran'.
Gooseberry *American gooseberry mildew*: 'Invicta', 'Greenfinch'.
Pear *Scab*: 'Jargonelle', 'Dr Jules Guyot'.
Raspberry *Spur and cane blight*: 'Malling Admiral'; *aphids*: 'Leo', 'Glen Moy', 'Malling Delight', 'Malling Joy'; *viruses*: 'Malling Jewel', 'Malling Promise'.
Strawberry *Grey mould (botrytis)*: 'Elsanta', 'Honeoye', 'Red Gauntlet'; *powdery mildew*: 'Cambridge Favourite', 'Red Gauntlet'; *verticillium wilt/red core*: 'Rhapsody', 'Troubadour'.

VEGETABLES

Brussels sprouts *Powdery mildew*: 'Braveheart', 'Rampart', 'Saxon'; *ringspot*: 'Cor Valiant', 'Rampart'; *white blister*: 'Saxon'.
Calabrese *Club root*: 'Harmony'; *downy mildew*: 'Harmony', 'China Pride'; 'Shogun'.
Carrot *Carrot fly*: 'Flyaway', 'Sytan'.
Chinese cabbage *Club root*: 'Trixie'; *downy mildew*: 'Emperor'; *virus*: various.
Corn salad *Mildew*: 'Jade'.
Courgette/marrow *Cucumber mosaic virus*: 'Supremo', 'Defender', 'Bush Champion', 'Petita', 'Tiger Cross'.
Cucumber *Mosaic virus*: 'Burpee Hybrid', 'Bush Champion', 'Slice King'; *downy and powdery mildews*: 'Burpless', 'Slice King', 'Tasty Green'.
Kale *Club root*: 'Tall Green Curled'.
Leek *Rust*: 'Autumn Mammoth', 'Verina'.
Lettuce *Grey mould (botrytis)*: 'Avondefiance'; *downy mildew*: 'Avondefiance', 'Dynasty', 'Little Gem', 'Musette'; *root aphid*: 'Avoncrisp', 'Avondefiance'; *virus*: various.
Onion *Downy mildew/white rot*: 'Norstar'.
Parsnip *Canker*: 'Avonresister', 'Tender and True', 'Cobham Improved Marrow'.
Peas *Wilt*: 'Ambassador', 'Hurst Green Shaft', 'Kelvedon Wonder', 'Sugar Snap'; *powdery mildew*: 'Amabassador', 'Kodiak', 'Oregon', 'Sugar Pod'.
Potato *Blight*: 'Cara', 'Estima', 'Maris Peer', 'Pentland Hawk', 'Wilja'; *common scab*: 'Arran Pilot', 'Golden Wonder', 'King Edward', 'Maris Peer'; *cyst eelworm*: 'Cara', 'Pentland Javelin', 'Sante'; *slugs*: 'Desiree', 'King Edward', 'Maris Piper'.
Spinach *Downy mildew*: 'Bergola'.
Swede *Club root/powdery mildew*: 'Marian'.
Tomato *Greenback*: 'Estrella', 'Shirley'; *fusarium wilt*: 'Estrella', 'Shirley', 'Pixie'; *tobacco mosaic virus*: 'Estrella', 'Shirley', 'Dombito', 'Pixie'; *verticillium wilt*: 'Estella', 'Pixie'.

ORNAMENTALS

Antirrhinum *Rust*: Coronette Mixed, Rust Resistant Mixed.
Aster *Wilt*: Carousel Mixed, Starlight Rose; *powdery mildew*: various.
Hollyhock *Rust*: various.
Pyracantha *Scab*: 'Orange Glow'.
Rose *Blackspot*: 'Alec's Red', 'Anne Harkness', 'Elina', 'Remember Me'; *powdery mildew*: 'Anna Livia', 'Flower Carpet; *rust*: 'Joseph's Coat', 'Maigold', 'Sweet Magic', 'Wedding Day'.

Understanding the problem

Despite our best endeavours plants may suffer from a pest or disease. Adverse environmental conditions and nutrient shortages, known as physiological disorders and mineral deficiencies respectively, can also cause unwanted symptoms.

PESTS

A pest is any creature that affects a plant adversely. Many different creatures such as birds, mammals, insects, and molluscs can act as pests. Some pests, like slugs, look more or less the same from birth to death. Others, like caterpillars, go through several different stages, sometimes with different common names. The different stages are not all necessarily capable of causing damage.

Some pests, such as slugs and certain aphids, attack a wide range of plants, while others, such as the lily beetle are quite specific. Although we tend only to notice pests when they are damaging the plants we want, they may also be living on weeds growing in the garden.

Spread and survival Pests can move from plant to plant; they can be transported in infested soil or on purchased plants. Potato cyst eelworms can survive in the soil as resting bodies for many years. Pests may overwinter on plants, in the soil, or in any protected nooks or crannies indoors and out.

Symptoms and identification If the pest is visible, identification is relatively easy – but remember that the presence of a creature does not mean that it is necessarily guilty. Often symptoms are all we have to go on because the pest is too small to see or it has already moved on.

Holes in leaves, stems, or roots, or plants disappearing completely are caused by pests with biting mouth parts: vine weevils, caterpillars, beetles, earwigs, fly maggots, larvae of sawflies, and midges, woodlice, slugs and snails, rabbits, and other mammals.

Curled leaves and distorted growth are caused by creatures that feed on plant sap, either by piercing the plant tissues (aphids, capsid bugs, leafhoppers, red spider mites, whitefly, and scale insects), or by living within the plants (eelworms).

DISEASES

Disease symptoms are caused by fungi, bacteria, and viruses. They are all parasitic organisms, which means that they take their food from other living creatures. Because they are mainly microscopic, they tend to be known by the symptoms they produce, such as "white rot" or "downy mildew", rather than by the name of the causal organism.

FUNGAL DISEASES The majority of plant diseases are caused by fungi. Fungi consist mainly of microscopic threads that grow through plant tissue, living or dead, to take food. Similar disease symptoms, such as rust, grey mould, and powdery mildew may be found on a variety of plants, which lead to the common belief that a disease on one type of plant will rapidly spread to others. This is not always so. Some diseases like grey mould can behave in this way; in many cases (with powdery mildews and rusts, for example) the similar symptoms are caused by different species of fungi on different plants, and they do not cross-infect.

Spread and survival Fungi spread from plant to plant mainly in the form of spores carried by wind, rain, contaminated soil, or infected plants. Fungi can survive the winter in living plants, plant debris, such as fallen fruits, or tough resting bodies in the soil that can persist for many years.

Typical symptoms include:
Leaf spots
Cankers and scabs
Silvering or yellowing of leaves
Wilting (wilts and foot rots)
Wet rots (damping-off of seedlings)
Powdery and fluffy moulds (mildews, grey moulds)

BACTERIAL DISEASES These are few but they are important and often difficult to control. Like fungal diseases they are spread by wind, rain, and on plant material, but they can only enter a plant through a wound caused by a pest or pruning, for example, or a natural weakness such as a leaf scar.
Typical symptoms include:
Soft rots and leaf spots
Cankers and galls

VIRUS DISEASES These are some of the most serious diseases and affect a wide range of plants. Once a plant is infected by a virus there is no cure. Viruses are moved from plant to plant by carriers, which include aphids, leafhoppers, eelworms, human hands, and secateurs. They also enter the garden on infected plants and cuttings taken from infected plants. It is advisable, where possible, to buy stock certified as virus-free, particularly for potato tubers, raspberry, strawberry, and blackcurrant plants.

Symptoms are very difficult to identify precisely, so try to check whether the symptoms are, in fact, caused by a pest, another disease, or a deficiency. Look for stunted growth; considerable reduction in cropping; mottled, mosaic or other patterns on leaves; malformed growth; and streaked flowers.

Virus control and prevention are similar for all plants:
- Grow virus-resistant cultivars and virus-free plant material.
- Break the cycle by removing all susceptible plants.
- Practice crop rotation.
- Dig up and burn or dispose of infected plants.
- Grow new plants from seed, rather than from cuttings.

Pest and disease problems can be tackled in various ways. Barriers and traps can be very successful. Biological and chemical controls can also be effective, but opt for one or the other – used together they may cancel each other out.

Barriers and traps

Much can be done to keep pests at bay by erecting barriers. Netting fruit bushes against birds is one obvious example. Tree guards placed round the trunks of young trees protect them from rabbits, deer, and scratching cats (see page 80).

Crop covers protect plants against small pests such as flea beetle, carrot fly, and cabbage caterpillars. The lightweight covers can be laid directly over the plants or draped over tunnel cloche hoops. The material must be well secured round the edges so that pests cannot penetrate. The usual materials are fleece and Enviromesh, a fine mesh plastic that lasts longer than fleece but gives less protection against the weather.

Plastic bottle cloches placed over individual plants will give protection from slugs and other pests. Use big bottles, so that the plants have room to grow. Cut off the bottom and remove the screw top for ventilation.

Root-fly barriers for brassicas can be purchased or made from 12cm (5in) squares of carpet underlay. Carrots can be protected from carrot fly by surrounding them with a 75cm (30in) high barrier of fleece or fine-mesh netting.

Grease bands round fruit tree trunks prevent pests such as winter moths and other overwintering pests, climbing up and later causing damage to blossom and fruits. Glue bands round pots act in a similar way against woodlice and vine weevils.

Saucers of beer or half orange skins placed cut side down will trap slugs, but they must be emptied regularly. Barriers of coarse grit around vulnerable plants may also keep them at bay.

Chemical sprays

Proprietary pesticides and fungicides can be very effective but rather than on a regular basis only use them when necessary to prevent a particular problem from getting out of hand. If regular spraying is required to keep a plant healthy, consider replacing it with a more resistant cultivar or a different, less vulnerable plant. There is a range of fungicides and pesticides on the market which do change from time to time. If you have a particular problem check with your garden centre or supplier for the most appropriate product. A few sprays are acceptable to organic gardeners, including those based on derris, pyrethrum, and sulphur. Before resorting to sprays see if any preventative method would work.

All garden chemicals should be used with great care and remember pesticides can harm beneficial insects as well as pests. Always read the manufacturer's instructions and follow them exactly. Abide by the safety advice given on page 261.

BIOLOGICAL CONTROL

Biological control is a means of controlling pests with a natural predator. The controlling agents are all tiny or microscopic creatures that are very specific in their action. The aim of biological control is to reduce pest levels and related damage rather than to eliminate them completely. Biological control is most effective where the agent is introduced when the pest level is low. There is no advantage in introducing the agent before the pests are present. As soon as the pests are seen, order the relevant biological control agent.

Before ordering check the following:

• That you have not used a pesticide within the last six to eight weeks that will harm the agent.

• That you can meet the required conditions of temperature, humidity, and daylight.

• The delivery date. Often the package containing the controlling agents must be opened on arrival. Try to use the agents as soon as they are delivered. Read the instructions carefully before opening the container. Some may be stored in the fridge for a short period.

BIOLOGICAL CONTROL AGENTS*

Pest	Predator/parasite	Optimum temp.
Whitefly	Encarsia formosa (parasitic wasp)	18–25°C (64–77°F)
Red spider mites	Phytoseiulus persimilis* (predatory mite)	17–25°C (63–77°F)
Mealybugs	Cryptolaemus montrouzieri (predatory beetle)	20–25°C (68–77°F)
Aphids	Aphidius matricariae (parasitic wasp) Aphidoletes aphidimyza (predatory midge larva)	Opt. day temp: 14–21°C (57–70°F); min. night temp: 16°C (60°F)
Vine weevil grubs	Heterorhabditis megidis/ Steinernema carpocapsae** (pathogenic nematodes)	Opt. soil temp: 14–25°C (57–77°F); min. 10°C (50°F)
Slugs	Phasmarhabditis hermaphrodita* (pathogenic nematode)	Opt. soil temp: 15°C (59°F); minimum 5°C (41°F)

* Only applicable under glass except where indicated
** Also suitable for outdoor use

Common pests and diseases

COMMON PESTS

Check with your garden centre or supplier for the most appropriate pesticide that is currently available.

Pest	Symptoms	Prevention	Control
Ants	Poor plant growth, wilts rapidly in dry weather	Move plants if nest established below them	Powders; glue or grease bands
Aphids *(greenfly, blackfly, etc.)*	Groups of aphids on shoot tips. Stunted growth, deformed shoots, leaves, and buds	Encourage predators such as ladybirds and lacewings	Spray with a suitable insecticide; biological control
Cabbage root-fly	Poor growth, wilting; white maggots eat the roots	Place barriers round stems of young plants	No chemical control currently available
Capsid bugs	Ragged holes in leaves at shoot tips	Spray susceptible plants with insecticide	Use an insecticide
Carrot fly	Yellowish or bronzed foliage; yellow maggots tunnel in the roots	Grow under fine net or fleece, or surround by barrier; sow late; use less susceptible cultivars	No chemical control currently available
Caterpillars	Holes in leaves, buds, and flowers	Cover with fine net or fleece	Remove by hand, use biological control, or spray with appropriate insecticide
Chafer grubs	Chews through roots, plant wilts	Regular digging to expose them to the birds	Difficult to control
Cutworms	Eat through below-ground stems on young plants	Regular digging to expose them to the birds	Difficult to control
Earwigs	Eaten petals on mainly dahlias, clematis, and chrysanthemums	Remove any debris under which they can hide	Trap in upturned pots stuffed with straw. They are also beneficial, so only trap if they are a nuisance
Eelworms	Distortion or discolouration of foliage and stems	Only buy healthy stock	Destroy infested plants; rotate crops
Flea beetles	Small round holes in leaves of young plants of brassicas, turnips, swedes, and wallflowers	Sow when there is a chance of rapid growth to get through the seedling stage quickly	Use an appropriate insecticide
Leaf miners	Silvery tunnels just beneath the surface of a leaf	None	Handpick infested leaves, squash larvae within leaves
Leatherjackets *(Crane fly larvae)*	Chews through roots, plant wilts	Regular digging to expose them to the birds	Difficult to control
Millipedes	Seedlings and soft plant tissues eaten	Remove any debris under which they can hide	Not easy to control
Red spider mites	A fine pale mottling of the leaves and silk webs on underside of leaves	Do not plant susceptible plants in hot dry places; damp down the floor of greenhouses	Difficult to control; use a biological control
Scale insects	Small scales on stems and leaves, sticky honeydew	None	Treat with appropriate insecticide
Slugs and snails	Any succulent growth eaten	Remove any shelter or rotting materials to discourage them	Slug baits, various traps, or biological control
Thrips	White mottling on leaves	None	Spray with appropriate insecticide
Vine weevil	Roots chewed through and plant wilts; notches cut out of leaf margins; plants growing in containers are worst affected	Remove and discard soil from roots of all plants entering the garden; use insecticidal potting compost	Difficult to control; insecticide drench or biological control for grubs in the potting compost
Whitefly	Sticky honeydew and sooty mould on leaves	None outside, sticky traps in glasshouses	Treat compost with an appropriate insecticide; biological control in greenhouses
Wireworms	Holes in potato tubers and other fleshy roots	Dig the soil to reveal to birds; lift potatoes as soon as possible	Difficult to control

Common pests and diseases

LARGER ANIMAL PESTS

These creatures can cause severe damage. Although there are preventative steps you can take, you may have to learn to live with them.

Pest	Symptoms	Prevention	Control
Birds	Eaten buds and fruit	Net the crops, fruit cages, use bird-scarers	None
Deer	Plants stripped of bark and leaves	Tall fence 2m+ (6½ft+), plant deer-proof plants, fit tree guards	None
Moles	Molehills, plants above runs wilting	None	Trapping or electronic repellents
Rabbits	Eaten leaves	Wire mesh fencing 1m (3ft) tall with 15cm (6in) sunk below soil level, fit tree guards	Trapping

COMMON PLANT DISEASES

Check with your garden centre or supplier for the most appropriate fungicide that is currently available.

Pest	Symptoms	Prevention	Control
Canker	Sunken and broken areas on the bark of trees and shrubs, sometimes bleeding	Immediately treat any outbreaks	Cut out and burn infected branches; spray with appropriate fungicide
Cucumber mosaic virus	Yellow mosaic patterning on the leaves	Destroy all affected plants	None
Damping off	Seedlings and cuttings rot at soil level and collapse	Use fresh compost and clean pots, do not over-water	Water with appropriate fungicide
Downy mildew	Yellowish discolouring on leaf surface and grey mould below	Improve air circulation between and through plants	Treat with appropriate fungicide (only lettuces)
Foot and root rots	Rot occurs around base of stem and plant wilts and dies	Good garden hygiene	None; burn infected plants
Grey mould *(Botrytis)*	A grey mould	Allow air to circulate between and through plants; remove all dead material from plants	Treat with appropriate fungicide
Honey fungus	Trees and shrubs die back; white mushroom-smelling threads between bark and stem; yellow toadstools at base.	Keep plants healthy	Dig up and burn infected plant
Leaf spots	Dark spots or blotches on leaves	Improve growing conditions	Collect and burn affected leaves; spray with appropriate fungicide
Phytophthora	Rotting at the base of woody plants	Improve drainage	Remove and burn plants
Powdery mildew	Leaves and stem covered in a white powder	Keep plants watered in dry weather; give plants good circulation of air	Burn badly infected plants; treat with appropriate fungicide
Rusts	Orange or brown spots	Improve the air circulation	Treat with appropriate fungicide
Sooty moulds	Black moulds growing on honeydew	Control aphids and whiteflies that cause honeydew	None
Virus infections	Stunted growth, distorted and discoloured leaves	Only buy healthy stocks; control aphids as they spread the disease	None; dig up and burn infected plants
Wilts	Foliage wilts and then dies back	Buy resistant plants	None; dig up and burn infected plants

Controlling weeds

A weed is a plant growing where it is not wanted. Weeds compete with crops for light, water, and nutrients and they also act as hosts for pests such as aphids and whitefly, and diseases, such as club root of brassicas. Identifying the weeds and understanding their means of survival is the first step towards controlling them. Annual weeds complete their life cycle in a season and are characterised by producing masses of seeds, so that the weed population in the soil is replenished from year to year. Every time the soil is cultivated weed seeds are brought to the surface where they germinate. Perennial plants live from year to year, and have roots or stems that persist underground. However, once the ground is cleared of perennial weeds they should not be a problem in the future, unless seeds are blown into the garden or they are imported with organic matter.

There are various ways of controlling weeds, but whichever one you employ, act before the weeds flower and set seed.

Handweeding

Most small weeds and many large annuals can be easily pulled out by hand. For those that break just above the ground and those that bring up a mass of soil, disturbing the roots of your plants, ease them out with a hand fork. Handweeding is easier when the soil is not compacted, and where mulches have left the surface friable.

Hoeing

Hoeing cuts weeds off from their roots just below soil level. You can use a hoe to weed between plants or rows of plants, or to clear an area for planting. It is one of the quickest ways of dealing with weed seedlings and annual weeds. The type of hoe is largely a matter of personal preference (see page 14), but keep the blade sharp. Hoe in warm dry weather so weeds wilt and die quickly; some may re-root if the soil is wet. Hoe shallowly to keep moisture loss to a minimum and to bring up as few weed seeds to the surface as possible. Hoe regularly when weeds are small and avoid nicking the stems of surrounding plants or damaging shallow roots.

Stale seedbed

This useful technique avoids weed seedlings getting a head start. Use it before broadcasting seed over an area, as for a lawn or wild-flower scheme, or prior to sowing slow-germinating seeds. Make the seedbed in the usual way, a couple of weeks before sowing. In cold weather, cover the area with fleece or plastic. A flush of weed seedlings will result that can be hoed off as shallowly as possible before sowing your chosen crop.

Flame weeding

This is a suitable method for controlling weeds in areas where hoeing or mulching are inappropriate, as on paths or gravel driveways. The weeds do not have to be burnt: pass the flame over them for a second or two until they change colour – usually to a brighter green. This indicates that the cell walls have burst. Seedlings and annuals are easily killed in this way, but perennials may need several treatments until the roots are exhausted. A flame weeder is a good way to kill weed seedlings on a prepared bed as it does not disturb the soil and bring fresh weed seeds to the surface.

Using chemicals

Most weedkillers are sold in a concentrated liquid form, which is applied after dilution with water. Apply the weedkiller with a sprayer if the area is large or with a watering can fitted with a dribble bar (see page 214) for small areas. Take care when using any weedkiller and avoid getting it on neighbouring plants – shield them with polythene if necessary. Always follow the safety instructions on page 261.

It is important to use the correct weedkiller for the job as they act in different ways:

Spot weeders are a handy means of killing isolated weeds and these are used straight from the container as instructed. They are particularly useful for treating perennial weeds in lawns and in close-planted beds and borders.

Contact weedkillers kill only the part of the plant they touch and are most suitable for clearing areas of annual weeds. They will not persist in the soil so planting can take place after use.

Systemic weedkillers are taken into the plant and down to the roots. They act against annual and perennial weeds, and can be used to clear ground prior to planting, although more than one application will almost certainly be necessary. These become inactive on contact with the soil, so once you are sure all perennials are dead you can plant.

Selective weedkillers are used mainly on lawns. They are designed to kill only broadleaved weeds, such as daisies and dandelions, and not the grass.

Residual weedkillers are taken in through plant roots. They are useful for clearing paths and heavily weeded areas, but you will not be able to replant for up to a year or until advised by the manfacturer's instructions.

Mulching and smothering

One of the best methods of suppressing weeds is to use a mulch to exclude the light. If weeds are kept in the dark when growing the roots will eventually become exhausted and die. Mulching materials include black plastic sheeting or organic matter like garden compost or bark (see page 32). Used locally around plants the soil should be cleared of weeds before the mulch is laid. This is also an excellent way of clearing weedy ground without recourse to chemicals as long as you are in no hurry to replant. It is not effective in eliminating or suppressing vigorous perennial weeds. These will always need to be removed first; or after the mulch is removed when they are weakened through lack of light.

Smothering weeds to clear the ground

First cut down tall weeds and grass with a strimmer or shears and remove excess material. Then exclude light completely by covering the area with heavy gauge black plastic tucked into the soil; thick overlapping layers of newspaper or cardboard; or old hessian-backed wool carpet. Weight the covering material down with bricks, and, for aesthetic purposes, cover with a thin layer of bark chippings.

The period of smothering depends on the weeds. Annual weeds will be killed in about two months during the growing season. Deep-rooted perennials may take up to two years. Take this time period into account when applying a mulch; newspaper and cardboard are unlikely to last more than a few months, whereas strong black plastic will last for years.

Weed control in paths and paving

Weedy paths and paved areas are a common problem and can be cleared using an appropriate weedkiller. You can also tackle the problem without chemicals, clearing the weeds by hand, or digging them out with an old kitchen knife. Even better, avoid weeds in the first place. Ask yourself the following questions:

Is a path necessary? A weedy path could indicate that it is rarely used. Individual stepping stones through a bed of plants or mown grass can be easier to maintain. Would another surface do? Concrete and well-laid paving slabs (see pages 241–44) give the least weed problems.

In an informal situation, such as in a vegetable plot, paths of old carpet covered in shredded bark or straw are easier to replace when they become weedy than makeshift paths of old bricks.

Does the path need relaying? Give all permanent paths firm, deep foundations to cover the soil and prevent weed seeds germinating; and lessen the chance of weed seedlings becoming established. A geotextile membrane is porous, and when laid between the foundations and the surface paving, gives extra protection and stops weeds growing between unmortared paving.

Retaining edges are essential for paths with a loose surface, such as gravel, to prevent soil spilling onto the path. Paving slabs, bricks and pavers must fit together closely; brush dry mortar into the cracks where they join to prevent them silting up with soil (see page 260).

How can weeds be eliminated? Tackle weeds that seed into paths as soon as possible, before they put down a good root system. A gravelled area can be hoed and weeds in between paving slabs removed with an old kitchen knife or special tool. Alternatively, use a flame weeder.

USING CHEMICALS SAFELY

1. Before buying, check a particular pesticide, fungicide, or weedkiller is suitable for the job in hand. Read the label carefully and, if in doubt, seek further advice.

2. Only use chemicals when necessary and do not spray beyond the immediate area of problem. For small outbreaks squash or handpick pests; remove infected leaves or fruits; fork out small patches of weeds and hand pull or hoe off scattered annual weeds.

3. Read instructions thoroughly before use, and follow them exactly.

4. Wear protective gloves and old clothes when mixing and applying chemicals.

5. Use a different sprayer for pesticides and fungicides from that used for weedkillers.

6. Dilute chemicals outside the house, not in the kitchen.

7. Never leave containers open and unattended when spraying.

8. Do not spray in windy weather, because weedkillers may drift on to garden plants and neighbouring gardens.

9. Spray in the evening or very early in the morning, when bees and beneficial insects are not flying about.

10. Avoid contaminating water features; many chemicals are fatal to fish and pondlife.

11. Thoroughly wash out spray equipment after use.

12. Wash hands thoroughly after using chemicals.

13. Never store diluted chemicals. Dispose of them safely according to the manufacturer's instructions.

14. Store all chemicals out of reach of children and pets, preferably in a locked cupboard.

15. It is illegal to acquire professional pesticides, fungicides, and weedkillers for garden use.

16. If chemicals get on the skin, wash off immediately with copious amounts of cold water.

17. Seek instant medical advice if a chemical is swallowed. Take the container with you for identification purposes.

THE YEAR
IN THE
GARDEN

One of the ways to achieve success in gardening is to plan ahead and do the various jobs at the right time. If you can do this you will not only save time, but also disappointments in the long term.

ROUTINE TASKS

Allocate a realistic amount of time each week to the garden – this can be anything from an hour or two to several days, depending on how many other commitments you have. A part of this time should be devoted to walking round the garden looking at the plants. This is the best way to get to know your garden and to keep on top of problems, including pests and diseases. Jobs like weeding, deadheading, and tying in wayward stems can be done as you walk. They will probably need to be done more frequently as the growing season gets under way, but the long summer evenings make this no hardship. At the same time, jot down what is happening each week in a five-year diary to keep a long-term record that can be referred to from year to year. Make a note of your plant successes and failures, the lateness or earliness of the season, any problems, or thoughts on how your garden could be improved.

Try not to forget the garden in winter. This is the time when you can check fences, plant supports, and tidy the shed. It is also the best time to plan any changes; while the bare bones of the garden are exposed it is easier to see the strong and weak points in its design. Winter is also the best time to plan planting schemes. You will have time to study catalogues and check on plant requirements to see if they can be matched within your garden, making reference, of course, to your gardening diary.

CLIMATE AND WEATHER

The reminders that are given on the following pages are a guide and should be treated as such. Always take the weather into account, and the lateness or earliness of the particular season before you plant, sow, or cultivate. Don't sow early crops in early spring if the weather is cold and the soil sodden; in these conditions seed will not germinate well, if at all, and you will compact the soil, damaging its structure, if you tread on it. Instead, wait until the soils warms and dries out in mid spring, when germination will be quicker and more regular.

If spring in your area tends to be wet and cold, protect a patch of soil with fleece, clear plastic, or cloches so you can advance the growing season (see page 23), or consider raising plants in modules under glass.

The further north you live the quicker winter comes and the longer it lasts, so you will need to sow and plant later in spring than you would if you lived further south. Winters tend to be harsher on the eastern side of Britain than in the west. The proximity of the sea will also affect your gardening. The associated winds tend to cut down the amount of frost, making the winters milder than further inland. However, the often fierce, salt-laden winds are not tolerated by all plants and must be taken into account. Get to know your local microclimates, which play such an important part in timing (see page 221). You can build up a picture of the microclimate in your own garden, finding the protected spots where fruit will thrive and plants can get ahead, and the more exposed areas. A maximum-minimum thermometer hung on a shaded wall will help you to monitor night frosts.

The year in the garden

MID WINTER   (NORTHERN HEMISPHERE = JANUARY; SOUTHERN HEMISPHERE = JULY)

VEGETABLES

- Clear and plan the vegetable garden.
- Order seeds.
- Inspect stored crops and remove any decaying vegetables.
- Harvest winter brassicas.
- Sow early radishes under cloches and cold frames until late winter.
- Sow peas in sheltered districts.
- Sow broad beans for an early crop.

FRUIT

- Plant new trees and bushes in suitable conditions.
- Prune newly planted fruits, bush fruits, and apples and pears (until early spring).
- Cut back summer-pruned laterals on red and white currants and gooseberry cordons (until early spring).
- Apply sulphate of potash to strawberries, raspberries, apples, and pears.
- Check supports and ties.
- Check fruit in store and remove any that are diseased or rotten.
- Cover strawberry plants with cloches or polythene tunnels at any time until early spring for an early crop.

- Take blackcurrant cuttings.
- Protect peaches and nectarines against peach leaf curl.
- Spray fruit trees and bushes with tar-oil if not done in early winter.
- Check for canker on apple and pear trees, and treat if necessary.

LAWNS

- Remove any accumulations of leaves.
- Check drains if water is standing on the surface for any length of time after rain, and drain persistently wet sites.
- Overhaul the mower and other lawn tools before the start of the new season.
- Continue aeration treatment.
- Lay turves in favourable weather.

ORNAMENTALS

- Plan the year's bedding and planting, and order seeds and plants from mail-order catalogues.
- If the soil is dry and weather fine, carry on with winter maintenance schedule of tidying the borders – removing dead material, weeding, top-dressing with well-rotted organic material.

- Take root cuttings of perennials.
- Cut out dead and damaged wood from trees and shrubs.
- Inspect stored bulbs, corms and tubers, and overwintering plants and remove anything that is decaying.
- Begin chrysanthemum cuttings under glass later in month.

GENERAL MAINTENANCE

- Check tree stakes and ties.
- Clean garden machinery and arrange for servicing and sharpening of mowers and other tools.
- Clear snow from trees and shrubs and garden structures if necessary.
- Clean and disinfect potting and propagation equipment such as pots and seedtrays.
- Clear fallen leaves from rock gardens and borders.
- Dig ground if conditions are suitable.
- Check fences, pergolas, and trellis. Make repairs and treat if necessary.

LATE WINTER   (NORTHERN HEMISPHERE = FEBRUARY; SOUTHERN HEMISPHERE = AUGUST)

VEGETABLES

- Rake in a balanced, general fertilizer two weeks before sowing early crops.
- If conditions are suitable sow in open ground: borage; red cabbage (until early spring); broad beans (until mid spring); summer cabbage (until late spring); salad onions (until early summer).
- Sow under cloches and frames: early bunching turnips; carrots, parsnips, and early beetroot (until early spring); bulb onions (until mid spring).
- Plant rhubarb crowns; shallots, garlic, and Jerusalem artichokes (until early spring).
- Top-dress over-wintered crops, such as onions, broad beans, spring cabbage, and asparagus when growth begins.
- Chit, or sprout, seed potatoes.
- Rub the sprouts off stored potatoes.
- Harvest broccoli, kale, and other winter brassicas.

FRUIT

- In suitable conditions continue planting trees and bushes.
- Treat canker on apples and pears.
- Protect blossom on fan-trained trees from frost with fleece or netting.
- Cut back the tips of summer-fruiting raspberries.

- Cut down newly planted raspberry canes if not pruned on planting.
- Mulch sweet cherries.
- Protect peaches and nectarines against peach leaf curl.
- Cover early-fruiting strawberries with cloches or polythene tunnels.
- Feed fruit trees and bushes.

LAWNS

- Disperse worm casts regularly on dry days.
- Complete all major turfing work.
- Apply a mosskiller in late winter if weather is settled; if still cold leave until early spring.
- Lightly top-dress if necessary.
- Towards the end of the season prepare for spring sowing, if soil conditions are suitable.
- Continue to aerate established lawns.

ORNAMENTALS

- Order seeds and plan borders, if not already done.
- Continue with winter maintenance when the weather allows.
- Prune late-flowering clematis.
- Cut out dead and damaged wood from trees and shrubs.

- Sow perennials in pots.
- Sow half-hardy annuals under glass.
- Continue to plant trees, shrubs, and bushes during mild, dry weather.
- Plant new perennials if weather permits.
- Plant lily bulbs.
- Pot on annuals sown in autumn.
- Start to force dahlia tubers under glass and take cuttings when ready.

GENERAL MAINTENANCE

- Check tree stakes and ties.
- Clear snow from trees and shrubs, and garden structures if necessary.
- Remove weeds as necessary.
- Continue to plant hedges if weather allows.
- Prune hedges, especially if overgrown, towards the end of the season.
- Check fences, pergolas, and trellis. Make repairs and treat if necessary.

EARLY SPRING (NORTHERN HEMISPHERE = MARCH; SOUTHERN HEMISPHERE = SEPTEMBER)

VEGETABLES

- Sow in open ground: chives, thyme, onions; Brussels sprouts (until mid spring); summer cauliflower, leeks, early beetroot, asparagus, summer corn salad (until mid spring); summer spinach (until late spring); peas (until early summer); autumn and summer lettuce successively (until late summer); endives and carrots (until late summer).
- Sow celery under cloches and in cold frames.
- Plant seakale, horseradish, onion sets (until mid spring); watercress, globe artichokes, and early potatoes (until mid spring).
- Hoe between over-wintered and perennial crops.
- Harvest broccoli, kale, and other winter brassicas; seakale (late mid spring); turnip tops (until mid spring); rhubarb (until mid summer); radishes (until mid autumn).
- Inspect over-wintered herbs regularly.

FRUIT

- Finish planting when soil conditions permit.
- Firm young trees and bushes lifted by frost.
- Feed established trees and bushes.
- Spray apples, cherries, peaches, nectarines, pears, plums and damsons where pests and diseases are known to be troublesome.
- Train new shoots of blackberries, loganberries, and other hybrid berries on to wires.
- Protect flowers on wall-trained peaches and nectarines; pollinate artificially if insects are scarce.
- Plant raspberries and strawberries.
- Prune autumn-fruiting raspberries.
- Mulch blackberries, raspberries, blackcurrants, and newly planted apple and pear trees.
- Prune plums and cherries as growth begins.

LAWNS

- Apply mosskiller if not done in late winter.
- On established lawns reseed worn areas, and repair ragged edges.
- Continue aeration.
- In warmer areas apply spring fertilizer in early spring if the weather is mild and settled.
- Begin to mow established lawns. Roll before mowing if turf has been lifted by frost.
- Rake seedbeds for new lawns after clearing weeds; apply preseeding fertilizer.
- Sow new lawns if conditions are suitable.

ORNAMENTALS

- Finish the winter clear up, including weeding, feeding, and mulching borders.
- Divide any overcrowded perennials.
- Plant new perennials.
- Sow half-hardy annuals; pot up any sown the previous season.
- Harden-off over-wintering hardy annuals raised under cover, and plant out.
- Sow hardy annuals outside.
- Plant out sweet peas.
- Order plug plants.
- If weather allows, remove winter protection from tender perennials and container plants.
- Deadhead bulbs regularly.
- Plant summer-flowering bulbs.
- Lift, divide, and replant snowdrops.
- Finish planting trees and shrubs.
- Prune bush and climbing roses.
- Repot or top-dress hardy plants in containers.

GENERAL MAINTENANCE

- Check tree stakes and ties.
- Weed regularly.
- Finish planting hedges.
- Control perennial weeds in paved areas, paths, and gravel drives.
- Look out for slugs and snails in beds and borders, and take control measures if necessary.
- Clean and make repairs to paths and paving if necessary.

MID SPRING (NORTHERN HEMISPHERE = APRIL; SOUTHERN HEMISPHERE = OCTOBER)

VEGETABLES

- Sow in open ground, spinach beet, and seakale, cardoons, broccoli, cauliflower and winter cabbage (including Savoys); leaf lettuce successively (until late spring); kale (until late spring).
- Sow under cloches and frames dwarf French beans, sweet corn, and celeriac.
- Plant second early and main crop potatoes, asparagus crowns; red cabbage and summer cabbage (until late spring).
- Stake peas.
- Thin spinach.
- Thin summer lettuce (until late summer).
- Apply fertilizer to potatoes.
- Prepare celery trenches at the end of this season.
- Harvest early turnips, spring lettuce, asparagus, and spring cabbage (until early summer); salad onions (until mid summer).
- Erect supports for runner beans.

FRUIT

- Remove greasebands applied in mid autumn.
- Thin shoots of established fan-trained peaches and nectarines; remove misplaced shoots of wall-trained plums and cherries (until early summer).
- Cut back the leaders of mature apples and pears grown as cordons, espaliers, and dwarf pyramids.
- Plant late-flowering strawberries.
- Prune young and established pyramid plums.
- Pinch off flowers on summer-fruiting strawberries, in their first year if planted in late autumn or spring.
- Ventilate strawberries under cloches and uncover plants in flower on sunny days to allow access for pollinating insects.
- Protect wall trees and soft fruit bushes against frost when in bloom.
- Begin to liquid feed fruit in containers regularly.

LAWNS

- Increase the frequency of mowing according to the weather and grass growth.
- Remove patches of coarse grass and reseed.
- Reseed any sparsely grassed areas.
- Sow new lawns.
- Check newly turfed areas and top-dress lightly, if necessary, to fill joints.
- Apply a spring feed in mid spring if not already done; a few days later apply weedkiller if necessary.
- Apply weed-and mosskillers.
- Rake out dead moss.
- Roll new lawns to firm in seedlings if required.

ORNAMENTALS

- Remove dead heads regularly from bulbs.
- Finish dividing and planting perennials.
- Stake and support emerging perennials.
- Prick out pot-sown perennial seedlings.
- Sow hardy perennials outside.
- Order plug plants.
- Prepare containers and hanging baskets with tender annuals, but keep under glass.
- Begin to liquid feed regularly plants in containers.
- Continue to sow tender annuals and pot up earlier ones.
- Take basal cuttings from perennials.
- Prune early-flowering shrubs after flowering.
- Tie in climbers and wall-trained plants regularly.

GENERAL MAINTENANCE

- Check tree stakes and ties.
- Weed regularly.
- Check recently planted trees and shrubs, and firm in if necessary.
- Mulch hedges and beds when soil is moist.
- Prepare ground for sowing early, leave for two weeks, and hoe to control annual weed seedlings.
- Remove suckers, as necessary, from roses, shrubs, and fruit trees.
- Control pests such as aphids as they appear.
- Water seedlings and established plants as necessary.
- Reinstate pump in pool after winter storage.

The year in the garden

LATE SPRING   (NORTHERN HEMISPHERE = MAY; SOUTHERN HEMISPHERE = NOVEMBER)

VEGETABLES

- Sow sweet corn, asparagus peas, basil, sweet marjoram, chicory, soya beans, marrows, courgettes, pumpkins, and squashes; ridge cucumbers (until early summer); runner beans, swedes, main crop beetroot (until early summer).
- Plant Florence fennel, sweet corn, New Zealand spinach, Brussels sprouts, leeks, celery, celeriac (until early summer), and Jerusalem artichokes.
- Earth up potatoes.
- Prepare the ground and plant leeks.
- Stake broad beans if necessary.
- Harvest lettuce sown previous late summer or early autumn; leaf lettuce (late spring onwards); early carrots and bunching turnips (late spring onwards); early beetroot (until mid summer); summer spinach.

FRUIT

- Plant out alpine strawberries by end of spring.
- Remove blossom from newly planted two- and three-year-old trees, spring-planted runners of summer-fruiting strawberries and perpetual strawberries.
- Mulch strawberries with straw to keep fruits dry.

- Protect strawberries from birds and frosts.
- Pick early strawberries under cloches.
- Tie in raspberry canes.
- Thin gooseberries.

LAWNS

- In late spring adjust the mower to the summer cutting height.
- Continue to treat lawn weeds and moss.
- Water new lawns during dry periods.
- Roll new lawns to firm in seedlings if required.
- During late spring apply a light dressing of nitrogen-rich fertilizer.
- Cultivate sites for new lawns. Leave rough over summer for autumn sowing.

ORNAMENTALS

- Remove dead heads and tidy herbaceous plants regularly.
- Continue to prick out perennials and annual seedlings.
- Thin seedlings of annuals sown outside.
- Pot on developing plants.
- Continue to stake perennials before they get too large.

- Harden-off and plant out tender annuals and bedding plants.
- Sow biennials.
- Move outside or plant up containers and hanging baskets once threat of frost is past.
- Plant out dahlias and chrysanthemums.
- Shear over vigorous alpines after flowering.
- Start taking softwood cuttings.
- Remove dead foliage of spring bulbs.
- At the end of the month plant or divide aquatics.

GENERAL MAINTENANCE

- Check tree stakes and ties.
- Tie in new shoots regularly.
- Weed regularly.
- Watch out for, and control, pests and diseases as necessary.
- Mulch where necessary.
- Water young and vulnerable plants in dry spells.
- Clean out garden pool if necessary.

EARLY SUMMER (NORTHERN HEMISPHERE = JUNE; SOUTHERN HEMISPHERE = DECEMBER)

VEGETABLES

- Plant marrows, courgettes, pumpkins, and squashes raised in modules under glass (early summer onwards); runner beans, winter cabbage, autumn, winter and summer cauliflowers, broccoli, tomatoes, outdoor cucumber, okra, sweet peppers, and basil; kale (early to late summer).
- Pinch out the growing points of runner beans if bushy plants are required.
- Pinch out broad beans when in full flower.
- Earth up potatoes.
- Stop cucumbers after 5–6 leaves.
- Support tomatoes.
- Remove the flowering shoots on rhubarb (early summer onwards).
- Hoe, water, and mulch growing crops.
- Continue to harvest crops regularly.

FRUIT

- Plant out melon seedlings in cold frames.
- Cut back laterals on red and white currant and gooseberry cordons and bushes (from early summer to mid summer).
- Harvest strawberries, summer-fruiting raspberries, dessert gooseberries, and cherries.
- Water bush and cane fruits as fruits begin to swell, and protect from birds.

- Ventilate protected strawberries on sunny days; remove protection when fruiting is finished.
- Peg down strawberry runners and remove those not wanted for propagation.
- Train in new shoots of blackberries, loganberries, and raspberries.

LAWNS

- Continue to mow regularly, raising blades during hot, dry weather.
- Remove any patches of creeping weeds before mowing.
- Control weeds if necessary.
- Water new lawns in dry weather.
- Spike the lawn to allow water to penetrate.
- Lightly top-dress and irrigate areas of heavy wear.
- Feed lightly towards the end of this season.

ORNAMENTALS

- Deadhead flowers as they go over.
- Water during dry spells.
- Prune early-flowering clematis.
- Continue to pot on pot-sown perennials.
- Remove the dead foliage of late-spring bulbs.
- Lift and divide bulbs if necessary.
- Plant out tender annuals and perennials in colder areas.
- Plant annuals to fill any unexpected gaps among

perennials or shrubs.
- Sow biennials outside in nursery rows.
- Plant or divide aquatics.

GENERAL MAINTENANCE

- Check stakes and ties.
- Tie in new shoots regularly.
- Trim hedges and topiary as necessary.
- Weed regularly.
- Watch out for pests and diseases, and treat as necessary.
- Mulch where necessary when soil is moist.
- Water young and vulnerable plants in dry spells.
- Clean out garden pool if not done in late spring.

MID SUMMER (NORTHERN HEMISPHERE = JULY; SOUTHERN HEMISPHERE = JANUARY)

VEGETABLES

- Sow Chinese cabbage, red cabbage for over-wintering, leaf lettuce, kale, spinach beet, and seakale; spring cabbage, main crop turnips and winter radishes (until late summer).
- Plant winter cabbage (including Savoys).
- Earth up Brussels sprouts if necessary.
- Protect cauliflower from the sun by breaking leaves over the curds.
- Pinch out the growing points of runner beans when they reach the top of the support system.
- Begin to blanch celery plants when they are 30cm (12in) tall by tying them up, then begin to earth up (repeat every three weeks).
- Watch for aphids, cabbage caterpillars, pea moth, and slugs, and treat as necessary.
- Hoe regularly and water in dry weather.
- Continue to harvest crops regularly.

FRUIT

- Prop up heavy cropping branches of fruit trees.
- Check ties on trained trees are not too tight.
- Train in new blackberry and loganberry shoots.
- Pick blackcurrants, red currants, and raspberries.
- Summer prune cordon, espalier and dwarf pyramid apples, pears and pyramid plums (until early autumn).

- Cut back unwanted laterals on the fan-trained cherries.
- Tie in replacement shoots on peaches and nectarines.
- Protect peaches and other fruits against birds, wasps, and earwigs.
- Cut out old raspberry canes after fruiting, tie in new ones, and remove unwanted suckers.
- Tidy up strawberry beds. Lift, and burn or discard plants which have given three crops.

LAWNS

- Mow regularly.
- Give final summer feed in mid- to late summer, followed by a final application of weedkiller if necessary.
- Apply base dressing of fertilizer to sites for new lawns towards the end of this season.
- Sow grass seed in late summer/early autumn during mild, damp weather.

ORNAMENTALS

- Deadhead flowers as they go over.
- Cut to the ground some of the early perennials so that they reshoot.
- Water hanging baskets and containers daily.

- Top up mulch where it has thinned.
- Continue to take cuttings.
- Take cuttings of pinks (*Dianthus*).
- Divide bearded irises after flowering.
- Collect seeds as required.
- Repot spring bulbs.

GENERAL MAINTENANCE

- Check tree stakes and ties.
- Tie in new shoots regularly.
- Continue to trim hedges.
- Weed regularly.
- Ensure that crops are picked regularly.
- Mulch where necessary.
- Continue watering and feeding.
- Watch out for and control pests and diseases as necessary.
- Take advantage of warm weather to remove plants, and repair and clean greenhouse.
- Construct paths, steps, plant supports, and erect buildings.

LATE SUMMER (NORTHERN HEMISPHERE = AUGUST; SOUTHERN HEMISPHERE = FEBRUARY)

VEGETABLES

- Sow onions for over-wintering; onions for spring salads, spring lettuce, winter spinach, and winter corn salad (until early autumn).
- Propagate sweet bay from cuttings of ripe shoots (until early autumn).
- Earth up kale, leeks, and winter cauliflower.
- Stop tomato plants when 4–5 trusses have set.
- Hoe between vegetable rows regularly, and water the crops in dry weather.
- Continue to harvest crops regularly and plan winter storage.

FRUIT

- Pick early apples and pears while under-ripe.
- Pick loganberries.
- Plant rooted strawberry runners.
- Prop up heavily laden plum branches.
- Protect ripening fruit from birds.
- Begin regular checks of apples, pears and plums for brown rot and remove and burn infected fruits.
- Cut back the pinched-out shoots on fan-trained plums (until early autumn).
- Cut out old fruiting laterals on established

fan-trained acid cherries.
- Ventilate protected fruit on hot days.
- After harvesting cut back old fruiting laterals on peaches and nectarines in the greenhouse.

LAWNS

- Raise the cutting height of the mower towards the end of this season, since the rate of growth will slow.
- Carry out renovation where necessary: scarify to remove matted growth or thatch, spike and top-dress, and seed-in sparse patches.
- Apply a lawn sand to control moss. Do not use mosskillers containing sulphate of ammonia at this time of year.
- Continue to seed-in new lawn sites.

ORNAMENTALS

- Continue to weed and water as necessary.
- Deadhead fading flowers, and cut perennials to the ground when necessary.
- Collect seed if required.
- Sow hardy annuals outside for the following year.

- Plant daffodil and crocus bulbs for next year.
- Continue to take cuttings.
- Divide or move bearded irises.
- Pot up rooted cuttings.
- Prune summer-flowering climbing and rambling roses.

GENERAL MAINTENANCE

- Check tree stakes and ties.
- Tie in new shoots regularly.
- Continue to trim hedges.
- Weed regularly.
- Watch out for, and control, pests and diseases as necessary.
- Mulch where necessary.
- Continue watering and feeding.
- Take cuttings of hardy plants as required.

The year in the garden

EARLY AUTUMN (NORTHERN HEMISPHERE = SEPTEMBER; SOUTHERN HEMISPHERE = MARCH)

VEGETABLES

- Sow lettuce in cloches and cold frames.
- Plant out spring cabbage and spring greens (early to mid autumn).
- Harvest spring-sown onions when the tops yellow and bend over.
- At the end of the season cut down asparagus foliage.
- Remove yellowing leaves and any "blossom" sprouts from Brussels sprouts.
- Clear away the debris from all harvested crops.
- Continue to earth up kale and leeks (until late autumn).
- Cover lettuce and winter salads with cloches from late in this season onwards.
- Ripen marrows, pumpkins, and squashes in the sun and store for winter use.
- Continue to harvest crops as necessary.

FRUIT

- Plan new plantings and order trees. Choose late-flowering cultivars for frosty areas.
- Harvest blackberries, raspberries and loganberries, plums, and damsons.
- Plant runners of summer-fruiting and perpetual strawberries by middle of season if possible.
- Protect autumn-fruiting strawberries against birds and slugs, and cover with cloches in cold weather.
- Cut back pinched-out laterals on fan-trained cherries.

LAWNS

- Raise the mower blades to the winter heights and mow as needed.
- Brush to remove early morning dew and encourage rapid drying in fine weather.
- Spike, scarify, and top-dress.
- Clear fallen leaves regularly because their accumulation can create conditions in which diseases may establish themselves.
- Sow new lawns.

ORNAMENTALS

- Continue to weed but only water if conditions are really dry.
- Deadhead flowers and cut back dead or dying stems of perennials.
- Start to lift and divide perennials if the weather is suitable.
- Finish sowing hardy annuals outside, and start under glass.
- Sow autumn-sown perennials in pots.
- Plant spring-flowering bulbs.
- Replant containers with winter bedding.
- Lift dahlias and other tender perennials, pot up and over-winter under cover.

GENERAL MAINTENANCE

- Check tree stakes and ties.
- Begin to clear leaves as necessary.
- Continue to water as necessary.
- Continue to clear weeds, and take pest control measures as necessary.
- Before winter, check electrical installations, the condition of fences, buildings, paths, and structures, and complete construction jobs.
- Clean out the cold frame or greenhouse.

MID AUTUMN (NORTHERN HEMISPHERE = OCTOBER; SOUTHERN HEMISPHERE = APRIL)

VEGETABLES

- Sow spring lettuce in cloches and cold frames.
- Plant rhubarb (until late autumn).
- Cut down asparagus, if not done in early autumn, and mound up the soil in the rows.
- Lift chicory for forcing (until late autumn).
- Cover winter spinach and winter corn salad with cloches for winter protection.
- Protect parsley with a cloche or move it under cover as a potted plant along with sweet bay, rosemary, and other less hardy herbs.
- Examine all stored crops regularly from this season onwards, and remove any decaying vegetables.
- Continue to harvest crops as necessary.

FRUIT

- Sow alpine strawberries in a cold frame or cold greenhouse.
- Prepare the ground for autumn planting.
- Order fruit trees and bushes for autumn delivery if not done last season.
- Repot or pot on fruit plants grown in containers.
- Tidy perpetual strawberry beds after fruiting by removing and burning old leaves and straw.
- Cover perpetual strawberries with cloches.
- Pick autumn-fruiting strawberries.
- Pick and store apples and pears as they mature.
- After leaf-fall, if secondary growth occurs, prune cordon apples and pears.
- Prune summer-fruiting raspberries and tie in young canes.
- Cut out old canes from blackberries, loganberries, and related hybrids after fruiting, and tie in new ones.
- Fix greasebands round fruit trees against crawling pests such as winter moth.
- Examine all stored crops regularly from this season onwards, and remove any that are decaying.

LAWNS

- Spike, scarify, and top-dress, if not done in last season.
- Lay turf lawns from this month onwards.
- Roll new lawns to firm seedlings if they appear loose.
- Mow new lawns when 3.75–5cm (1½–2in) high.

ORNAMENTALS

- Collect any late seed.
- Continue to lift and divide clumps of perennials if weather allows.
- Clear up dying and dead herbaceous material ready for winter.
- Sow autumn-sown perennials in pots.
- Sow hardy annuals, including sweet peas, under glass.
- Plant out biennials, such as wallflowers and sweet williams.
- Plant tulip bulbs.
- Protect plants of borderline hardiness if necessary.
- Plant trees and shrubs.

GENERAL MAINTENANCE

- Check tree stakes and ties, and make sure they are secure for winter.
- Stop watering, except for containers in dry periods, but continue weeding.
- Plant hedges.
- Clean and store canes, stakes, and other supports.
- Clear fallen leaves from rock gardens, lawns, beds, and borders.
- Protect pools from leaves with a net.
- Check gutters and drains for blockages.
- Improve drainage where necessary by digging a soakaway.

LATE AUTUMN (NORTHERN HEMISPHERE = NOVEMBER; SOUTHERN HEMISPHERE = MAY)

VEGETABLES

- Sow broad beans for over-wintering.
- Protect late cauliflowers from frost.
- In sheltered districts, complete sowings of lettuces.
- Trim the outer growths of globe artichokes, detach suckers from the plants, and grow on in pots in a cold frame or cold greenhouse until planting out in the following mid spring.
- Dress soil with lime if required.
- Harvest winter crops as necessary, including leeks and winter brassicas.

FRUIT

- Check supports and repair if necessary.
- Check that the fruit cage is closed and check the condition.
- Inspect stored fruit, and ripen pears at room temperature.
- Prune blackcurrants between now and late winter.
- Shorten unwanted laterals on red and white currant and gooseberry cordons between now and late winter.
- Shorten leaders on red and white currant and gooseberry bushes between now and late winter.
- Prune apple and pear espaliers and dwarf pyramids.

LAWNS

- A final mow may be necessary if the weather is mild.
- Do not mow in wet or frosty weather.
- Apply autumn (high-phosphate) fertilizer.
- Clear up fallen leaves and make leafmould or add them to the compost heap.
- Continue laying turfs when conditions are suitable.
- Prepare sites for sowing new lawns next spring.

ORNAMENTALS

- Order and buy bare-rooted trees, shrubs, and roses.
- Plant if weather is suitable; if not temporarily heel in bare-rooted plants.
- Take hardwood cuttings.
- Part-prune roses to prevent wind-rock during winter.
- Continue to tidy borders when weather permits.
- Finish lifting and dividing clumps of perennials if weather allows.
- Pot up sweet peas under glass.
- Protect tender plants outdoors against frost.

GENERAL MAINTENANCE

- Check tree stakes and ties.
- Protect vulnerable plants in containers by moving to a protected position and wrapping in straw, bracken, sacking or old carpet and covering with bubblewrap or polythene.
- Plant hedges when weather is suitable.
- Begin to dig beds and borders.
- Clear up fallen leaves and make leafmould or add to the compost heap.
- Remove pump from pool, service, and store over winter.
- Install pool heater.

EARLY WINTER (NORTHERN HEMISPHERE = DECEMBER; SOUTHERN HEMISPHERE = JUNE)

VEGETABLES

- Plan next year's crop rotation and order seeds from catalogues.
- Continue to inspect stored produce and remove any that is decaying.
- Protect celery and globe artichokes with straw, bracken, or fleece against frost.
- Lift and trim swede roots for packing in boxes to produce shoots as spring greens.
- Harvest chicons from forced chicory.
- Winter digging can start now (until late winter).
- Protect bay, rosemary, and marjoram from severe winter weather.
- Apply lime if required.
- Continue to harvest winter crops as necessary including leeks and winter brassicas.

FRUIT

- Take strawberries in pots into the greenhouse for fruit in early spring.
- Check fruit in store and remove any that are diseased or rotten.
- Spray all fruit trees and bushes with tar-oil winter wash when dormant.
- Continue to prune bush and cordon fruit (until late winter).
- Continue planting in suitable conditions.

LAWNS

- Complete leaf clearance.
- Continue turfing if weather is suitable.
- Dig over areas to be seeded in the spring.
- Clean and overhaul mowers and other lawn equipment.

ORNAMENTALS

- Plan displays for next year.
- Order seed and plants for next year.
- Deadhead winter-flowering container plants.
- Take root cuttings.
- Continue maintaining beds if weather allows.
- Plant trees, shrubs, and roses if weather allows.

GENERAL MAINTENANCE

- Check tree stakes and ties.
- Control weeds as necessary.
- Plant hedges if weather allows.
- If not done in early winter, protect vulnerable plants in containers by moving to a protected position and wrapping in straw, bracken, sacking or old carpet and covering with bubblewrap or polythene.
- Clean, oil, and repair tools and tidy the garden shed.

Glossary

Abort Failure to develop properly; usually refers to flowers or their parts.

Acid Describes soil with a pH below 7.

Adventitious buds Growth buds that arise without any direct relation to the leaves, usually in response to a wound.

Adventitious roots Roots that develop from stems.

Aeration The process of spiking a lawn in order to allow air into the soil and relieve compaction.

Alkaline Describes soil with a pH over 7.

Annual A plant that completes its life cycle within one growing season.

Anti-desiccant Chemical used as a spray to reduce water loss when transplanting trees and shrubs in the dormant season. Especially useful with evergreens and conifers.

Apex The tip of a stem, hence apical bud, the uppermost bud on the stem, and apical shoot, the uppermost stem on a system of branches.

Apical bud The bud at the shoot tip.

Apical dominance Used of a terminal or apical bud which inhibits the growth of lateral buds, and grows more rapidly than they do.

Axil The upper angle between a leaf, or leaf-stalk, and the stem from which it grows.

Bacteria Parasitic or saprophytic single-celled micro-organisms. Many are beneficial, but some cause disease.

Bare-root plant A plant lifted from the open ground (as opposed to a container-grown plant).

Bare rootstock Rootstock lifted from the open ground to be used for bench planting.

Base dressing Fertilizer applied immediately before sowing or planting.

Bedding plant A plant used for temporary garden display, usually in spring or summer.

Bench grafting Grafting on to a rootstock that is movable – that is a pot-grown or a bare rootstock.

Biennial A plant that completes its life cycle over two growing seasons.

Blanching The exclusion of light from an edible vegetable to whiten the shoots.

Blindness A condition in which a shoot or bud fails to develop fully and aborts.

Bloom Either a blossom, or a natural white powdery, or waxy, sheen on many fruits and leaves, or an abnormal white powdery coating of fungus on galled leaves.

Bolting Producing flowers and seeds prematurely.

Bonemeal Bones ground to a powder, sterilised, and used as a fertilizer.

Bottom heat The warmth, usually provided artifically, from under the compost in, for example, a propagator.

Bract A modified, usually reduced, leaf that grows just below the flower head.

Branched head A branch system on a tree in which there is no central leader shoot.

Brassica Collective term for cabbages, cauliflowers, turnips, and related vegetables.

Break The development of lateral shoots as a result of pruning a shoot to an axillary bud.

Broadcast To distribute seed evenly over the entire seedbed, as opposed to sowing in rows.

Bud The embryo shoot, flower, or flower cluster, hence growth bud, flower bud.

Bud burst The period of the end of the dormant season when new buds begin to swell and produce leaves or flowers.

Budding A method of grafting using a single growth bud rather than part of a stem with several buds.

Bulb An underground storage organ that consists of swollen fleshy leaves or leaf bases, which enclose the following year's growth buds.

Bulbil A small bulb, formed in the leaf axil on a stem, or in the inflorescence.

Bulblet Very small bulbs that develop below ground on some bulbs.

Cap A hard crust on the soil surface.

Carpeting plant A plant whose stems take root as they spread; also known as carpeter.

Catch crop A rapidly maturing crop grown between harvesting one vegetable, and sowing or planting the next on the same ground.

Central leader The central, vertical, dominant stem of a tree.

Chelated Describes a special formulation of plant nutrients, which will remain available in alkaline soils.

Chitting The germination of seeds or sprouting of potatoes prior to sowing and planting.

Chlorophyll The green pigment present in most plants, by means of which they manufacture carbohydrates.

Chlorosis The abnormal yellowing or whitening of foliage when a plant fails to develop normal amounts of chlorophyll.

Climber A plant that climbs by clinging to objects by means of twinging stems with hooks or tendils or, more generally, any long-stemmed plants trained upwards.

Clone A plant propagated vegetatively, with identical characteristics to its parent.

Compost, garden Rotted organic matter used as an addition to or substitute for manure.

Compost, seed and potting Mixtures of organic and inorganic materials, such as peat, coir, sand, and loam, used for growing seeds, cuttings, and pot plants.

Conifer A tree or shrub that bears its seeds in cones.

Contact insecticide An insecticide that kills pests by direct contact.

Contractile roots Roots of bulbs and corms that contract in length, thereby pulling the organ deeper into the soil.

Cordon A normally branched tree or shrub restricted by spur pruning to a single stem.

Corm A solid swollen stem-base, resembling a bulb, that acts as a storage organ.

Cotyledon A seed leaf; usually the first to emerge above ground on germination.

Crock The use of small pieces of clay flower pot placed, concave-side down, in a pot or container over the drainage hole to facilitate drainage.

Crown Either the basal part of an herbaceous perennial plant from which roots and shoots grow, or the main branch stem of the tree.

Cultivator A tool used to break up the soil surface to improve its texture. A rotary cultivator, or rotovator, has revolving tines or blades and is power-driven.

Current year's growth/wood The shoots which have grown from buds during the present growing season.

Cutting A detached piece of stem, root, or leaf, taken in order to propagate a new plant.

Some of the best plants for a
garden are attractive in more
than one season of the year,
such as this *Passiflora caerulea*.

Right: Shrubs, annuals and perennials provide both colour and interest as they spill out over an informal path.

Below: A well-balanced garden with flowers, herbs and vegetables, as well as plants in pots and under glass.

Deciduous Describes a plant that loses all its leaves at the end of the growing season.

Deadhead To remove the spent flowers or the unripe seedpods from a plant.

Dibber A tool that is pushed into the soil to make a planting hole.

Dicotyledon A flowering plant that produces two seed leaves at germination.

Die-back The death of branches or shoots, beginning at their tips and spreading back towards the trunk or stem.

Disbudding The removal of surplus buds or shoots that are just beginning growth.

Dot plant Bedding plant used to give height or contrast to carpet plant arrangements.

Double leader Two shoots competing as leaders on a tree, each trying to assert apical dominance.

Dressing A material such as organic matter, fertilizer, sand, or lime that is incorporated into the soil. A top dressing is applied to the surface only, without being dug in.

Dribble bar A sealed, perforated tube attached to a watering can spout that enables weedkiller or other liquid to be dribbled on to plants or soil.

Drills Straight furrows, narrow and shallow, in which seeds are sown.

Dwarf pyramid A tree pruned to form a pyramid-shaped central-leader tree about 2m (6ft) high.

Earth up Mounding earth around the base and stems of a plant, e.g. potato.

Espalier A tree trained against a support with a vertical main stem and tiers of horizontal branches.

Etiolation The blanching of foliage and lengthening of stems caused in green plants by insufficient light.

Evergreen A plant that retains its foliage for more than one year.

Eye Used to describe a growth bud, particularly of roses, vines, and potato tubers.

Fallowing Allowing land to remain uncropped for a period.

Family A group of related genera. For example, the genera *Poa* (meadow grass), *Festuca* (fescue), and *Agrostis* (bent) all belong to the family of grasses *Gramineae*.

Fan A shrub or tree in which the main branches are trained liked the ribs of a fan against a wall, fence, or other support system.

Fertilizer Material that provides plant food. It can be organic, i.e. derived from decayed plant or animal matter, or inorganic, i.e. made from chemicals.

Flowers of sulphur Pure yellow sulphur in finely powdered form, used to reduce the pH of some soils.

Flushes Irregular successive crops of flowers and fruit, as on perpetual strawberries.

Foliar feed A liquid fertilizer sprayed on to, and partially absorbed through, the leaves.

Foot The base of the main stem of a herbaceous plant.

Forcing The hastening of growth by providing warmth and/or excluding light.

Friable Describes a fine, crumbly soil with no hard or wet lumps.

Frost-lifting The loosening and lifting of plants in the soil after hard frost.

Fungicide A substance used for controlling diseases caused by fungi and some bacteria.

Gall An abnormal outgrowth of plant tissue.

Genus (plural genera) A group of allied species in botanical and zoological classification.

Germination The development of a seed into a seedling.

Grafting Propagation by uniting a shoot or single bud of one plant – the scion – with the root system and stem of another – the stock or rootstock.

Growing point The extreme tip of roots or shoots.

Growth bud A bud that gives rise to a shoot.

Habit The natural mode of growth of a plant.

Half-hardy A plant unable to survive the winter unprotected but not needing all-year-round greenhouse protection.

Half-standard A tree grown with 1–1.2m (3–4ft) of clear stem.

Harden-off To acclimatise plants raised in warm conditions to colder conditions.

Hardy Describes a plant capable of surviving the winter in the open without protection.

Heeling in The storing of plant material upright or inclined, in a trench which is then filled in with soil and firmed.

Herbaceous perennial *see* Perennial.

Herbicide Synonym for weedkiller.

Hormone weedkiller Chemicals which, when applied to weeds, affect their growth, often causing the stems to extend rapidly before the plant collapses and dies.

Host A plant that harbours, or is capable of harbouring, a parasite.

Humidity The amount of water vapour in the atmosphere. Relative humidity is the amount of water in the atmosphere, relative to it being saturated, at a particular temperature. (Warm air will hold more water than cool air.)

Humus Fertile, organic matter that is in an advanced state of decay.

Hybrid A plant produced by the cross fertilization of two species or variants of a species.

Inflorescence The part of a plant that bears the flower or flowers.

Insecticide A substance used to kill injurious insects and some other pests.

Larva (plural larvae) The active immature stage of some insects. The larva of a butterfly, moth, or sawfly is known as a caterpillar, a beetle, or weevil larva as a grub, and a fly larva as a maggot.

Lateral A side growth that develops at an angle from the main stem of the plant.

Layering Propagating by inducing shoots to form roots while they are still attached to the parent plant.

Leaching The removal of soluable minerals from the soil by water draining through it.

Leader shoot The shoot that is dominating growth in a stem system, and is usually uppermost.

Leaf axil *see* Axil.

Leaf-fall The period when deciduous plants begin to shed their leaves.

Light The glass or plastic covering, or lid, of a cold frame.

Lime A compound that contains calcium or calcium with magnesium, added to the soil to reduce acidity.

Line out To plant out young plants or cuttings in temporary positions.

Glossary

Loam A fertile soil with balanced proportions of clay, sand, and organic matter.

Long Tom A pot about half as deep again as a normal pot.

Maiden A one-year-old tree or shrub.

Manure Bulky material of animal origin added to soil to improve its structure and fertility.

Mature A plant that can produce flowers and, hence, reproduce sexually.

Micro-organisms A microcopic animal or plant organism that can cause plant disease. Micro-organisms are beneficial when decomposing plant and animal residue to form humus.

Mole plough A plough pulled through the soil to form a drainage tunnel.

Monocotyledon A flowering plant that produces only one seed leaf.

Mosaic A patchy variation of normal green colour; usually a symptom of virus disease.

Mound layering An alternative term for the technique of stooling.

Mulch A top dressing of organic or inorganic matter, applied to the soil around a plant.

Mutant (or Sport) A plant that differs genetically from the typical growth of the plant that produced it.

Naturalised Describes plants grown in natural surroundings, where they increase of their own accord, and need little maintenance. Also plants established in an area, although they are not native to it.

Nitrate A fertilizer containing nitrogen that can be natural, such as potassium or sodium nitrate, or synthetic, such as calcium nitrate.

Nymph The active, immature stage of some insects and mites.

Offsets Small bulbs produced at the base of the parent bulb; also a young plant developing laterally on the stem close to the parent.

Organic matter Matter consisting of, or derived from, living organisms. Examples include farmyard manure and leafmould.

Ornamental A plant grown for its decorative qualities.

Over-winter Refers to the means by which an organism survives winter conditions.

Pan A hard layer of soil beneath the surface.

Parasite An organism that lives on, and takes part or all of its food from a host plant; usually to the detriment of the latter.

Perennial A plant that lives for more than three seasons and usually much longer.

Perlite A neutral, sterile, granular medium derived from volcanic rock. Used as a rooting medium, and in potting, cutting, and seed composts.

Pesticide A chemical used to kill pests or to control pests and diseases.

Petiole The stalk of a leaf.

pH The degree of acidity or alkalinity. Below 7 on the pH scale is acid, above it is alkaline.

Phosphate (or Phosphatic fertilizer) Fertilizer with a high proportion of phosphorous.

Photosynthesis The process by which a green plant is able to make carbohydrates from water and carbon dioxide, using light as an energy source and chlorophyll as the catalyst.

Pinching (or Stopping) The removal of the growing tip of a shoot.

Planting mark The slight change in colour on the stem of a bare-root plant, indicating the depth at which it was formerly planted.

Plunge outside To bury container plants up to the pot rims in ash, peat, or sand beds to protect the roots from frost in winter.

Pollination The transference of pollen from the male to the female parts of the flower.

Potash (K2O) A component of all balanced fertilizers, supplying the mineral potassium, which is essential for plant growth.

Pot-bound The condition reached by a pot plant when its roots have filled the pot and exhausted the available nutrients.

Presser board A piece of flat wood with a handle used to firm and level compost.

Pricking out The transplanting and spacing out of seedlings.

Propagation The production of a new plant from an existing one, either sexually by seeds or asexually, for example, by cuttings.

Rambler Roses producing long, flexible basal canes, trained on walls, fences, and screens.

RCCB (Residual Current Circuit Breaker) A safety device that cuts off power to electrical equipment if there is any leakage of current to earth.

Recurrent flowering The production of several crops during one season more or less in succession.

Relative humidity *see* Humidity.

Renewal pruning Pruning to maintain a constant supply of young shoots.

Resistant Describes a plant that is able to overcome completely or partially the effect of a parasitic organism or disorder. It also describes a pest or disease that is no longer controllable by a particular chemical.

Rhizome A creeping horizontal underground stem that acts as a storage organ.

Rod The main, woody, stem of a vine.

Rootball The soil or compost ball formed among and around the roots of a plant.

Root cutting A piece of the root of a plant used for propagation.

Rootstock *see* Grafting.

Rose (spray head) The water can or hose attachment producing a fine spray.

Rosette A small cluster of overlapping leaves, often close to ground level.

Rotovator *see* Cultivator.

Runner A rooting stem that grows along the surface of the soil, as in strawberries.

Run-off When spraying the point at which a plant becomes saturated, and further liquid runs off on to the surrounding area.

Sap The fluid in living plants that transports nutrients to various parts of the plant.

Scab A roughened, crust-like, diseased area.

Scarifying The process of vigorously taking a lawn in order to remove thatch.

Scion *see* Grafting.

Scramblers Climbing plants that do not twine or bear tendrils, clambering up by pushing through surrounding trees and shrubs. e.g. the so-called climbing roses.

Seedcoat The tough protective layer around a seed.

Seed dressing A fine powder applied to seeds before sowing to protect them from pests or diseases.

Seedheads Faded flower heads that have been successfully fertilized and contain seeds.

Seed leaf (syn. cotyledon) The first leaf or

leaves produced by a germinated seed. Self-sterile describes a plant whose pollen cannot fertilize its own female parts.

Self-sterile Describes a plant whose pollen cannot fertilize its own female parts.

Semi-evergreen Describes a plant intermediate between evergreen and deciduous. It bears foliage throughout the year, but loses some leaves during the winter.

Sepal The outermost, leaf-like structures of a flower.

Shrub A perennial plant with persistant woody stems branching from the base. If only the lower parts of the branches are woody and the upper shoots are soft and usually die in winter, it is known as a sub-shrub.

Silt Very fine soil formed from clay.

Snag A short stump of a branch left after incorrect pruning.

Soakaway A pit into which water drains.

Soil profile Used to describe a cross-section of soil from surface to bed-rock, showing layers as sub-soil, top-soil.

Species A group of closely related organisms within a genus. Abbreviations: sp. (singular) or spp. (plural).

Spit The depth of a normal digging spade, roughly equal to 25cm (10in).

Spore A reproductive body of a fungus or fern.

Sport *see* Mutant.

Spot-treat To treat a small defined area or a particular plant, usually with weedkiller, fungicide, or pesticide.

Spp. *see* Species.

Spreader A substance added to a spray to assist its even distribution over the target.

Spur A slow-growing short branch system that usually carries clusters of flower buds.

Subsp. Abbreviation for sub-species.

Stamen The male reproductive organ of a flower, comprising a stalk with an anther.

Standard A tree or shrub grown with 1.5–2m (5–6ft) of clear stem.

Station sowing The individual sowing of seeds at a predetermined spacing in the site in which they will grow until pricking out or harvesting.

Stock *see* Grafting.

Stool The base of a plant, such as a cane fruit that produces new shoots.

Stopping *see* Pinching.

Strike To take root, usually of cuttings.

Strike off To remove excess compost above the rim of a pot or seedtray.

Sub-lateral A side-shoot growing from a lateral shoot.

Sub-shrub *see* Shrub.

Sub-soil *see* Top-soil.

Sub-species A category intermediate between a variety and a species.

Succulent A condition in certain plants that has developed as a response to a lack of readily available fresh water. A succulent plant is capable of storing relatively large quantities of water.

Sucker A shoot growing from a stem or root at or below ground level.

Suckering plant A plant that spreads by means of underground shoots or suckers.

Sump Synonym for soakaway.

syn. Abbreviation for synonym.

Tap root The primary vertical root of a plant; also any strong-growing vertical root.

Terminal bud, shoot, flower The uppermost, usually central, growth on a stem. (*see* Apex.)

Thatch On a lawn, a layer of dead or living organic matter, along with debris, found between the roots and foliage of the grass.

Tilth A fine, crumbly surface layer of soil. It is produced by weathering or careful cultivation.

Tine The prong of a fork, rake, or other tool.

Tolerant Describes either a plant that can live despite infection by a parasitic organism, or a fungus that is unaffected by applications of a certain fungicide.

Top dressing *see* Dressing.

Top-soil The upper layer of dark fertile soil in which plants grow. Below this lies the sub-soil, which is lighter in colour, lacks organic matter, and is often low in nutrients.

Transpiration The continual loss of water vapour from leaves and stems.

Trace elements Food materials required by plants only in very small amounts.

True leaves Leaves typical of the mature plant as opposed to simpler seed leaves.

Truss A cluster of flowers or fruit.

Tuber A swollen underground stem or root that acts as a storage organ, and from which new plants or tubers may develop.

Turgid Plant material that contains its full complement of water, and is not therefore limp or under stress.

Union The junction between rootstock and scion or between two scions grafted together.

Var. Abbreviation for the botanical classification varietas (variety); it refers only to naturally occurring varieties.

Variety A distinct variant of a species; it may be a cultivated form (a cultivar) or occur naturally (varietas).

Vegetative growth Leaf and stem growth as opposed to flowers or fruit.

Vermiculite A sterile medium made from expanded mica. It is light, clean, and moisture-retentive, and is used in seed, cutting, and potting composts.

Virus Disease-causing organism, not visible to the naked eye, that may live in plants and less often in the soil.

Watering-in To water around the stem of newly transplanted plants to settle soil around the roots.

Water shoot A vigorous, sappy shoot growing from an adventitious or dormant bud on the trunk or older branches of a tree.

Water stress A variable condition of wilting in which plant material is losing water faster than it can take it up.

Water table The level in the soil below which the soil is saturated by ground water.

Weedkiller, contact action A weedkiller that kills only those green parts of plants with which it comes into contact.

Weedkiller, residual A weedkiller that acts through the soil, and remains effective for a period ranging from a few weeks (short-term residual weedkillers) to several months (long-term residual weedkillers).

Weedkiller, translocated or systemic A weedkiller that is absorbed through the leaves and stems and is carried via the sap-stream to kill the whole plant.

Wetting agent A substance added to composts, and included in sprays that allow greater contact with water.

Wind-rock The loosening of a plant's root system by strong winds.

Index

Page numbers in italic indicate photographs. Under main headings, subheadings for general information appear first, followed by subheadings for any species or cultivar names. Glossary entries are followed by 'g'.

Index

Index

Acknowledgements

The publishers would like to thank the following individuals whose photographs appear in this book:
Front and back cover: Garden Picture Library/Mark Bolton; 1 Octopus Publishing Group Ltd/Howard Rice/Hyde Hall; 2 Octopus Publishing Group Ltd/Sue Atkinson; 19 top Octopus Publishing Group Ltd/Stephen Robson; 19 bottom Octopus Publishing Group Ltd/Stephen Robson; 20 top Octopus Publishing Group Ltd/Sue Atkinson; 20 bottom Octopus Publishing Group Ltd/Sue Atkinson; 37 left Octopus Publishing Group Ltd/Stephen Robson; 37 right Octopus Publishing Group Ltd/Stephen Robson; 38 Octopus Publishing Group Ltd/Paul Barker; 55 left Octopus Publishing Group Ltd/Howard Rice; 55 right Octopus Publishing Group Ltd/Howard Rice/Hyde Hall; 56 top Octopus Publishing Group Ltd/Stephen Robson; 56 bottom Octopus Publishing Group Ltd/Stephen Robson; 73 Octopus Publishing Group Ltd/Sue Atkinson; 74 left Octopus Publishing Group Ltd/Howard Rice/Wisley; 74 right Octopus Publishing Group Ltd/Sue Atkinson; 91 Octopus Publishing Group Ltd/Stephen Robson/Susan Campbell; 92 top left Octopus Publishing Group Ltd/Sue Atkinson; 92 top right Octopus Publishing Group Ltd/Stephen Robson; 92 bottom Octopus Publishing Group Ltd/Paul Barker; 109 Octopus Publishing Group Ltd/Paul Barker; 110 top Octopus Publishing Group Ltd/Howard Rice/Hyde Hall; 110 bottom Octopus Publishing Group Ltd/Howard Rice/Cambridge University Botanical Garden; 127 top Octopus Publishing Group Ltd/Sue Atkinson; 127 bottom Octopus Publishing Group Ltd/Howard Rice/Wisley; 128 top Octopus Publishing Group Ltd/Howard Rice/Cambridge University Botanical Gardens; 128 bottom Octopus Publishing Group Ltd/Sue Atkinson; 145 Octopus Publishing Group Ltd/Howard Rice/Cambridge University Botanic Garden; 146 top left Octopus Publishing Group Ltd/Howard Rice/Hopley's Plants; 146 top right Octopus Publishing Group Ltd/Sue Atkinson; 146 bottom Octopus Publishing Group Ltd/Paul Barker; 163 Octopus Publishing Group Ltd/Stephen Robson; 164 top Octopus Publishing Group Ltd/Stephen Robson; 164 bottom Octopus Publishing Group Ltd/Stephen Robson; 181 Octopus Publishing Group Ltd/Stephen Robson/Preen Manor; 182 top left Octopus Publishing Group Ltd/Stephen Robson; 182 top right Octopus Publishing Group Ltd/Stephen Robson; 182 bottom Octopus Publishing Group Ltd/Stephen Robson; 199 Octopus Publishing Group Ltd/Steve Wooster; 200 top left Octopus Publishing Group Ltd/Stephen Robson; 200 top right Octopus Publishing Group Ltd/Sue Atkinson; 200 bottom Octopus Publishing Group Ltd/Stephen Robson; 217 top Octopus Publishing Group Ltd/Paul Barker; 217 bottom Octopus Publishing Group Ltd/Sue Atkinson; 218 top left Octopus Publishing Group Ltd/Sue Atkinson; 218 top right Octopus Publishing Group Ltd/Sue Atkinson; 218 bottom Octopus Publishing Group Ltd/Sue Atkinson; 235 top Octopus Publishing Group Ltd/Paul Barker; 235 bottom Octopus Publishing Group Ltd/Stephen Robson; 236 top left Octopus Publishing Group Ltd/Stephen Robson; 236 top right Octopus Publishing Group Ltd/Sue Atkinson; 236 bottom Octopus Publishing Group Ltd/Paul Barker; 253 top Octopus Publishing Group Ltd/Sue Atkinson; 253 bottom Octopus Publishing Group Ltd/Sue Atkinson; 254 Octopus Publishing Group Ltd/Stephen Robson; 271 Octopus Publishing Group Ltd/Howard Rice/Meredith Lloyd-Evans; 272 top Octopus Publishing Group Ltd/Paul Barker; 272 bottom Octopus Publishing Group Ltd/Stephen Robson.

The publishers would also like to thank Selina Mumford for her editorial help.